Incredible but TRUE

Eight spies landed in the United States to carry out a devastating plan of death and destruction . . .

THEY CAME TO KILL was originally published at $4.95 by Random House, Inc.

ABOUT THE AUTHOR

EUGENE RACHLIS was born in Roxbury, Mass., and educated at Boston University. He has been a staff editor for the *New York Times Magazine*, and was managing editor of the *Woman's Home Companion*.

Co-author of the book *Peter Stuyvesant and His New York*, Mr. Rachlis has written a number of books for young people, as well as having published articles in many of the nation's leading magazines.

Mr. and Mrs. Rachlis live in New York City with their two sons, and spend their summers on Shelter Island, not far from where four of the German saboteurs landed who are mentioned in THEY CAME TO KILL.

THEY CAME TO KILL

The Story of Eight Nazi
Saboteurs in America

EUGENE RACHLIS

POPULAR LIBRARY · TORONTO

POPULAR LIBRARY EDITION
Published in December, 1962

© Copyright, 1961, by Eugene Rachlis
Library of Congress Catalog Card Number: 61-6269

Published by arrangement with Random House, Inc.
Random House edition published in October, 1961
Two printings

Published simultaneously in Toronto, Canada, by
Random House of Canada, Limited.

DEDICATION:

> *To my mother and father*
> *with love and gratitude*

Printed in Canada

CONTENTS

"... *they would have stilled the machines and endangered the lives of thousands of defense workers ... they came to maim and kill.*"

—J. Edgar Hoover, Director, F.B.I.,
  March of Time radio broadcast, July 9, 1942

PART I
SCHOOL FOR SABOTAGE

Chapter 1
Code Name: Pastorius

At eight o'clock on the evening of June 12, 1942, Lieutenant Commander Lindner of the German submarine *U-202* noted in his log that he was twenty miles off the coast of Long Island, due south of East Hampton, and about a hundred miles east of New York City. He was wrong, but not by very much. The *U-202* was actually opposite Amagansett, another summer resort town three miles to the east. An error so slight was of itself testimony to a remarkable display of navigational skill. Lindner had taken the *U-202* more than three thousand miles in fifteen days, the last two of them from off Nova Scotia in exceedingly heavy fog, to a shoreline he had never seen. Now, with fog still pressing sullenly about him, Lindner ordered the *U-202* submerged, and the power switched from her Diesel engines to silent electric motors. As the submarine moved slowly north toward shore, Lindner spoke briefly to a short, thin-faced man, wearing khaki Navy work clothes, and walked to the mess room. In a few minutes he was joined by the thin-faced man and three others dressed like him, and by two of the submarine's crew. In curt, concise sentences Lindner described the *U-202*'s position and estimated the time it would take at her present rate of speed to reach a point offshore from which the two sailors could safely launch a boat. Landing these four men was Lindner's assignment, and now that it was all but complete, he was understandably anxious for it to be done right. He was a combat officer with a fine record—on his last mission he had sunk three Allied ships off Greenland—and had not been entirely enthusiastic about a voyage in which he had firm orders to avoid enemy action. Lindner was looking forward to getting rid of his passengers and returning to the open Atlantic, to a submarine commander's proper business of seeking out merchant convoys to torpedo.

What Lindner had to do now was risky. The fog had killed his hope of examining the shoreline by day and basing his plans for the landing on what he saw. The lack of visibility could be an advantage, of course, but it also called for supreme caution. Lindner was as concerned about getting his rubber boat and his sailors back to the *U-202* as he was about landing the four men. He ordered the two sailors to inflate the boat and attach a towline to it, and he gave one of them a flashlight and a rocket. If they were not hauled back after tugging a few times on the towline, they were to blink the flashlight, doubtful help in a fog like this; the rocket was to be discharged only if they ran into trouble on shore. The sailors left the mess room while the others continued talking. At 11:00 P.M. they heard a soft scraping sound; the submarine had touched the ocean floor. Lindner ordered the *U-202* raised and moved forward again. When she scraped bottom the second time, he ordered her to the surface and turned her parallel to shore. He opened the hatch and called the thin-faced man to the deck. "What do you think of the night, Dasch?" he asked. "Christ, this is perfect," the man answered. They were some fifty yards from the beach and could not see it.

The thin-faced man went below and told his three companions to make a final check of their pockets to see that they held nothing of German origin. The men made nervous, perfunctory pats at their clothing; one of them had a small bottle of German brandy, another a pack of German cigarettes, but neither was brought out. Just before midnight, Lindner came down from the deck to say that the rubber boat was inflated and alongside, and his sailors ready. He joined the four men in a drink and left to go topside again. The four men followed a few minutes later, one of them carrying a large sea bag. When they were on deck, sailors below handed up four solidly built wooden crates, which looked like so many fruit cases, each about two feet long, eight and a half inches deep and a foot wide. The men placed them carefully in the rubber boat to assure a proper balance. The man with the sea bag stepped into the stern of the boat and was followed by the others, holding paddles. Then came the two sailors with their paddles, and last of all, the thin-faced leader.

With the weight of the six men and the four boxes, the boat sat heavily in the water, but rowing was not difficult at first. As a sailor on the *U-202* payed out the towline, the boat moved swiftly away. In a few minutes the submarine was completely out of sight and the sound of surf rose from a murmur to a roar.

Suddenly, in the overwhelming darkness, the men in the small boat lost all sense of direction. The sound of breaking waves seemed to come first from the left, then the right. Despite the weight, the boat was now being tossed about on the huge waves, and the ocean spray was soaking the men. One of them, trying to keep his balance, knocked his cap into the water; the others knelt low and paddled harder. Then, in a moment of frightened silence, they heard the surf straight ahead. The waves about them rose higher and threatened to swamp the boat. The leader shouted an excited and not very encouraging, "Come on, boys, let's go to it," just as a wave struck, nearly capsizing the boat and causing two men to drop their paddles in the water. But the force of the wave had also been enough to get them over the breaking surf. It was followed by another, which propelled them forward so fast they did not realize they were aground until the wave had receded.

The two sailors immediately leaped out and pulled the boat beyond the water's edge. The four men followed. Two of them quickly began unloading the boxes; the man hugging the sea bag walked a few yards inland and put it down before he returned to help. The leader ignored the unloading of the boat as he walked a wide circle of the beach around them. Satisfied, he came back and urged that the boxes and bag be moved up into the dunes at once. He led the way for about a hundred yards, as two men carried boxes and one dragged the sea bag. The two men dropped their boxes beside a fallen sand fence and returned to the boat as the third man opened the bag, pulled out a raincoat and stretched it flat on the wet sand. Then he reached into the bag and withdrew damp and wrinkled civilian trousers, jackets, vests, shirts and socks, four pairs of shoes, two short shovels of the kind the military calls entrenching tools, and a small canvas bag, all of which he dropped on the raincoat. By the time the sea bag was empty the others had returned with the last of the boxes, and the thin-faced man from an exploration beyond the dunes. He had seen what appeared to be a tall beacon tower; this disturbed him, and he urged the others to change quickly from their wet Navy uniforms to the civilian clothes. He himself stripped to his trousers, put on a shirt and tie, a red sweater and a brown fedora, and ran back down to the two sailors, who were struggling to turn the boat over to drain it.

He helped them finish the job, and then told them to be ready to go as soon as one of the men brought down the sea bag with its discarded military clothing. He stood quietly for a moment, ankle-deep in the water, breathing hard; he had put in too much physical effort too soon after the confining and sedentary weeks on the submarine. When his breath came more normally, he shook hands with the sailors, thanked them for their help, and turned to join the others. He took a few steps, paused while staring into the fog, and then walked back to the sailors. He told them not to wait for the sea bag after all, but to return to the submarine at once. The two sailors needed no urging; they tossed their paddles into the boat, seated themselves carefully and tugged hard on the towline. Seconds later there was a reassuring tautness on the rope, and they were off the beach and out of sight beyond the breaking waves.

Four nights later, on Tuesday, June 16, some eight hundred and fifty miles to the south, German submarine *U-584* approached Jacksonville, Florida. It was a beautifully clear night, and through the periscope of the submerged submarine, the shoreline was distinctly visible. In the mess room, Lieutenant Commander Deeke and a short, handsome man with a head of thick brown hair examined a chart of Florida's Atlantic coast. Toward midnight, Deeke penciled a circle around Ponte Vedra, a strip of beach about seven miles south of Jacksonville. This done, he ordered the submarine closer to shore under electric power. As she moved in, the *U-584* passed within a few yards of a lightship; this amused Deeke. Only when he heard the unmistakable sounds of airplanes overhead, probably on night training from the Jacksonville Air Base, did Deeke order his periscope withdrawn. Soon after midnight the planes were gone. By then the *U-584* was some fifty yards from shore, and Deeke ordered her to the surface.

On deck, he and the brown-haired man looked about them. The sea was calm, the night warm and, if anything, too bright. Deeke's instructions had been identical to Lindner's, and he now proceeded to carry them out in almost the same way. A rubber boat was inflated and held alongside the submarine; in view of the short distance to shore and the absence of large waves, Deeke put a single sailor in charge. Soon three more men came on deck, wearing swimming trunks and, incongruously, Navy jackets and work caps. From below they lifted four boxes of the same size and construction as those on the *U-202*, a shovel, and three small blue canvas bags. Working swiftly, the four men placed themselves and their cargo in the rubber boat, the sailor followed and started paddling expertly toward shore. Within a few minutes they were on land. The sailor was told not to wait, and as soon as his passengers and their possessions were on the beach and their caps and jackets in the boat, he scooped up a handful of sand, filled a pocket to bulging with his undeniably superior souvenir, and yanked at the towline.

The four men on shore watched the rubber boat skim toward the submarine, and remained where they were until the submarine itself slowly turned toward the open sea. They were pleased to see that a man was stationed at the deck gun during this maneuver. Soon the gunner went below, and the submarine submerged. On shore, the brown-haired man led the others some three hundred yards from the waterline to the stumps of three easily identifiable palm trees. They quickly dug four holes, desposited the boxes and filled the holes. They looked about them one last time as one man walked to the water to throw the shovel into the outgoing tide. Then, as calmly as if they were on a swimming party, they picked up the three canvas bags and walked leisurely along the beach toward Jacksonville.

About an hour later, as the night was beginning to fade to gray, the men stopped and chatted briefly. The brown-haired leader and a tall, broad-shouldered young man continued to walk north; the other two sat down on the beach and waited quietly. By the time the sun was up, the two hikers were back; they had been as far as Jacksonville Beach without having seen anyone. At about 11:00 A.M., after they had taken occasional dips in the surf and had been gently warmed by the sun, the four men changed to the civilian clothes which were in their bags, and walked to the highway just beyond the beach.

At a nearby gasoline station, the tall young man asked about the bus schedule to Jacksonville. He returned grinning;

one was due shortly. It came a few minutes later; the young man bought four tickets from the driver, and in less than forty-five minutes the four men were in the center of Jacksonville. The young man and one of the others went directly to the Hotel Mayflower. After registering, he had his hair cut, bought a suitcase, some clothes, toilet articles and a wrist watch. His companion limited himself to a suitcase and clothes. The other two men registered at the Hotel Seminole and also went shopping. When the four met that evening, they were in excellent spirits, and carried on a lively, though muted, conversation as they dawdled through dinner and many drinks.

Commanders Lindner and Deeke, at that moment speeding to join the wolf packs of which they were normally members, had not been told the identity of their passengers, the contents of the wooden crates, or the purpose of their landings. But both were experienced hands and quite possibly had made good guesses.

By the morning of June 17, 1942, six months and six days after Adolf Hitler declared war on the United States, he had placed on enemy territory eight men skilled in the techniques of military and industrial sabotage, and with them the weapons and plans to mount a two-year program of destruction of essential war industries.

The relative ease with which eight fully equipped and thoroughly trained enemy agents were landed at predetermined locations on the American coast was, without question, a reflection of Germany's supremacy on the Atlantic in 1942, and of the seamanship of her submarine commanders. Yet the landings were only details, although important ones, in a bold and imaginative adventure meticulously conceived by a small group of men in the Abwehr (literally, Defense), the German Military Intelligence Corps.

This group, called Abwehr II, had practically created sabotage as a formal military discipline, and since September 1939 had been applying it effectively throughout most of Europe. Offhand, formal sabotage sounds like contradiction. Ever since an unknown Frenchman tossed his wooden shoe, or *sabot*, into an unfriendly piece of machinery, thus creating a certain amount of havoc as well as a new word, sabotage has been equated with spontaneous or improvised destruction. The idea of taking the haphazard out of sabotage by training men in its tools and techniques originated in Nazi Germany. By December 1941, when Abwehr II was called on to begin preparing a sabotage operation against the United States, the tools and techniques were ready.

There was no reason why they should not have been. As Germany under Adolf Hitler moved inexorably toward World War II, the officers of the High Command of the German Armed Forces had mastered the lessons of World War I with appalling thoroughness. Among other things, they had learned the value of sabotage, which had hampered their military and industrial efforts in that war. The activation of a special section of Military Intelligence, distinct from spying and concerned only with sabotage, was a natural step for the German Army.

Abwehr II was run by Colonel (later General) Erwin von Lahousen, an Austrian with particular talents for organization and intrigue, two essential qualities in a job of this kind. He was also a realist who recognized that, as another Abwehr officer had said, "the perpetration of any considerable act of sabotage on the enemy country is among the most difficult tasks of a secret service." Lahousen's standards for success were high. His fellow officer described them as secretly putting out of action an enemy mechanism or organization so thoroughly that "the extent of the damage done and the period which must elapse before it can be repaired are of decisive significance. Only when these two are of considerable proportions can it be said that an act of sabotage has had any operational value in the military sense or has been really effective from the industrial point of view."

Achieving Lahousen's standards was, of course, the goal of Abwehr II. At the working level, this meant assignments to destroy communications lines, basic industries, warships, airports and railroads. Each assignment had its own special problems; but each one also had a constant basic problem: the means of secretly getting enough explosives, and men trained in their use, to the objective. Abwehr II had solved these difficulties in the past, and its officers saw no reason why they could not again, even in a mission against the United States, which meant sending agents into a country three thousand miles away, in which it would be almost impossible to protect them.

The plans had to be made faster than Abwehr II may have liked; American sabotage carried a sense of urgency from the moment it was conceived, because the demands for action were coming from Hitler himself. He wanted to inaugurate a continuing reminder to the United States of its vulnerability to German power. In the overall German strategy for conquest of the West, such a reminder was needed at this time. In the little more than two years between Hitler's march into Poland and the Japanese bombing of Pearl Harbor, there had swiftly come to Germany the heady feeling that no goal was unattainable. On the Continent itself, the crunch of Storm Troopers' boots was a grating reminder to the defeated and a rhythmic chant to the victors of what had been accomplished by Hitler and his generals. Resistance movements had not yet attained the effectiveness which was later to slow the conqueror's march to total victory in France, Holland and Norway. Instead, there were mass arrests of Jews, Socialists, Communists, democrats, intellectuals and antifascists. While the concentration camps were being filled, and the enormous land gains consolidated, the Luftwaffe's bombs over Great Britain and the U-boats' torpedoes in the Atlantic were added evidence of Germany's superiority to the best its enemies could show. If progress on the Russian front and in Africa was perhaps not as swift as some had anticipated, this was no cause for alarm in late 1941; the spring and summer offensives would remove all doubts.

The actual entry of the United States into the war represented a new, if not totally unexpected or alarming, element. It was not assumed in Germany that this would lead to an immediate military clash; for one thing, the Japanese had forced America's attention to the Pacific. As far as Europe was concerned, it would be some time before the United States could do more than it had done while at peace, which was primarily to supply arms and equipment to Great Britain. A realistic sabotage plan had to take this into account. By design, and by the nature of sabotage itself, it would be both a military and a propaganda effort. A factory blown up in secret and put out of operation for months is a superb military achievement; it is also a propaganda victory. Carried out often enough, such destruction can cause the civilian population to doubt the capabilities of its leaders and, as Hitler had proved in the past, to accept the inevitability of defeat. A successful sabotage operation in the United States would be Germany's way of saying that, busy as it was, it had the means to injure at will, even from an overwhelming distance.

The quicker this was said, the more effective its impact.

Incredibly, Germany was without a single reliable agent in the United States when war was declared. Abwehr II had had strict orders to stay out of the United States during the years of uneasy peace. The German Foreign Office, on the advice of its American experts, had been responsible for this decision, which was based on the sound theory that whatever chance there was of keeping the United States from entering the war would be destroyed by the discovery of German-sponsored sabotage. Actually, Abwehr II did not altogether obey its orders; for a brief period it maintained a group in Mexico which claimed to be in constant communication with members of a pro-Nazi underground movement in the States who were ready to sabotage munitions factories and ships. But before Germany and the United States went to war the Foreign Office discovered the operation, and even this tenuous potential was disbanded.

Nor could Abwehr II use as sabotage agents the spies employed by Abwehr I—which had no restrictions on its spying activities in the United States—for the simple reason that they had been taken out of action. As the result of an amazingly successful roundup by the F.B.I. early in 1941, the most important German spies were in jail. The coup had been organized the year before, when a naturalized American named William Sebold returned from a trip to Germany and told the F.B.I. that he had been forcibly recruited as a spy. Under F.B.I. guidance, he continued that role—he was set up as a consulting engineer in the old Knickerbocker Hotel Building off Times Square in New York—and was able to bring thirty-three Nazi agents into a well-planned trap. The sudden loss of so many reliable men was one of the reasons why Abwehr II was under pressure to give priority to an American sabotage mission.

Although the demand for speed may have seemed excessive, because finding the right men was bound to take time, Abwehr II had all necessary facilities for the project. In the Berlin suburb of Tege, Abwehr II had established a laboratory where explosives experts experimented to find new and improved products in their own special line of business. In general, the installation resembled any up-to-date chemistry laboratory, its work benches crowded with retorts, Bunsen burners, Erlenmeyer flasks and test tubes, white-smocked men watching and making notes. But against one wall a large table seemed quite out of place; its display of suitcases, hair brushes, vacuum food containers, oil cans and cigarette lighters made it look like a counter in an American supermarket or drug store. All these objects contained samples of the laboratory's craftsmanship. Built into each one was a chemical or mechanical detonator, with an accurate timing device, a special explosive mixture or, quite often, both.

The Abwehr II experts were pardonably proud of their achievements and their ability to solve special problems. They had developed, for instance, a detonator which worked by air pressure and was especially useful in sabotaging aircraft because it could be set to go off only when a plane reached a specified height. Another one, which looked like an ordinary cigarette lighter, could be set for delays of as long as forty days.

The proper use of these and other weapons was taught by laboratory experts at Quenz Farm, the site of the Abwehr school for sabotage, forty miles west of Berlin. Quenz Farm had been the training site for a number of special projects involving pro-Nazi civilians of many nations, and the prospects of its use for an American assignment would not require any extra preparations. Here, too, Germans with language skills or foreign experience were trained in the techniques of military sabotage. Most of these men were used in variations of Homer's Trojan Horse, which after thousands of years is still the model for what the French call *ruse de guerre*. Disguised as civilians or, more often, as soldiers of the country scheduled for invasion, they would apply their learning to make things easier for the troops that followed them. Once an entire platoon in Russian uniforms, supplied with proper military paybooks and even letters from home, drove Red Army vehicles hundreds of miles behind the Russian front on a sabotage mission which made a major German advance possible.

With its laboratory and its school, all Abwehr II lacked for a proper start on the new assignment was a plan and the men to carry it out. German Military Intelligence knew with a fair degree of accuracy the location and importance of American factories, railroad lines, waterways and power installations; its experts could map a program which would keep the most ambitious saboteur busy for many months. As for manpower, it was available among the thousands of repatriated Germans who had returned from years of residence in the United States. Many had the proper requisites—they spoke English and had a wide knowledge of the country—and in a number of instances were indebted to Germany for their return passage. Nor would finding them be difficult. All returning Germans had to fill out forms which eventually reached the files of a variety of agencies, among them the Nazi Party's Ausland Institut. This was concerned with foreign countries, but more specifically with the Germans who had lived in them and had come back to the homeland. Its records had been used in recruitment for many Abwehr assignments. Now they would be studied again.

The man Lahousen selected to do the recruiting was named Walter Kappe. He was a loyal Nazi, of course, and he had lived in the United States for twelve years. He was familiar with the Ausland Institut records, and he was possessed of remarkable energy and intelligence. Kappe applied himself to his assignment with passionate vigor, and as he began choosing his men, the operation became his own creation. From the start, it reflected his personality and character.

Walter Kappe was just turning thirty-seven when he was put in charge of the sabotage operation against the United States, and it was by far the most important job he had ever held. He was not only aware of that but he also knew that its success would assure even greater responsibility and correspondingly greater reward. For Kappe, this was incentive enough. He was an ambitious man who had always fallen just short of the power he sought, and found it impossible to attribute his failures to his own shortcomings. In this he was one with much of his own generation of Germans, for whom failure was a commonplace that could be blamed on depression, inflation, Jews, foreigners or Communists. For these men, the Nazis held the promise of personal and national fulfillment. Unlike some of his contemporaries, though, Kappe did not allow himself to be swallowed into the anonymous legions of the Nazi bureaucracy. He had a taste for high living which could only be indulged by people of means or position, and he meant to have both. Although he was quite fat—he was five feet ten inches tall and weighed two hundred and thirty pounds—he considered himself rather rakish and something of a lady's man. Kappe's preoccupation with pleasures of the flesh was curtailed, however, when he took his new assignment, because it occupied nearly all his waking hours.

For the past twenty years, Kappe had lived as if to prepare himself for just such a position. In 1922, when he was seventeen, he had left the University of Göttingen to join the Deutsche Freikorps, the so-called Free Corps which was organized to fight Communists and ended up as the nucleus of Hitler's Storm Troopers. He was also for nine months a member of the Black Reichswehr, the illegal German Army which existed in defiance of the Versailles Treaty. Then, logically, he joined the newly formed Nazi Party.

This decision, like the ones that preceded it, kept Kappe in the mainstream of the rootless young men who came to the Nazis along the same unmarked road. With them he roamed the country looking for jobs, and when none were to be found sought trouble instead. The Germans called these roving bands the Wandervögel, Wandering Birds, a name which, in the Middle Ages, applied to young craftsmen who moved from town to town looking for work. The Wandervögel after World War I had nothing but the name in common with their predecessors. Few had skills to offer, and even if they had, there was rarely work available. They traveled in such large numbers that civic authorities were forced to house them to keep them off the streets, and their hostels became recruiting grounds for activists of the right and left. Communists fought nationalists with arguments and fists as both sought signatures for their membership cards. The Wandervögel hostels provided the first political lessons for many men who were later to hold responsible positions in the Nazi Party and German Government.

In 1923, when the Beer Hall Putsch in Munich failed and Adolf Hitler went to Landsberg Prison to dream and write of revenge, many Nazis temporarily laid aside their swastikas. Germany would be theirs one day, but for the moment they would keep their thoughts under cover and make do in the Germany that existed. This was not an answer for many young men and women; however bright the dream, each day's awakening to unemployment and worthless money was the reality. In the twenties, thousands of them emigrated to the United States. Walter Kappe, Wandervögel, Nazi, unskilled and jobless, was among them. In June 1924, he received a passport, and six months later he boarded the *S. S. Orduna* for New York.

In June 1925, Kappe was in Kankakee, Illinois, working in a farm implement factory. To his fellow employees he was a stubborn and bull-headed man, but also a lively one. He made a mark as a kind of shop cutup, taking great pride in being the first to tell a new joke and to know all the words of a new song. But factory work was not for Kappe, and by the end of the year he was casting about for something more suitable to his talents and disposition.

Journalism seemed made to order for him, and he wrote application letters to the German-language newspapers in Chicago. It is hard to see what qualifications he offered, but he was accepted at the Chicago *Abendpost,* where he fulfilled his reportorial duties with great energy, but in his own fashion. This often meant supplementing his wages by slanting stories for a price. His co-workers considered him completely unscrupulous. He also had a tendency, when drunk, to moods of petulance and strange assertions of superiority. He poured soda water into white wine to give the impression he was drinking champagne, and posed as a Prussian aristocrat, complete to heel-clicking arrogance. But these quirks were only expressed outside the office, and the *Abendpost* did not fire Kappe until 1930, when he wrote a crudely offensive article about a local Jewish businessman.

Kappe moved to Cincinnati then, and became active in various pro-Hitler groups. Soon he and his friends evolved the idea of a single national organization built along Nazi Party lines. The base for such a group existed in a national club called Teutonia, and late in 1932, Teutonia and the local pro-Hitler clubs came together under the name of Friends of the Hitler Movement.

In January 1933, the Nazis were no longer a movement but the German Government. That month, Kappe was among half a dozen Nazi leaders who called a convention of the Friends of the Hitler Movement in New York. There, with the swastika proudly displayed and the Horst Wessel song to provide the proper musical accompaniment, the name was changed to Friends of New Germany, and Walter Kappe was named Press and Propaganda Chief. Three years later the American version of the Nazi Party became the Amerikadeutscher Volksbund—the German-American Bund —and Fritz Kuhn became the American Fuehrer.

Kappe promptly made a strong effort to move in on Kuhn's position. As editor of the Bund newspaper, *Deutscher*

Weckruf und Beobachter, he had a unique forum to lead an attack on Kuhn, but an open declaration of war might have turned out disastrously. Instead, Kappe instigated whispering attacks against Kuhn. But Kuhn had the strength, and when the showdown came, it was Kappe who was forced to resign.

On June 12, 1937, he left the United States to return to Germany, where his American experience brought him closer to the eminence he sought. He was made propaganda director of Station DJB in Berlin, which broadcast to North and South America. When war came he served on the Rhine's West Wall fortifications during the Polish campaign and briefly, as a lieutenant of infantry, in the French campaign. By 1941, as many Nazis sensed that war with the United States was inevitable, a good deal of thought was given to the potential usefulness of Germans who had lived in the United States. The Ausland Institut had their records; what was needed most was a considered judgment of their talents for all aspects of the German war effort. This was a job made to order for Kappe. He loved to talk, and a large part of the work was addressing groups of repatriated Germans. He loved to plot, and when it turned out that he would be transferred to the Abwehr as a first lieutenant, he was certain he had come to his true career. When, late in 1941, he was given the specific assignment of finding and training men for sabotage in America, there was no question in his mind about his ability to do so.

Lieutenant Kappe maintained a small unit free of the usual military chain of command. He operated from a third-floor office at Rankestrasse 8, Berlin, under the front of a nonexistent publication called *Der Kaukasus.* Here Kappe kept his files, interviewed potential saboteurs, and worked on the innumerable details of his assignment. For one thing, he had to study existing reports on the United States, and in the course of this he became an expert on the Sebold affair. Kappe considered Sebold's defection and the subsequent loss of Abwehr I's American agents the result of an error in personnel management, which he did not intend to commit. And although Sebold had indirectly caused Kappe's promotion, the lieutenant's public expression was, of course, one of scorn for the traitor. He invariably referred to Sebold as "that son of a bitch" and on one occasion told friends that "there is no stone big enough for him to hide under." He added ominously, "We will get him." Kappe was aware that the Abwehr had to act quickly, but the memory of the Sebold case was a reminder to act carefully.

In making his plans, Kappe had the help of Abwehr technicians and experts on various aspects of United States industry, and together they compiled an impressive list of objectives to guide the men Kappe was about to recruit. Foremost among the railroads selected to be crippled was the Chesapeake and Ohio—an astute choice, since the line is one of the leading coal carriers in the United States. Damage to bridges, tunnels or major switching points along its lines would delay production in the steel mills and war-material plants to which it hauled coal from the mines of West Virginia and Pennsylvania. Still, although destroying transportation facilities was important, damage to a basic industry was even more desirable. Kappe and the experts chose light metals, the key to American airplane production. The specific targets were three plants of the Aluminum Company of America at Alcoa, Tennessee, Massena, New York, and East St. Louis, Illinois, as well as the Philadelphia Salt Company's cryolite plant in Philadelphia, which supplied important raw material for the manufacture of aluminum. Information about the best ways to cripple the aluminum works came from an engineer who had toured them not too long ago as an official representative of the I. G. Farbenindustrie.

One other kind of sabotage was planned: scattered nuisance bombings which Kappe expected to have a great propaganda impact. For these the policy of Nazi anti-Semitism was the controlling factor; bombs were to be placed in department stores owned by Jews, and timed to create the greatest possible panic. Kappe also suggested the locker rooms of major railroad stations for similar bombings, but a series of explosions aimed especially at American Jews struck him as particularly appropriate.

The sense of humor for which Kappe was noted in Kankakee showed in an inspired flash of irony when he chose the code name for his project. He called it Operation Pastorius, after Franz Daniel Pastorius, the leader of the first community of immigrant Germans in the United States, thirteen families of Mennonites and Quakers who settled in Germantown (which is now part of Philadelphia) in 1683. The humor may not have been understood by all of Kappe's

21

colleagues; nevertheless, Pastorius became the official name of the sabotage operation in the spring of 1942, when Kappe was preparing his own group of immigrants to land in the United States.

Chapter 2
Most Likely to Succeed

The eight men who changed from German Navy fatigue uniforms to American civilian clothes on barren beaches those two mornings in June 1942, performed the simple act with a profound sense of relief and achievement. Relief at having survived the Atlantic crossing, achievement at having completed the last leg of what was, for each of them, a return trip to the United States. It was not a homecoming in any sentimental sense. None of them had ever expected to see the United States again, although three had ties in the country which could be called emotional; one had a mother and father in Chicago, one a mistress and a wife in New York, the third had sisters and a brother. All had left the United States for Germany in ways which indicated to Walter Kappe, as he narrowed his list of choices for Operation Pastorius, that their fidelity was to the Fatherland and to Hitler. They were back on American soil with crates of high-powered explosives and efficient detonators, and the plans to use them, because Kappe, who prided himself on his knowledge of men and their capabilities, had found them the best qualified for his purpose.

Kappe began his recruitment by screening the Ausland Institut records carefully, then designating candidates for personal interviews. Sometimes he traveled great distances to meet potential recruits. He often went in civilian clothes on the pretext of delivering morale speeches to repatriated Germans in war factories, but he always found time for confidential talks with one or two men. Some of the men he sought were already in Berlin; others were called from other cities to the offices of *Der Kaukasus*. Once he made a choice, Kappe had to proceed through Nazi Germany's bureaucracy to transfer the men to his unit. He got men released from service on the Russian front, from work benches at Volkswagen and other war-production factories, from guard duty at a prisoner of war camp, from war-supporting civilian jobs in Berlin. That he was able to do this was an indication of the importance which the High Command attached to the sabotage project.

It was not, however, as easy to find the right men as Kappe had expected. Many Germans had left the United States simply because they were misfits, which made them useless for this operation. For every one who came back because of a strong sympathy for the Nazis and, after 1939, a sincere desire to help Germany win the war, there were hundreds who just wanted to leave a strange country and regain the warmth and familiarity of a now prosperous homeland. For every one who had traveled widely in the United States, or had lived among native Americans, there were many more who had never moved out of Yorkville, the German-American neighborhood in New York City, or a similar close-knit community. But in spite of these personnel difficulties, Kappe found twelve men to take the sabotage course at Quenz Farm.

A variety of circumstances was to cause this number to be reduced to eight, and in this final group, differences in personality, temperament and intelligence were obvious from the start. At the same time, they had a great many things in common, most of which had provided the basis for Kappe's choosing them. All were young; at thirty-nine, George John Dasch, already slated to lead one of the landings, was the oldest; Herbert Haupt, a tall, broad-shouldered twenty-two-year-old, was the youngest. All had lived in the United States long enough to be familiar with American customs and manners; Dasch had been there nineteen years, Haupt from early childhood. All of them had been in many parts of the country, so their knowledge of America was not limited to just one city or a section of it. Each spoke English fluently, although some had German accents stronger than Kappe might have liked; yet he could reassure himself that in most cities of the United States an accent was not necessarily a liability. Each man had a trade in which there were many job opportunities and an itinerant tradition; they could find work wherever their assignments carried them in the United States. All of them had at least the equivalent of a high-school education and the intelligence to absorb rudimentary chemistry lessons. And the records of all of them had been carefully examined for Nazi loyalty.

If among these eight, and the four others who did not get

to the United States, there were men who lacked imagination, Kappe was not necessarily dismayed. For this operation some followers would be needed, men who were short on original thought but long on loyalty. It would be up to Dasch and to Edward John Kerling, whom Kappe selected to lead the second group, to make the actual sabotage plans from his outline, and to see that the others carried them out. As it happened, Kappe had less trouble finding leaders than followers. Both Dasch and Kerling were in Berlin, and eager for the assignment.

Kappe had met George Dasch in June of 1941, months before he was recruiting for Operation Pastorius. Dasch was thin-faced, underweight, with premature flecks of gray in his black hair and abnormally long arms for his five-feet, eight-inch body. On the basis of what he knew of the man's background and personality, Kappe was impressed enough to remember him when he was needed. Dasch had two qualities which fascinated Kappe and which he could not help finding irresistible—a glib intelligence and the manners of an American. During his nineteen years in the United States, Dasch had worked as a waiter, and had taken the opportunity to observe and imitate those surface characteristics of Americans which are exhibited in public places. Most of that time his ambition had been to become part of the life on the other side of the lunch counter or at the elegantly set dinner table, the waited-upon instead of the waiter, and he watched and heard and remembered the gestures and the language of those he envied. Although Dasch had worked at some rather exclusive resort hotels and some expensive restaurants, he retained best such expressions as "scram" and "blow my stack," "snooks" as a term of endearment, and a few tired phrases that he misused—as "a sight for sore eyes" to describe someone whose clothes were torn and disheveled. Kappe could not have noticed such lapses since his own years in the United States had been mostly among German-speaking residents. Dasch's seeming ease with English and his familiarity with many American cities and towns, including Long Island resorts, were desirable qualifications. Furthermore, Dasch's files at the Ausland Institut and his work in Germany since his return gave evidence that he was first-rate material for Operation Pastorius.

Behind those qualifications and files were a number of misrepresentations and omissions. Dasch was a strangely complicated man whose life up to now had been one of unfulfilled aspirations. He firmly believed the best things in life were, or ought to be, free. This had not turned him to crime; rather, his was a consistently immature inability to connect his actions with their consequences, and he was, therefore, invariably confused and irritated when the bills fell due. An early example of this occurred when he was sixteen years old, and had already tried and abandoned studies for the priesthood. In December 1918, a month after the Armistice, Dasch was discharged from the German Army, in which he had served as a clerk for the last year of the war. He returned to his home town, Speyer am Rhein, and became an interpreter for the French Army of Occupation, a job which became increasingly difficult as antagonism grew between the townspeople and the troops. Quite understandably, Dasch sided with his countrymen in most disputes; quite understandably, the French resented this. "The French were trying to put me in prison for my activities," he recalled, as if the action were that of a heartless and uncomprehending parent, "and I was forced to flee."

The flight brought him to unoccupied Germany for the next few years and to jobs as he could find them. They were scarce, and in 1922 he stowed away on a ship bound for Philadelphia. For the next five years, in New York, he had the dregs of the jobs in hotels and restaurants—fry cook, busboy, soda fountain clerk—eventually reaching the status of waiter. In 1927, though, he felt, as did so many others in the year of Charles Lindbergh's dramatic achievement, that his future lay in aviation. He applied for work at the Curtiss plant on Long Island but was turned down. Whereupon he joined the Army Air Corps. Dasch's length of service was exactly one year, one month and ten days. He then bought his way out, an accepted procedure in the prewar Army, and was given an honorable discharge with a character rating of excellent. During his hitch he saw Brooklyn, the Panama Canal, San Francisco and Honolulu. But he did not learn to fly. He left the service on the West Coast and became a waiter in San Francisco and then night manager of a hotel in Sacramento. There he took flying lessons at a local airport, but soon became disillusioned at his prospects. The self-discipline and the cost of getting in the flying hours necessary for a pilot's license were more than he could manage. From

Sacramento he moved to the Biltmore Hotel in Los Angeles, and then back to New York and another series of hotel and restaurant jobs.

About this time Dasch began to feel that, after all, he might not be destined for anything more in the United States than a life as a peripatetic waiter. In 1930, he had saved enough money to make a two-month visit to Germany in the spring, to help finance his brother's trip to America, to get married in the fall and then go to Europe again, this time to take his wife on a five-month tour of Germany, France, Switzerland, Italy and Austria. Whatever the United States had failed to fulfill of Dasch's vision, it had provided him with more material reward than most people had at the time. Yet it rankled that his lot was not much better than that of a servant and that most of his income was determined by the whim of a paying customer. "I was never satisfied," he said of this period. "I hated the tipping system and felt it was degrading."

The sense of degradation prodded him to seek a way out once more. Marriage, too, had brought with it an ambition to settle down and to become an American citizen. His wife, Rose Marie Guilli—whom he never called anything but Snooks—was from western Pennsylvania. She was a hairdresser who had also done her share of wandering from job to job and who now wanted nothing more than a fixed residence.

Dasch became a salesman for the Mission of Our Lady of Mercy in Chicago, selling sanctuary supplies to Catholic churches and institutions in Belleville, Peoria and Springfield, Illinois. He moved to a St. Louis suburb and was ready to enter the mainstream of the American middle class. But the manager of the mission was fired, and the new manager brought in his own salesmen and, Dasch said, "found ways and means to bring my work to an end."

Dasch and his wife returned to New York and its hotels and restaurants. He made no more attempts, in this country, at least, to break out of the only occupation at which he could earn a living.

Notwithstanding his disappointment in the United States, Dasch completed his requirements for citizenship in June 1939, and was supposed to go to court in September for the final swearing-in ceremony, which he said he had been "dreaming and hoping for" during his years in America.

When his name was called, Dasch was not in the courtroom for the simple process of achieving that dream. He was doing his best to get to Nazi Germany—to see, as he said later, if he could find there the dignity and pride in work which had eluded him in the United States.

The precise steps which led to Dasch's sudden change would be hard to determine under the best of circumstances, and he never made them clear. Until the summer of 1939, he said, he had felt that the Nazi movement consisted of the "old militarists and supernationalists" who had once brought Germany to war and defeat; he had watched "with sorrow" as Hitler took power. Then his mother came to America to visit, and he turned to her to confirm his views. "To my surprise," he said later, "my own mother even praised the work of Hitler. . . . I said to myself that perhaps I had been wrong all along; perhaps I had a prejudiced mind that had been closed to the truth." His mother returned to Germany in August. When war came on September 3, Dasch had made up his mind to go back, too.

Then, in 1940, Dasch was surprised, as he had been in the past and would be again in the future, to learn that there was a price to be paid for his decision; he had to register as an alien. He was dejected. "It was a private insult," he said, "and only my wife could soothe my hurt feelings." After all, "I still felt like an American even if I hadn't gone through with the final legal formalities." Whether it was the Alien Registration Law and its effect on his pride, the years of waitering, mother love, a new-found patriotism or the promise of Hitler, Dasch now put all his energy into returning to Germany. With a persistence he had not shown in his previous efforts at breaking out of his waiter's uniform, he began to pester the German Consulate in New York. "Several times a week I checked . . . to see where I stood," he said. "Each time they always told me I was still on the waiting list. But I kept after them. I was anxious for the trip." One day a consulate employe told Dasch that a reason for the delay was that he was not known as a Nazi. "That," he says, "got my fighting Dutch up. I went to Washington to the German Embassy and stated my claim there." What arguments he used to prove his fidelity to Hitler are not known, but "after prolonged cross-examination, it was proposed . . . that I return to New York and await further developments."

The wait was not long. In December 1940, he was called

to the consulate. What he had said, and what the German Embassy had written, must have been impressive. About the middle of January he and his wife received German passports. She was eager to make the trip with him but because of the Neutrality Act could not get an American passport for travel to a war zone. A few days later Mrs. Dasch became quite ill, a matter which caused Dasch some concern but which did not turn him from his intense desire to get to Germany. For the rest of January and early February, Mrs. Dasch was bed-ridden. In mid-February, Dasch brought her to the Bronx Hospital for a hysterectomy. There were complications, and the recuperation period was a long one. On March 21, Dasch visited her with the news that she had only one more week in the hospital, and when he returned home that evening a telegram was waiting; he was to report to the German Consulate as soon as possible. He was there before it opened the next morning. His sailing orders were ready; he was to take a bus that evening to San Francisco, where he would board the Japanese liner *Tataku Maru*. The speedy turn of events did not confuse Dasch at all. "I thought of my wife in the hospital," he said, "and at the same time I also remembered the hell I had raised with the Consul for the chance of going home. So, therefore, I reached the quick decision to sail."

The day was spent getting the proper papers from the German Consul, the Japanese Consul, the shipping line. He sent telegrams to his sisters and brother to meet him at his older sister's house. He urged them to "go to Snooks at the hospital the next day and explain the circumstances of my sudden departure." He did not find the time to make a fare-well visit or telephone call. His brother drove him to the bus terminal, and at six-thirty Dasch was on his way to Germany. The real sense of leaving America did not come until a week later, though, on March 27, when the *Tataku Maru* passed through the Golden Gate: "I said goodbye not only to San Francisco, but also to a country with its people who had been kind, good and understanding, but also on the other side, cold and rude to me."

After the ship left Honolulu some of the more ardent Nazis began to organize programs of songfests and propaganda speeches. "I naturally joined them," Dasch once said. "The whole business was distasteful to me," he said another time. Whatever course he followed, he did recall that some pas-sengers beat him up for having his hands in his pocket while everybody raised theirs to heil Hitler. He also says that he was reprimanded by a self-appointed trial board and told that he would be reported in Berlin. There is no evidence that any report was made. It is also conceivable that the incident never took place; one of the passengers did not remember it at all, and Dasch later exchanged letters and Christmas cards with most of the passengers, which would indicate a fairly harmonious relationship.

The ship reached Yokohama on April 11. The next day, by train and ferry, the travelers moved westward, joined by Germans from Japan, China and other Far East points. By the time they reached the Manchurian-Russian border, there were a hundred in the party. On May 13, 1941, they arrived in Berlin, which was reveling in German victories. Flags fluttered from all public buildings, and Berliners, especially those in uniform, laughed easily on the streets and in cafés, restaurants and night clubs. For most of the Germans from abroad who entered the city that day this was the end of a long journey, and so it must have seemed to George Dasch. But its consequences were still to come; for him the arrival in Berlin was a beginning.

The newcomers were assembled in the ballroom of the Russische Hof Hotel. After the welcoming speeches, which hailed them as heroes for having returned to the Fatherland in its time of need, paper work dominated the day. Endless forms had to be filled out, for the Ausland Institut, for the Gestapo, for the rationing board, the local police, the Foreign Office. Dasch, quite naturally, though with a boldness he had not often shown, lied about his experiences in the United States. After all, he was in Germany to improve his place in life. There was no mention of his occupation as waiter; instead he had been a salesman for an export-import company and had secretly provided Germany with many commercial benefits. He did not have to exaggerate his travels in the United States, of course.

Dasch got no immediate indication as to how well he had completed his forms. Like the other repatriates, he was given twenty-five marks and told to report within two weeks to the Ausland Institut. He spent the time visiting his family in Speyer. There was a letter from his sister in New York telling him that Snooks had sailed April 26 on the Spanish liner *Marquise de Camille*. (She never did arrive; the ship was stopped by the British and its passengers were interned at Bermuda for the duration of the war.) Dasch did some checking on his wife's whereabouts, but his prime objective was the right kind of job. In his search he ran into the bureaucratic walls of Nazi Germany, and came early to two conclusions: "that you have got to know someone if you wish to go somewhere," and "it was a great handicap to me that I was not a member of the party."

Logically enough in a country at war, he sought a place in the military. Apparently he was beginning to believe his new account of his life, for he seems to have offended a colonel in the Third Army at Wiesbaden with his ideas of what he considered a rightful place in the service. "What do you think," the colonel asked, "we fry an extra fish for you?" Dasch put this down as a sign of the obtuseness of the military mind and decided to try Dr. Joseph Goebbels' Ministry of Propaganda. To an officer in the American Division he bluntly announced that Nazi propaganda in America was all wrong and that, from his knowledge of the country, he could put it right. The officer politely suggested that there was, perhaps, something for him as an interpreter in the Army.

Dasch was disappointed, but he remembered that a cousin of his had married a man named Reinhold Barth, who was working as an Army interpreter. Barth directed Dasch to a Nazi Party office, where at last he found a sympathetic audience and was given a letter to an officer at Army headquarters.

"When I reached that office," Dasch said, "I was told that this officer was not with the General Staff any more and for that reason I could not have entrance to the building . . . after much pleading, he asked one of the noncommissioned officers to take me to the fourth floor to a certain room. When we got there, we were told that the officer we were supposed to see had moved and no one could tell us where.

"So this noncommissioned officer told me that he would take me back downstairs again. So I asked him kindly to give me the letter for a moment. At this very moment I stood in front of a door and knocked at the door and walked right in and closed the door behind me. A staff officer with red stripes, I think he was a colonel, approached me and asked me what I wanted. So I told him that I had a great deal of trouble getting in there and that I was anxious to get the contents of this letter known. I requested him to open the letter, which he refused, for the letter was not addressed to him. I begged him to do so and finally tore the letter open and handed the letter back to him so that he could read the contents. After reading it, he merely said to me, 'Come right in, old man.'

"Outside the noncommissioned officer on the door stood shivering. The staff officer advised him to go right back where he came from and took me into the office of a Captain Spies. There I was treated very cordially. After he read the letter, he requested me to sit down and smoke a cigarette and he cross-examined me as to what I knew about America . . . I was then requested to return the following day . . . to meet the person who handled the cases of this office for the United States."

Dasch must have seen his triumph in grander terms than the Army did, but the next day, June 3, 1941, he did meet Walter Kappe. After a lengthy interview, Kappe decided that Dasch's American experience, or rather, Dasch's version of it, was worth keeping on tap. Kappe had the influence, and used it, to place Dasch at Sonderdienst Seehaus, which monitored foreign broadcasts. For the next six months Dasch listened to American news broadcasts, which he translated into German for distribution to government officials. He was "quite pleased" at the lightness of his tasks, the pay and the extras, and perhaps most of all, the status he had acquired. "I did not suffer under the Nazis at all," he said. "In fact I was sitting pretty." This comfortable posture lasted until December. Dasch had been in touch with Kappe off and on during this period at the Seehaus, but now there came a message from his sponsor, freighted with mystery and intrigue, and including a statement for Dasch to sign, pledging himself to secrecy about all that he would soon be told.

Kappe was starting to recruit for Operation Pastorius, and George John Dasch, whose American manners and speech had impressed him so, was his first choice. At the end of February 1942, Dasch was transferred from the Seehaus to Abwehr II.

Kappe did not meet Kerling, who was to lead the Florida section of Operation Pastorius, until March 1942, but when he did he was immediately impressed with Kerling's strength of character and his intense loyalty to the Nazi cause. In eleven years in the United States, Kerling had not once been tempted to apply for American citizenship. Although he worked as a domestic in fashionable homes, he had made no effort to acquire the smoothness of American speech or manner which Dasch cultivated. Kerling was thirty-two, strong and well proportioned—about five feet, nine inches and a hundred and seventy pounds—and had the kind of masculine good looks the Nazis thought were an Aryan monopoly: brown, wavy hair, which he parted in the middle; heavy brows over calm gray eyes; and an ingratiating smile. His intelligence—his almost immediate comprehension of the problems involved in Operation Pastorius—made him one of Kappe's favorites from the start.

Kerling was born in Wiesbaden on June 12, 1909. By the time he was ready to enter Freiburg University, he was one of Germany's disaffected youngsters who were turning in increasing numbers to Hitler's National Socialism. He became a member of the Nazi Party in June 1928. For the rest of his life, this early show of allegiance was to give him the special status which Hitler bestowed on the so-called Old Guard, the first hundred thousand members of the party; Kerling's membership card was numbered in the seventy thousands. In some cases, as in Kerling's, the early joiners were later rewarded with inexpensive medals and jobs in the regime's sprawling bureaucracy, but at the time he signed up his immediate satisfaction, aside from attending meetings and taking part in street fights, was the uniform in which he could strut for his last nine months at Freiburg. In March 1929 he suddenly left the university and came to the United States, but he never gave up his party membership. He arranged with friends in Germany to pay his dues regularly, which, until the Nazis actually took over Germany, was a strong expression of faith.

Under the circumstances, the reasons why Kerling remained in the United States as long as he did are as obscure as his reasons for coming at all. Certainly the jobs he found were not such as to compel enthusiasm. He spent two years at his first place of employment, a Brooklyn packing company, where he smoked hams. This was balanced, nicely enough, by two years as a shipping clerk at a Jewish-owned packing company in Manhattan which did not handle ham. He was still working there when he married Marie Sichart, a native of Munich who had gone to the United States in the mid-twenties. She had worked as a cook in a number of households and evidently had not given much thought to German politics until she met Kerling. Not long after they were married, though, she too became a member of the Nazi Party. The political union joined, the Kerlings decided to seek employment as a couple, he as butler or chauffeur, she as cook. To acquire experience, he drove for Ely Culbertson, the bridge expert, for a short time. This was followed by an equally brief period as chauffeur for a wealthy manufacturer with homes in Mt. Kisco, New York, and St. Petersburg, Florida.

Then the Kerlings found jobs together in expensive suburbs of New York—Greenwich, Connecticut, and Short Hills, New Jersey—but they learned almost immediately that politics was not enough to keep them bedfellows. Petty bickering led to noisy quarrels. They just "couldn't get along," Mrs. Kerling said later. They did not divorce, as Kerling wished, but did go their separate ways.

In 1936, Kerling visited Germany for a month to see the Olympic games, which some Germans in America seemed to consider a personal triumph for Hitler; entire delegations of Bundists attended them.

When he came back to the United States, Kerling met a young lady who was to give him, for a while, the illusion of love which he did not have at home.

The beginnings of the affair are not quite clear. Abigail Johnson* was a New Englander who visited Germany as a tourist in the thirties. She was not a Nazi, nor even sympathetic to the party, and it is hard to see what she and Kerling had in common. Yet there was something romantic about his appearance, and the fact that he was married may have added a fillip of excitement. Miss Johnson's family objected to Kerling, but this did not stop them from seeing each other. She permitted him to cut, and keep, a lock of her hair. He apparently promised that he would get a divorce and marry her. But the Kerlings never divorced, and the romance ran its course, ending on a bitter note. Miss Johnson accused Kerling of giving her the "runaround," and he departed. She seems to have recovered from the emotional wounds more rapidly than he. A few years later she was married, while he was still writing her long letters recalling their times together as an "outstanding point in my life amongst you Americans."

* *This is not her real name. To use it now would be a disservice; she was not involved in the sabotage plot.*

The phrase "you Americans" is significant. Kerling was always the stranger in the United States, and when, soon after he and Abigail Johnson parted, he did find a woman to share his bed and his hopes, she was of German parentage. Her name was Hedwig Engemann, and she was working as a waitress in Miami early in 1940, when Kerling arrived there in a particularly unhappy frame of mind.

The fall before, just after the war in Europe began, Kerling and several friends had decided to dash to the aid of Germany, and had bought the yawl *Lekala,* anchored in Baltimore, for the bargain price of less than $2,000. As they were sailing her to New York, the Coast Guard intercepted the *Lekala* off Atlantic City. In view of the American Neutrality Act, there was certainly ground for suspicion. The *Lekala* was ordered to proceed to the Coast Guard station on Staten Island, where Coast Guard, F.B.I., Immigration and Customs officials searched her for possible violations of the law. For three weeks, while the Nazis fumed and threatened, the *Lekala* was held at Staten Island. Finally the boat was released, but on condition that she be sold. Kerling decided to sail her to Florida for disposition, whereupon the Coast Guard ordered that the *Lekala* report to every Coast Guard Station between New York City and Miami, a procedure which alone would have discouraged the most reckless of adventurers.

Not all of the *Lekala*'s crew was that reckless. When the Coast Guard held the boat for nine days at Wrightsville, North Carolina, two of the men decided to return to New York. Early in January, the *Lekala* arrived in Miami with some rather dispirited sailors, who now began to defect one by one. One of the last to leave was Herman Neubauer, a former cook and a loyal Bundist.

Kerling remained, though he was dispirited too; instead of dashing to Germany, he had had to proceed at a snail's pace to Miami, harassed by government officials and newspaper headlines.

The boat market was not booming at all that year, and it was not until May that Kerling finally found a customer. For most of that time he had the *Lekala* to himself. But he was not lonely after he met Hedy Engemann, who came to the boat with him their first evening together and, by her own account, "every day, practically" after that. Hedy fell in love with Kerling and was not at all distressed that her lover was married. For four months they enjoyed the Florida climate, the comforts of the *Lekala*, and each other. In these circumstances, Kerling's strong urge to return at once to help his country in its hour of need weakened. Finally, at the end of April, with the sale of the boat imminent, Hedy decided to go back to New York and wait for Kerling. He followed a month later.

Perhaps the pleasures of life with Hedy reminded him of the earlier romance; or it may have been guilt. In Washington, on his way from Miami to New York, he took time to write Abigail Johnson a long birthday letter. The letter is a strange mixture of lies, half-truths, self-pity, rationalizations and Nazi sentiment. It was, like the others he wrote her, probably an accurate reflection of his feelings—especially his political ones—at the time. But before he could discuss politics, he had to reassure Abigail about his feelings for her. "After all," he wrote "you haven't been to me just another girl. If so I would not write you. . . . I would give a lot to know what you are doing, to know that you are happy. I don't want to bring back unpleasant memories, Abby, but there has been a time when we both have been very happy. I haven't been it since."

After these expressions of his warmed-over emotions, Kerling managed to convey the Nazi version of the war. "We know we have to fight in Europe," he said, "not for the fun of it, but to live, not to save some sort of government or some ideals. It's just for room. You may not understand this here, and it looks like America once more wants to save English 'democracy' which at present, is more brutal as dictatorship in Russia. Abby, let us hope we don't have to fight each other. In any case don't let us hate each other, even in war. Well, Abby, the last eight months haven't been any too peaceful for me. . . . I haven't done a stroke of work all this time just using all my time to find a way out, in order to get home to help my country. So you see, at present, I am not as carefree as usual."

Whatever he had been in Washington on June 4, the day he wrote that letter, he was carefree by the time he was back in New York the next day. At least he was as far as Hedy Engemann was concerned. She had found a job as waitress at the New York World's Fair and was happy to spend all her spare time with Kerling. Nor did the presence of Mrs. Kerling in New York upset the arrangement at all. In fact, when Kerling told her that he had taken a mistress she did not particularly object but seemed to consider, in view of what had happened to her own feelings about him, that it was perfectly proper for him to do so. Thus from the time Kerling returned from Miami in early June of 1940 until he boarded the *S.S. Exchordia* for Germany late in July, New York had its compensations for him.

In Germany, his low-numbered Nazi membership card helped him get a job without delay. He was sent to an Army listening post in Deauville, France, where he translated English-language broadcasts into German. It was a short-term project, and in three months Kerling was back in Berlin, this time in the Ministry of Propaganda as the stage manager of theaters which produced the frequent propaganda-filled shows which Goebbels felt were the proper entertainment for German audiences. The job demands could not have been heavy; Kerling had time to write long letters to Abigail Johnson, to Hedy Engemann and to his wife.

For eighteen months Kerling managed his theaters, and, as he wrote to Abigail Johnson in December 1940, he was "very happy to be home again during these great times." The German soldiers were invincible, he said, and "here in Berlin you would not know that we are in a war—even I have been surprised when I returned. . . . You have been in Berlin in peacetime—it has not changed much and the occasional visits of British planes don't worry anybody. We know we have not started the bombing of civilians, the English did it for months. . . . I have a very interesting job here at present. But I burn to get back in the Army again."

Although she responded with the news that she had married, Kerling wrote again a few weeks before Germany and the United States were at war. "Don't think for a minute that we here are foolish enough to condemn you all in a— bunch. . . ." he said. "We know the power of propaganda well enough to know that you are at present only prey of a small group of Jews. The time will come when you once more find out that you have been fooled into a war which is not yours. . . . I only hope—and for your sake, Abby, I wish that this awakening won't be too hard for you. . . . You have no idea in America what your soldiers would have to put up with. I know America well. I know what you can put up against us, but please believe me, Abby. I feel sorry for the American soldier, for your brother, if he should have to fight against the German Army. . . .

"I am here in Germany and doing my duty. . . . I haven't had one minute of regret. . . . We sacrifice for a better future which Germany has deserved. Our young soldiers who have fallen on the fields in Russia have paved the way for a better world, perhaps for you too. . . . I hope you will be spared the worries of having your husband or your brother in the field. This is my wish for your Christmas, Abby. I want to see you happy and laughing as I remember you ever."

Kerling's own unique part in paving the Nazi way for a better world was only a few months away at the time he wrote. In March 1942, Walter Kappe came to visit Kerling at his office in the Propaganda Ministry, and they talked for about two hours. Kerling had not met Kappe in the United States, though he had been vaguely aware of him as a Bund official. In Berlin there was no mistaking Kappe's authority. He knew about Kerling's activities in Germany and in the States as well. Among other things, Kappe asked Kerling if he would like to return to the United States. This was a stock joke among many Germans who had returned from America, to which the stock response was yes. It was a safe reply because it was always assumed to be a form of humor and even those who meant it, which in Nazi Germany was treason, could say it with complete safety. Kerling played the game; he answered yes.

A week later Kappe was back, and this time his questions were more pointed. When Kappe specifically asked whether he would take part in a military mission to the United States, Kerling's immediate response was affirmative. "I couldn't say no," he later explained. "It would look like I was a coward and tried to stay in a place where I could earn money while the others are fighting." From Kappe's circumspect discussions, Kerling had the impression that Operation Pastorius was to be in the nature of a commando raid and carried out in Army uniform. This was an appealing idea.

Kerling had tried hard to return to Germany, when it seemed to him all loyal Germans must, to find his duty and to serve his nation. His duty actually found him, and for a while, at least, Edward John Kerling was doing what he most wanted to do. On the basis of his known ability and his past records, he was one of Kappe's happiest selections.

Those two, then—Dasch, who had returned to Germany almost on impulse, and Kerling, who had wanted so desperately to return because he had to stand on the side he had long ago chosen—were the men Walter Kappe trusted most with the mission he was directing. On them, more than on any of the others in Operation Pastorius, would be the responsibility for its success or failure. Under the Abwehr system of training they would now begin to work and live closely with the men whom they were to lead back to the United States.

Chapter 3
Campus on the Farm

Quenz Farm, the school which matriculated Kappe's men for an intensive training course in sabotage, had been a rambling and rather luxurious German farm owned by a wealthy Jewish shoe manufacturer. Under Abwehr supervision, it had become an efficient, if somewhat incongruous, military campus. Its isolation, and the innocent appearance characteristic of farms, especially old ones, made it ideal for projects that had to be carried out in secrecy. Quenz Lake, for which the farm was named, lies in a wooded section of countryside outside Brandenburg, a German city of no particular distinction except that it is the capital of the Prussian province of the same name, which in turn has been immortalized in the title of the six concertos Johann Sebastian Bach dedicated to the Duke of Brandenburg in 1722. The gate to the farm was a good fifteen-minute walk from the Brandenburg bus line's last stop, itself well beyond the city limits. The main farmhouse, a solid, two-story, twelve-room stone building—so well appointed that one of the new arrivals was convinced that it had been a country club—stood more than a hundred yards from the gate and a high stone wall which faced a narrow dirt road. The other buildings—a barn, a garage, two smaller houses for farm workers and their families, a greenhouse and some scattered sheds—were more or less grouped to the side and rear of the main house and were barely visible from the road.

To a passing German—a hiker, say, from Brandenburg— the picture could only have been one of pastoral serenity. The illusion would have been heightened, especially after the years of tight rations and ersatz diet, by the reassuring farm sounds and smells which carried to the road. Cows, pigs, chickens and ducks roamed the grounds of the Quenz estate, and so did the children of the tenant couple who maintained the livestock, the greenhouse and a small vegetable garden. But behind the stone wall soldiers stood on guard each day; and at night, when the noises had subsided and rural calm had set in, a sergeant in civilian dress patrolled the property with a sawed-off machine gun on his arm and three well-trained and extremely vicious German shepherd dogs by his side. Although the sabotage school was, as a high Abwehr officer has said, "completely hidden from the outside world," no one was disposed to take unnecessary chances.

The vast fields of the estate, most of them long since fallow, were ideal for the kind of training the Abwehr sponsored. On them had been constructed bridges of various styles and materials and lengths of railroad tracks, and there was room to spare for rifle and pistol ranges. The men in Operation Pastorius were not expected to use the latter except as extracurricular activity, but when they arrived the bullet-splattered targets still held the evidence of previous students' marksmanship, or lack of it. The lake was available for training in boat handling and a nearby airport for practice in parachute drops, but Kappe's class used the lake only briefly and the airport not at all. A makeshift gymnasium on the ground floor of one of the smaller farmhouses was equipped with parallel bars, weight-lifting devices, a boxing ring and a few wrestling mats for training in judo, and a nearby field was used for group calisthenics, soccer matches and hand-grenade throwing.

The floor above the gymnasium was divided into a lecture room large enough to hold twenty men and an instructor, and a laboratory which was quite adequate for its purposes— the theory and structure of explosives, fuses and incendiary bombs and a study of the techniques of invisible writing. The main farmhouse was an excellent dormitory which included a recreation room and ample dining facilities, enough for officers and men to eat separately. The students were assigned downstairs rooms; instructors and the sergeant who acted as night guard lived upstairs. The greenhouse and the gardens supplied the class with fresh fruits and vegetables and occasional flowers to brighten the dinner tables. The garage and storage buildings were not used, at least during this three-week period. No cars were kept on the premises, but there were a few bicycles for the men to pedal along the country roads on their Sundays off, looking, as far as anyone could tell, like so many farmhands enjoying their time away from the fields.

All in all, the farm at Quenz Lake was its own natural, thus perfect, disguise for the unique institution it had become. By the time Kappe and his students arrived to employ its facilities it had the fresh-scrubbed but well-worn look of an established college welcoming classes at the start of a new semester.

Kappe had been purposely vague in his interviews with most of the men, so that—except for Dasch, who had worked with Kappe since March—none of those who came to Quenz Lake had a clear idea of why they were there or whom they would meet. They started to arrive on April 7, 1942, the Tuesday after the long Easter week end. At the end of the week, Kappe, his twelve students, two instructors and an assistant from the Abwehr laboratory in Berlin, and four observers—two from the Army and two from the Navy—were in residence. Not until Sunday evening, when the men were assembled in the farmhouse after dinner, did Kappe actually use the word "sabotage." By that time it may not have come as a complete surprise to his audience. There certainly could not have been any doubts left by Monday morning, when the men attended their first classes in the theory and practice of explosives.

The twelve students were divided into four-man teams that morning. Besides Dasch and Kerling, Kappe named as group leader a man whom everybody called Dempsey, at his own request, because he had been a boxer in the United States. After only a week, Dempsey was called away to train a German middleweight for a forthcoming match with an Italian, and Kappe indicated to the others that he would be sent to the United States in the fall with another group. The men hated to see him go; he had made the off hours pleasant with detailed accounts of his boxing career, which appeared to be one spectacular success after another, and with stories of famous fighters, all of whom were deeply indebted to him for their proficiency.

Dempsey's stories had provided almost the only light moments, because the Quenz schedule, under Kappe's direction, was an arduous one. Reveille sounded at 7:00 A.M. for calisthenics until seven-thirty, when beds were made and rooms put in order. Breakfast lasted from eight to nine, but it was not as leisurely as the hour would indicate. During that time, each man had to read an American publication and talk about its contents. Nearly current issues of *Life*, *Collier's*, the *Saturday Evening Post*, the *New York Times* and the *Chicago Tribune* arrived regularly. They were not only sources of information about the United States but also represented an unspoken assurance that Germany still had friends there who could get this material abroad without any trouble. Kappe insisted that all conversations at the school be held in English, except for those with the two explosives experts, Dr. Walter Schulz and Dr. Helmuth Koenig, who could speak only German. After breakfast came three intensive hours of classroom lectures, laboratory work and applied study on the equipment scattered around the fields of Quenz Farm. This was followed by lunch and another hour of reading. The afternoons were given over to more class work and to the sports program, and most evenings to long sessions, led by Kappe and Dasch, on American slang, recent American laws and news events, and the lyrics of standard American songs.

At least two evenings a week Kappe accompanied his students to a country tavern a few miles from the farm. It was not unusual, as they walked down the deserted country road, for all of them to break out into "The Star-Spangled Banner," "Oh! Susanna" or any one of a number of old favorites whose words one of the men recalled. At the tavern Kappe kept his own drinking to a minimum in order to watch the effect of alcohol on the others. It was his practice, after the men had a number of drinks, to suddenly ask sharp questions about what they had learned in class or about the fictitious autobiographies they had started to rehearse. Most of the men held their drinks well, or at least did so when they realized what Kappe was doing.

Classes were conducted by two superbly talented men. Drs. Schulz and Koenig had achieved recognition at the Abwehr laboratory for their work on a number of tiny but effective exploding devices and for their development of simple formulas for explosives and time fuses made from ordinary materials. Schulz and Koenig alternated their class work; Schulz specialized in practice, Koenig in theory. Both men, with Kappe, directed field exercises in the proper placement of the explosives in tracks, bridges and towers. The laboratory assistant to the two doctors was an elderly man, whose name nobody ever caught, who prepared the materials for each lesson and cleaned up afterward with the unobtrusive efficiency of a family retainer.

Koenig started with basic chemistry, but taught no more than was essential to the understanding of explosives and incendiaries. The first classes were devoted entirely to incendiary mixtures and methods of igniting them. The students learned that a combination of Chile saltpeter and sawdust, or one of aluminum powder and plaster of Paris, made effective incendiaries. All that it took to set them off was a fuse consisting of a tablespoonful of a mixture of potassium permanganate, flour and sulphur. Altogether, Schulz and Koenig explained four simple formulas for light-burning mixtures, which could be ignited by a simple match or fuse, and three for hard-burning mixtures which required special fuses. The charm of all these mixtures was that the materials to make them were readily available at nearly any drug store.

Early in their studies it was impressed on the men that sabotage most often requires the saboteur to be some distance from the scene of his work at the precise moment of its success. Toward this end they were to be supplied with the most efficient mechanical and electrical timing devices the Abwehr laboratory had developed. But since theirs was also a long-range program in which they might not receive fresh supplies, the students were given thorough instructions in making their own chemical and mechanical fuses. Again the emphasis was on the use of common materials. Some of the devices had the flavor of macabre Rube Goldberg inventions. One consisted of a glass test tube half filled with dried peas over which water was poured nearly to the top. A loose cork disk with a brass screw in its center attached to a piece of wire was floated on the water. Another cork with a brass screw in its center and a groove for the wire to pass through was then fitted to the open end of the tube. The wire from the inner cork and one from the screw in the outer cork were then run to an electric battery. The expansion of the peas caused by their soaking in the water forced the floating cork toward the one in the neck of the tube. When the brass screws met, an electrical contact was made. Under Schulz's tutelage the men were able to work out accurate time schedules based on the size of the test tube, the number of peas and the distance between the two corks.

An almost childishly simple method was used to ignite a mixture of calcium chlorate and powdered sugar, which in turn fired both light-burning and hard-burning mixtures. For this a small medicine bottle half full of sulphuric acid was capped with a piece of paper held securely in place by paraffin. When the bottle was inverted, the sulphuric acid ate through the paper and fell to the ignition mixture, causing it to burn. Time was controlled by the kind of paper used to cap the bottle. Ordinary bond paper was good for four to six hours, a post card for ten to twelve and a playing card for up to twenty-four hours, long enough for the slowest man to be far from the scene. In practice, the ignition mixture was put inside an ordinary paper bag which was partially buried in the burning mixture. The inverted medicine bottle was then tied inside the mouth of the paper bag.

Another device was based on the principle of land mines. This consisted of a piece of rubber tubing the diameter of garden hose and three-quarters of an inch long. At each opening were fixed metal plates which were soldered to wires leading to an electrical connection. Between the two plates rested an ordinary thumbtack. Pressure on the top plate immediately caused contact to be established. The men learned that this device was especially effective under rugs, in a door jamb and in elevator shafts.

All told, ten homemade fuses were explained. Koenig carefully drew the designs on the blackboard, listing the ingredients and each step of the process while his chalk kept pace with his words. The men were encouraged to take notes and copy the blackboard illustration. Then they walked next door to the laboratory, where under Schulz's direction they built the devices and experimented with time-control variations. Before the students left the laboratory, the two doctors walked among the men, gathered all the notes they had taken and solemnly burned them. It had been impressed on the students from the first day that they had to memorize their lessons.

Fuses, however well designed, are but the means of setting off an explosion or fire at the target selected for sabotage. When satisfactory progress in the making and use of fuses was evident, the two professors turned with obvious pleasure to the use of explosives. Power lines, railroad yards and factories presented separate problems; how much of a given explosive to use and where it was to be placed for highest effectiveness under varying circumstances called for special instruction. Schulz and Koenig devoted these classes to an explosive of their own invention, because it was the one the men would carry to the United States in large quantities. It was a stable material which came in yellow brick-size blocks that looked very much like something manufactured by modern toymakers to bring out the creative instincts in children. The stability of the explosive was such that it could be dropped, cut, hammered, burned or drilled full of holes without going off. Only a special detonator, which itself required intense heat, caused it to explode.

The form of this explosive most favored by Drs. Schulz and Koenig was chipped and painted black so that it resembled a lump of coal. A cavity held the detonator. The disguise was almost too good; it had once been the cause of embarrassment to Abwehr II. For months after the war began, British merchant ships had refueled at the Bulgarian port of Varna on the Black Sea. Abwehr agents there decided to mix some of their own lumps of exploding coal with the stock that the British normally purchased. This was a fairly simple accomplishment; when it was done an Abwehr agent remained near the docks to see the coal poured into the hold of the next British ship to arrive. The captain of that ship was not in desperate need of fuel, however. He examined the Bulgarian coal and decided it was of too poor a quality for his boilers. Soon after he left port, an Italian freighter entered and her captain, obviously less choosy, agreed to buy the lot of coal. The Abwehr agent, realizing what was happening, dashed to friends on the Bulgarian Security Force and confessed what had been done. He managed to stop the sale, and thus save a friendly vessel and his own face, but the cost was an exorbitant price for several tons of Bulgarian coal.

It is unlikely that the men at Quenz Farm heard this story, since they were being groomed for success, not failure, with this explosive. Its possibilities, as explained and then demonstrated by Schulz and Koenig, were impressive. In time, the men became as fond of the pieces of coal as their inventors. One day, in conducting lessons on the best way to blow up railroad tracks, the professors took one group to a field where a length of track had been laid out. A piece of the coal bomb weighing less than two pounds was then set off. It blew away a large piece of rail and left two twisted ends pointing grotesquely upward. Schulz and Koenig closed the day's lesson by showing how a simple mine device could set off the detonator when a train ran over the track. They also explained that since two pounds was sufficient for a steel rail, less was needed for wooden objects, more for heavier steel targets. An expert saboteur, they added, did not necessarily seek complete destruction of his target; in many cases, weakening it to the point of uselessness was more effective.

Testing under conditions simulating those in the United States took the place of written examinations. From time to time during the day, and often after dark, individuals or teams were given written instructions to destroy or weaken certain structures in the fields. Schulz, Koenig and Kappe acted as guards. The men had to find the objects—wooden posts buried in the sand or iron tracks hidden by vegetation—bypass the guards, examine the wood or metal to decide whether it required an explosive or an incendiary, determine the precise amount needed to do the job efficiently, and get away safely. They were then graded on the plans they suggested for destroying the target.

By the end of the first week most of Kappe's students were showing a decided talent for their studies. Two, however, did not. One man who had been assigned to Dasch, and who made so little impression on the others that they could only remember his nickname, Scotty, was a heavy drinker. Another, Ernest Zuber, who had been in Dempsey's group, had arrived at Quenz Lake directly from ten months on the Russian front. He seemed to be still shaken from his battle experience and found it difficult to concentrate. Scotty and Zuber showed such consistent inability in the classroom and in field tests that Kappe had no choice but to dismiss them.

With their departure, and Dempsey's, the two remaining men in Dempsey's group—Heinrich Harm Heinck and Richard Quirin, two stolid machinists—were simply put under Dasch. Kerling's group—which included Herbert Haupt, the youngster of the enterprise; Werner Thiel, a machinist; and, by coincidence, Hermann Neubauer, Kerling's old fellow sailor from the *Lekala*—remained intact. Although Dasch's team was now five men, Kappe was not disturbed. He had made another decision, in which the extra man was to play an important role. Kappe now planned that when these two groups, and those scheduled to follow, were established, he would go to the United States himself to direct all sabotage personally.

Kappe may not have had official approval for this; his immediate orders were to carry out Operation Pastorius. Yet, given his ambitions, the prospect of supervising from Chicago a vast sabotage underground against the entire United States was a stirring one. Success in such an effort would, after the ultimate victory of the Third Reich, bring rewards ample even for a man who once aspired to take over the German-American Bund.

To prepare the way for his eventual American leadership, Kappe chose one of Dasch's men, Ernest Peter Burger, a stocky, flabby man who had been a Storm Trooper. In addition to his responsibilities for sabotage, Burger was to establish a front in Chicago, either as a commercial artist or as a violin instructor, for both of which he considered himself qualified, and to indicate his address with classified advertisements in the *Chicago Tribune* on the first and fifteenth of each month. There was an assumption that the *Tribune* would be received regularly by the Abwehr and that this method of communication would be continuing notice that all was well when Kappe was ready to leave for America.

The other men were told about Burger's front and that it would serve as a central communications point when necessary, although not all of them were aware of its significance to Kappe's future plans. Some of them were dismayed that Burger was to be responsible for their safety. In their first week at Quenz Lake, the men had begun to learn about each other, as well as about sabotage. What they had come to know of the man they called Pete Burger did not evoke the same trust that Kappe so patently gave him.

Before he was enrolled in Operation Pastorius, Burger had been a prisoner of the Gestapo for seventeen months. His fellow students knew this, and it seemed logical to them that Burger would carry a grudge which might one day hurt them. They did not understand what Kappe and Burger knew so well: the Gestapo and the Army, especially Army Intelligence, were bitter rivals; the enemy of one was the friend of the other. The feud between the Gestapo and Intelligence was undoubtedly the most intense of the many which went on within Nazi Germany. The two groups had drawn an agreement—rather scornfully called the Ten Commandments by both sides—which established the Abwehr's responsibility in Military Intelligence and the Gestapo's in civilian activities, but the Gestapo, under Heinrich Himmler, ignored the agreement. Before the war ended Himmler took over Military Intelligence, and until he did so, he encouraged the friction between the two agencies as a means of achieving his ambition. Army ordnance experts, for instance, were not permitted to study parts of the bomb which was recovered by the Gestapo after the Munich Beer Hall explosion in November 1939, in which Hitler and other party leaders were nearly killed.

Quite often the rivalry manifested itself in public, to the entertainment of many Germans, most of whom hated the Gestapo. Open display of friction by shouted insults and fist fights was considered a bad example to the German people, and dance halls and other public places frequented by one side were put off limits to the other, but this did not prevent brawls. At a Berlin night club one evening in May 1942, two Luftwaffe officers, each wearing an Iron Cross, asked the band leader to play an American tango. Dancing had hardly started when a civilian walked over to the band leader, flashed a Gestapo badge, and ordered him to stop playing an enemy song. The frightened musician pointed to the Air Force heroes. As the Gestapo agent walked grimly toward their table, the two officers rose, shouted the room into silence, and announced that they were about to throw out a "Gestapo rat." They did so with great ceremony and to the applause of the audience, after which the band struck up the tango again, to more cheers.

Under conditions which gave rise to such quarrels, Burger's persecution by the Gestapo all but guaranteed his loyalty to the Abwehr. He also had a great deal more to offer. At thirty-five, he could show Nazi credentials unmatched by anyone connected with Operation Pastorius, even Edward Kerling, the veteran of nearly twenty years' party service. Burger had been an active participant in Hitler's first attempt to seize power, the Munich Beer Hall Putsch of 1923; his membership in the party was almost as old as Hitler's, and he was proud of it. As far as he was concerned, his later problems with the Gestapo were not the fault of Hitler or of Nazi principles, but of certain evil men—businessmen and profit seekers, as he described them—who had perverted the aims of the original revolution. He never lost faith that Hitler and the Nazi Party would return to those earlier, and to him nobler, principles.

When Burger joined the sabotage training program he was not at his physical peak. In his Storm Trooper years his face had had a taut grimness; now, though he was not quite fat at a hundred and fifty pounds and five feet, eight inches, his facial muscles had begun to soften and there was a puffiness under the eyes. In the twenties he had alternated studies at a technical school with street fighting, at which he was adept. In late 1926 or early 1927, after a particularly bloody battle, it seemed appropriate that he leave Germany for a brief period. The Bavarian courts had been dealing rather lightly with Nazis while harshly punishing their opponents, but he may have been too zealous a brawler even by Nazi standards. Whatever the reason, he applied for a visa to the United States, where he arrived in February 1927.

For the next six years he worked in various machine shops in the Midwest, joined the National Guard, first in Michigan and then in Wisconsin, studied English privately and at night schools, and became a United States citizen. The only break in his residence came when he returned to Germany in the summer of 1929. Whether the prospects of Nazi victory seemed bleak or he was still considered too troublesome is not clear. He did not stay long. Back in the United States there was work again, and the pleasures of drilling with National Guard, and once, helping to break a milk strike in Racine, Wisconsin, which may have been exhilarating to an old Storm Trooper. But the depression brought layoffs, brief jobs on a road gang, and then no jobs at all. Soon after Hitler took over, Burger's parents wrote him that he could now return to Germany in complete safety. They sent him money for a ticket, and in the fall of 1933 he was back home, back in the Nazi Party and, better yet, appointed aide-de-camp to Ernest Roehm, who was then, and for a few more months, Hitler's closest friend and chief of the Nazi Storm Troopers.

This high estate ended violently in the blood purge of June 30, 1934, when Roehm and his key subordinates were killed. Before the purge ended most of those who were identified with Roehm were dead, many of them suicides. Burger escaped because a few days before the fury erupted he had been lent as aide-de-camp to the chief of the Medical Division of the Storm Troopers, who for some reason was allowed to live. But the party's Old Guard was in disgrace and those who were linked with Roehm underwent a long period of degradation. One night a passing S.S. man shouted an insult at Burger, who promptly shot him off his bicycle.

Despite his relationship with Roehm and his bravado about it, Burger survived, although in a position of less importance than he had held before the purge started. He was assigned to a minor post in the party's domestic propaganda division in Berlin, but a good mind—and a faith that the purge represented only a passing phase in Nazi development—brought him greater responsibility. To help him do his new job better he signed up for courses at the University of Berlin, where he came under the influence of Professor Karl Haushofer, the father of geopolitics, which gave a specious intellectual justification to Hitler's land grabs. Haushofer had become a favorite of Rudolph Hess and of Hitler himself, and he took a "fatherly interest in me," as Burger said. A week after he graduated, in July 1939, Burger married his secretary, and not long after that he was assigned to do a study on Czechoslovakia for Haushofer. His confidential report was passed on to Hess himself. The report, whatever it contributed to geopolitical theory, contained some uncomplimentary observations on Gestapo activities in Czechoslovakia, but it was well received by Burger's mentor. In November 1939, he was assigned to do a similar report on Poland, which by then was under German domination. He was more diligent than before; after sending back one confidential report, which must have been seen by the Gestapo, he found a growing lack of cooperation among Nazi officials in the conquered nation. On March 4, 1940, he was arrested.

Among other charges, he was accused of falsifying government documents. It was enough to keep him in Gestapo hands, theoretically pending trial. Either the Gestapo was too strong or Burger's friends in power could not reveal their association with him. At any rate, no one came forward immediately to get him out of trouble. Eventually some pressure was brought and the charges against him were dropped, but, presumably for the sin of getting caught, he was not returned to Haushofer's good graces. In July 1941, he was a private in the Infantry, guarding Yugoslav and British prisoners of war outside Berlin.

But a man with Burger's intelligence and connections among high party officials could not be kept in such a subordinate position for long. When Kappe came across his name on a list of Germans who had lived in the United States, Burger's future was determined. In February 1942, Kappe interviewed him, and early in April, Burger was released from guard duty and on his way to the sabotage school at Quenz Lake. It was not the appropriate reward for a man of his devotion and service to the Nazi Party, but it was far from the death or disgrace which had come to many of his friends who had also been caught in the crossfire of party battle. It was, in a sense, his chance for redemption, away from the Gestapo, away from those he felt had betrayed his revolution.

Most of Burger's colleagues were unsophisticated in the ways of the Nazi regime. Even after Kappe addressed them on the depths of Gestapo-Abwehr animosity, and cited their instructor Dr. Schulz as having undergone as degrading an experience with the Gestapo as Burger, they could not see why Burger should want to work for Germany. Dasch accepted him most readily. But Burger, the disciplined Nazi, found Dasch overtalkative, inattentive at class and altogether too lackadaisical as a leader. They worked closely, but no friendship or real trust developed.

After the final grouping was fixed, Dasch's unit worked quite apart from Kerling's, except during sports and calisthenics and occasional field problems which required the participation of all students. Thus the members of one group did not have a chance to become well acquainted with members of the other. In addition, soon after the men arrived, Kappe had started to rehearse them in the aliases and fictional life stories they would use in the United States. Before the course was well along, the men were not only calling each other by their aliases but had, for the most part, forgotten the real names of all but one or two friends in their own group. Such friendships were formed swiftly. Some were based on common experience; Heinck and Quirin had been recruited together from the Volkswagen plant in Braunschweig and had both been in the German-American Bund, although not in the same chapter, in New York. One pair renewed an old friendship; Kerling and Neubauer were glad to see each other again. Dasch and Werner Thiel, a machinist in Kerling's group, had met on their trip home via San Francisco and Yokohama. Kerling befriended Thiel, who was the most slow-witted member of his foursome, and Thiel became quite dependent on his leader. Neubauer and Thiel, like Heinck and Quirin in Dasch's group, were of the *lumpen*, the clods which had moved or been moved with millions like themselves to an acceptance of Hitlerism with all its excesses.

As these relationships grew, two of the nine students went their own way socially. One of these was Joseph Schmidt, a freebooter by conviction. He had been assigned to Dasch, but it was soon apparent that he was not one to take orders, because he considered himself a leader of men, and that he did not think highly of Dasch. He once told Burger that Dasch would have to be killed in the United States if he did not show that he was more than just a favorite of Kappe's. Schmidt had left the Rhineland in the midtwenties and for fifteen years had farmed, fished and trapped by himself in Alberta, Canada, and supplemented his income by selling wood alcohol to local Indians. It was the kind of free life he enjoyed, but it ended when Canada went to war. Late in 1941 he was back in Germany. Except for his independence, Schmidt seemed to be a promising student, even though Kappe rejected as impractical his suggestion that he go on his own to start forest fires in Canada.

The other lone wolf was not one by choice, but because he was isolated by the developing pattern of friendships. Herbert Haupt, the tall, broad-shouldered young man in Kerling's group, was gregarious by nature, but he had unwittingly offended by his youth, his extraordinary good looks— Burger said he had "Greek classical features"—and a tendency to show off by wearing flashy jewelry and using a lot of American slang. The others thought him too frivolous for a project as serious as this, and it was hoped, even suggested, that Kappe not send him to the States. Kappe invariably replied that Haupt's physical capacities—he was a muscular hundred and ninety pounds and nearly six feet tall, and had had boxing lessons—made him an asset, and that it would be up to Kerling to control him. Kappe's defense of him did not help, and Haupt found himself isolated.

The feeling that Haupt would not make an altogether trustworthy associate, especially in difficult situations, was warranted. The logic which moved Haupt from Chicago to a school for sabotage in Germany is of the kind that reaches its highest form of expression in the children's game in which one box, when opened, reveals another box which in turn reveals another, and so on to the tiniest box of all, which does not open. For Haupt the progression began as simply as opening that first box. It is doubtful that any of the other men gathered at Quenz Lake could have summed up their reasons for leaving the United States as forthrightly. "I was associating with a girl named Gerda Stuckmann," he said, "and my folks objected to my going with her, and her folks objected to her going with me, because I was younger, and she became pregnant and I didn't know what to do, so I talked to two friends of mine and left for Mexico." Haupt was only twenty-one at the time, and Gerda Stuckmann Melind had been a widow for four years. He was also scheduled to register for the draft. Nothing made more sense than Mexico.

Up to the time of these problems, life had not put too many demands on Herbert Haupt. He was born in Stettin, Germany, on December 21, 1919, and was brought to Chicago when he was five. At ten he became an American citizen by virtue of his father's naturalization. He went to school the required number of years, did not show any special talents or aptitudes, and quit high school in his sophomore year to work as an optician's apprentice at the Simpson Optical Manufacturing Company, where he worked diligently, if without distinction, for two and a half years. When his problems came to a head, his closest friend, Wolfgang Wergin, who worked with him at Simpson's, decided to make the trip with him. Haupt told his mother, who was ill and in a hospital, that he was going on vacation, and told Gerda Melind that he was taking a short trip to California. On June 16, 1941, with about eighty dollars each, Haupt and Wergin got into Wergin's 1933 Chevrolet and drove south.

In Mexico City they found, to their surprise, that as foreigners they could not get jobs without work permits. They wandered aimlessly and watched their money dribble away (although sometimes it was more than a dribble; Haupt could not resist buying an oversized silver ring decorated with the Mexican eagle which opened to reveal a tiny box). About three weeks after they arrived they met a man named Hans Sass, who seemed full of information and sympathy for two all but broke Americans of German descent. Their new friend suggested they move to his rooming house, and then introduced them to an official from the German Consulate. It apparently did not occur to Haupt or Wergin that, as American citizens, they could have sought help at the American Embassy. When the German official suggested that there was work for young Germans in a Japanese monastery and that the Consulate would pay their fare, it seemed a perfectly natural thing to accept the offer. On July 26, Haupt, Wergin, Sass and a dozen other Germans from several Central American countries departed for Yokohama. Another box had opened for Haupt.

The monastery turned out to be a labor camp, and Wergin and Haupt, used to working conditions in a modern American shop, were dismayed at what they saw. For the only time in their strange voyage, they rebelled. After a few days the German officials abruptly told them that they would have to earn their living and that, as a matter of fact, there happened to be a German liner at Kobe, where they could learn to work as seamen. "There wasn't anything else to do," Haupt recalled. "We would be vagrants in Japan; we could not get any more money." Wergin and Haupt, among others, took a three-week course on the liner.

Not long afterward, they were put aboard a German freighter, and learned that it was bound for Germany and they were expected to work their passage. Haupt did duty as an oiler and as a lookout in the crow's nest. Shortly before reaching France, he sighted a British naval blockade and his warning enabled the vessel to run past it safely.

Haupt and Wergin arrived at Bordeaux on December 11, the day Germany declared war on the United States, and German officials kept them aboard ship for three days. When it was decided that they represented no danger to Germany, Haupt and Wergin were given a pass to Paris, and after further questioning were shipped to Saarbrucken. At last they were permitted a certain amount of freedom. Wergin went to some relatives in East Prussia and Haupt to his grandmother's at Stettin. He was reconciled to the fate which had brought him there, and even somewhat pleased; he now considered becoming a pilot in the Luftwaffe.

But that turned out to be considerably less easy than his coming to Germany in the first place. The Gestapo was not entirely convinced about his story, which sounded too naive to be true. And, as in Mexico, Haupt found he needed a work permit before he could look for a job. In March he received a medal and commendation for successful blockade running, and a few days later a letter from Walter Kappe, who identified himself as editor of the magazine *Der Kaukasus*. Kappe suggested that Haupt come to Berlin to discuss an article about his trip to Germany. Haupt borrowed train fare from his relatives; it was the first chance he had been given to earn some money. Kappe got Haupt's story of the trip and a good deal more. Two weeks later, Haupt was recalled to Berlin. This time Kappe turned the conversation to Haupt's problems in Germany, the continued questioning by the Gestapo, the difficulties in finding work. Then Kappe "pointed out that the only thing left for me to do was to return to the United States and I agreed with him." Nor did Haupt disagree when Kappe indicated that certain unspecified duties for Germany might be expected of him in the United States. Once more Haupt went back to Stettin. At the end of March he was told to report to Kappe's office after Easter, and this time to bring all his belongings with him. Within a few days, Haupt was on his way to Quenz Lake. He had come a long way from Chicago and Gerda Melind's trouble.

The men's personal relationships—or lack of them—did not affect their work at Quenz, where they operated as teams to Kappe's satisfaction. Only once did he find a reason for a change in plans. Early in the course it had been decided that the men should be trained in the assembly and handling of collapsible boats, which they would use for the landing in the United States and keep for future needs. Most of the men were landlubbers and had no enthusiasm for this part of their training. They had seen the high surf on the Atlantic coast and were not at all sure that Quenz Lake presented the same problems. Kappe dismissed the protests; the boats, he said, would be easy to navigate on the surf when the weight of the explosives and other equipment was added to the weight of the occupants. Then one day, for no apparent reason, a collapsible boat holding Kerling and Haupt split in two on the lake. The sight of the two men floundering in the water, unable to swim in their heavy uniforms, made Kappe relent. Kerling had the presence of mind to pull off his boots and trousers, but Haupt nearly drowned, and by the time Kappe and others reached them in another boat, the two men were blue with cold. That evening Kappe went to Berlin. He returned the next day to announce that the Navy would land the men with its own boats and sailors, and that if sabotage in America required work on water the problem would just have to be solved as it came up.

The decision was in keeping with what had been stressed throughout the training—self-preservation as a basic principle of sabotage. On the theory that he who misses and gets away will live to hit another day, the emphasis in classrooms and field tests had been on sound planning and the proper use of the timing devices. It was also the reason for a concise, but thorough, indoctrination in secret inks the day before classes ended at Quenz Lake. The safest way of communication was by regular mail and with invisible writing. Like the incendiaries, explosives and fuses, the secret inks were based on simple, available ingredients. Laxatives, aspirin, cigarette ashes and glycerin were the bases for most of them, or for making the writing visible when needed. The simplest method of all required no special formula. A piece of paper was thoroughly soaked in water. The excess water was run off and the paper was placed flat on a glass surface. On top of it was put a dry sheet of paper. A letter was then written on the dry sheet with a normal black pencil with pressure enough to reach the wet sheet. The dry sheet was then destroyed and the wet one allowed to dry, after which a camouflage letter was typed on it. When the sheet was immersed in water again, the original penciled letter appeared.

The men were fascinated by the seeming magic of words appearing on blank sheets of paper, and the day spent practicing with different inks was more carefree than usual. It also marked the close of basic training at the sabotage school. On Wednesday, April 29, the men were started on their final examination, a twenty-four-hour field test of the knowledge they had gathered since their arrival. In addition to Kappe, Schulz and Koenig, the Abwehr sent fifteen additional officers as observers.

The nine men now left of the original twelve knew that failure here would remove them from Operation Pastorius. As they received their test instructions in invisible ink from Kappe at noon, none was predisposed to fail.

They were placed in groups of two or three for the final examination. The targets varied for each group; after reading their instructions, the men were to proceed to the assigned site after dark, determine the best means for its destruction, go to the laboratory to prepare the fuses and explosives needed to do the job, return to the site and place their charges where they would do the maximum of damage. Land mines which set off harmless firecrackers were distributed throughout the fields; others, to trigger tear gas bombs, were placed in the rooms of some of the targets. The observers acted as guards and were supplied with firecrackers which they were to explode if they caught any of the students in obvious errors.

It was a grim game. Burger and the would-be lone wolf Joseph Schmidt worked together to destroy an imaginary oil tank which for purposes of the test was placed in the cellar of one of the farm buildings. They were among the high scorers who managed to place their explosives without being seen and without stepping on a mine. Others were less fortunate. Heinrich Heinck set off one firecracker and was immediately besieged by more gleefully thrown by the acting guards. One man was overwhelmed by tear gas as he entered the house he was supposed to blow up. Dasch and Richard Quirin were seen by guards as they started to place a carefully prepared fuse made from a watch, its timing nicely controlled for a fixed hour by dry cells. The fuse was so well made that the accident of their being seen was not counted heavily against them.

All in all, the test was considered a successful demonstration of the men's ability to use the tools and methods of modern sabotage. One of the purposes of the test was to determine the men's reactions in a sustained effort, and all had performed well; even those who had been observed or had stepped on mines had reacted coolly under the guards' simulated attacks. On May 1, as his graduates left Quenz Farm on furlough before the final phases of their preparation, which would take place in Berlin, Kappe was satisfied that the Abwehr's school for sabotage had produced nine men fully capable of carrying out Operation Pastorius. He agreed with Dr. Schulz, who had proudly announced, "Never since the school started have I had a bunch so eager."

Chapter 4
Postgraduate Course

The furloughs were generous, considering that they followed just three weeks of work; Dasch and Kerling were told to report back to Kappe in Berlin on Monday, May 11, the others a day later. Kappe needed these ten days to attend to the inevitable problems involved in transporting his group from Berlin to the United States, but the men were not aware of what form their final preparations would take, nor of the details of the trip in store for them. They were delighted with the vacation and took it, each in his own way, to round off as best they could the lives they had made since returning to Germany.

Dasch visited his parents in Speyer and restrained his normal loquaciousness; he did not talk about his assignment, but said he was being transferred to Chile. He wanted the days to pass quickly; he was eager to go back to Berlin and get on with the project. Schmidt made a brief visit to his parents near Cologne but returned to Berlin early to enjoy its night clubs and the women who frequented them. Kerling visited his parents in Wiesbaden, but not altogether happily; he had growing doubts—not about the assignment, its goals or his own ability, but about the quality of some of his colleagues —and he wanted a chance to discuss them with Kappe. Peter Burger spent his vacation with his wife; he told her he was going to the United States, but nothing about what he would be doing there. As added insurance against a future that would be uncertain at best, he taught her one of the methods of invisible writing he had so recently learned and gave her a password by which she could recognize a genuine message from him. He also saw her moved from their apartment in Berlin to his parents' home in Bavaria. Young Haupt had none of Burger's concerns for either the present or the future. He visited his grandmother in Stettin, loafed, and returned to Berlin ready for more high adventure.

The remaining four men, of whom Kappe expected nothing more than ability to follow their leaders, had no strong emotions about their assignments. They did as they were told, as they must have done all their lives. If any of them was aware that this vacation might be the last with his family he did not show it. Heinrich Heinck and Richard Quirin returned to Braunschweig, where their wives and children still lived in the government-run housing unit of the Volkswagen plant. Quirin moved his wife and daughter to the home of his parents-in-law, and told his wife he had been called by the Army. Heinck also saw to his family's comfort. They both returned to Berlin to rejoin Dasch's unit with a lethargy which was characteristic of them.

These two men had led such similar lives that it is easy to see why they became friends. Both had attended trade schools and become machinist's apprentices. In 1927, when jobs were increasingly scarce in the Berlin area where he grew up, Quirin went to the United States on money borrowed from an uncle. That same year, Heinck, working on the Hamburg-American Line's *S.S. Westphalia* as an oiler and machinist's helper, jumped ship in New York. They each remained in America for twelve years.

Quirin did so legally, first at the home of another uncle in Schenectady, New York, where he worked as a tinsmith, studied English at night school, moved on to the maintenance department of General Electric, and applied for American citizenship. With the depression he was laid off at General Electric, and he wandered to New York City, where he worked as a house painter and discovered Yorkville. Here it was easy enough to forget the difficulties of a new language and the desire for a new citizenship. In time, when the German-American Bund was formed, Quirin joined and found some comfort in the uniform of the Ordnungs Dienst, the Bund's version of the Storm Troopers. When he heard that Germany was paving the way back for those who wanted to return, his German-born wife was homesick, Hitler was in power and the promise of the Third Reich was high. In 1939, he was a machinist at Volkswagen.

Heinck, whose stay in America was illegal, remained in New York and rarely left the company of other German nationals, even at work, as he progressed from busboy to handyman to elevator operator and finally to his own trade as machinist. He, too, found gratification in the uniform of the Ordnungs Dienst and in the stirring speeches on German nationalism. When noncitizens were ordered to leave the Bund, he continued to attend its social functions, and applied for membership in the Nazi Party in Germany. He also took advantage of Germany's offer to pay his passage early in 1939, and later that year found himself at a work bench next to Quirin's.

When Kappe interviewed both men on one of his talent hunts for the sabotage mission, he was impressed by their knowledgeable, uncomplicated approach to their work and their stubborn devotion to duty. They did not strike him as likely to let their imaginations carry them beyond the job at hand. And there was no question of their devotion to the Nazi Party. Two months after Kappe had spoken to them at Braunschweig, their papers were being processed for transfer to the school at Quenz Lake. They made the trip together and, not surprisingly, arrived at precisely the time they were supposed to, the only members of the whole group to do so.

Hermann Neubauer and Werner Thiel were the other two men who gave Kappe the feeling that he had done well to balance his groups more or less evenly between individualists and those who would work with them. These two members of Kerling's group were as eager to obey orders, to please their superiors, and to forgo responsibility as Quirin and Heinck. Like them, they had absorbed the lessons at Quenz Farm thoroughly and unquestioningly, and like them had dutifully seen to the care of their families, and returned to Berlin for the instructions still to come. They were essentially the same kind of men, the ballast in Kappe's operation.

Neubauer had gone to the United States in 1931, when he was twenty-one. He had had some training as a cook and found employment in restaurants and on ships, but did not stay very long in any single job or city. In 1934 he worked in concessions at the Chicago World's Fair and in several hotels, became a member of the Bund, and later of the Nazi Party. In 1939 he joined Kerling in his efforts to sail the *Lekala* to Germany. After that, he worked in hotels in Miami and married Alma Wolf, a German-American girl he had known in Chicago. When they went to Germany in 1940, Neubauer was drafted almost at once. Three days after Hitler's invasion of Russia, an artillery shell exploded near Neubauer's billet and embedded shrapnel in his face and leg. The doctors removed as much of the shrapnel as they could, but the pieces over his right eye were too close to the brain to risk an operation and the others were not considered serious. He now carried a metal fragment as big as a lima bean in his cheek and smaller scraps in his forehead and leg.

In March 1942, at a medical center in Vienna, he received a cryptic note from Walter Kappe. "Soldier Herman Neubauer," it said, "I ask you if you would like to go on a special assignment to a country where you have been before." Neubauer, who had expected to be sent off to the front once more, replied immediately. Three weeks later his company commander gave him train fare to his home in Hamburg, and from there to Berlin, with orders to report to Kappe at the editorial offices of *Der Kaukasus*.

Thiel was a machinist who went to Detroit in 1927, at the age of twenty. He found work at the Ford plant and then at General Motors. By 1930, work had become a hit-and-miss affair—a few weeks with Fisher Body, a few with Chevrolet. He decided to try New York, and there, with machinists in even less demand, he found a job as a handyman, then spent three years as a porter at the Home for the Aged and Infirm on Central Park West. Just across the park was Yorkville, the Friends of New Germany, and its successor, the Bund. They made up for demeaning work. The prospect of a better job took him to Hammond, Indiana, where he helped found a chapter of the Bund. Then the work ran out and there began a series of jobs in East Chicago, Los Angeles, San Diego, San Francisco, Hammond again, and Fort Myers, Florida. By then, what he heard of Hitler's Germany sounded promising. He applied for passage at the German Consulate, and met Dasch on the return trip to Germany. He found steady work in a war plant in Berlin, and for eight months lived what he called "a normal working man's life."

That was ended abruptly early in March 1942. Kappe and Dasch introduced themselves to him after Kappe had spoken to foreign workers at Thiel's plant. The first interview was followed by another a week later, at which Kappe talked, according to Thiel, about how nice it would be "for some of us fellows who knew the United States to go back and do something." On April 1, Thiel left his job at the war plant, went home for the Easter holidays, and reported for duty at Quenz Lake two days later.

The two men who were to lead these dutiful followers received their special instructions on May 11. The information was not elaborate, but rather details of the kind to which Kappe attached great importance. Off and on since the start of classes at Quenz Lake, he, Dasch and Kerling had discussed how much money they would need to operate for two years. Estimates as high as hundreds of thousands of dollars, because of the possibility of bribes, had been made by Kerling. Dasch was more modest; when Kerling finally suggested $25,000 a man, Dasch thought $15,000 was enough. In Berlin, Kappe told them that he had reached a decision; the money would be delivered to them in the false bottoms of small canvas bags before they left the city. Each group leader would be given $50,000 for general expenses, travel, the establishment of fronts, the purchase of materials, and bribes, if needed. In addition, the men were to have $9,000 each, of which the group leader would hold $5,000. Each man would receive the other $4,000 in a money belt which Dasch had designed, plus $450 in cash for his immediate use. The money would be in genuine American bills—there were enough risks in the operation without adding the chance of being caught passing counterfeit currency—and the denominations would be no larger than fifty dollars. This would mean bulky packages, but would avoid the trouble and suspicion of changing larger bills.

After lunch Kappe gave each of his group leaders a standard-sized man's white handkerchief, then took a bottle of ammonia from his desk, opened it, and let the fumes penetrate the cloth. Within seconds, numbers, letters and then whole words appeared in red. Each handkerchief held the name and address of a mail drop in Lisbon and two reliable sources for help in the United States. In addition, Kerling's handkerchief had the address of Dasch's brother in New York, who would hold mail for him, while Dasch's had that of Haupt's uncle in Chicago, who would hold mail for Kerling. The two leaders were to communicate with each other through these addresses until Burger set up his business front in Chicago and even after, if they found it expedient to have more than one place to write. The Lisbon address was for them to use only when they wrote to Kappe. For that purpose, the invisible inks they had learned to make at Quenz Lake were not sufficient. Kappe gave each man a watertight tube containing four or five match sticks tipped with a grayish substance. Under the guidance of a young woman in Kappe's office they were instructed to write lightly with the match sticks. The writing disappeared as soon as it dried, whereupon the young woman took the blank papers to a small box-like machine and turned on a light. Under the glow of an ultraviolet bulb, the writing reappeared.

This was not the most efficient means of getting word back to Germany, Kappe knew, but it was practical. He had planned originally to give Quirin and Heinck a brief course in radio transmission and to equip them with a short-wave set. Heinck had once built receiving sets as a hobby, but neither he nor Quirin was particularly qualified to use a transmitter and Kappe decided there was not enough time to train them. Short-wave transmission would have to wait for another sabotage group. Meantime, communication with Kappe was to be kept to a minimum—observations in the United States which would help in planning future sabotage groups, the location of new war plants, the need for more money or explosives, reports on any untoward behavior by the men on the mission.

Kappe's passion for detail extended to the exact arrangements for a meeting between Dasch and Kerling as soon after they arrived in the United States as possible. On the basis of the promised dates for the departure of the two groups, and the Navy's estimate of the time to cross the Atlantic, he suggested that the two men meet on July 4. It may well have been a safe date in itself, but Kappe's pride in his own humor suggests that he chose American Independence Day as yet another of the little jokes with which he amused himself. After some discussion, Dasch and Kerling agreed to meet between noon and 1:00 P.M. in the grill room of the Hotel Gibson in Cincinnati, a hotel and a city they both knew well. If one of them didn't show up, they were to try again between six and eight that evening, and if that failed, the same times the following Sunday, and then each Sunday thereafter until they met or were convinced that something had gone wrong. Dasch and Kerling agreed with Kappe that Cincinnati was ideally located. It was near Chicago and not too far from eastern Long Island and Jacksonville, where, Kappe now informed them, the two landings would be made. It was also a central point from which they could assign men to study target sites.

Dasch and Kerling agreed not to undertake any sabotage before they met in Cincinnati. In fact, Kappe insisted that they not hurry even after the meeting; it was more important that they establish themselves securely, with respectable fronts for all the men. Neither he nor the High Command expected results for perhaps as long as six months, he said, although he suggested that two or three months was more reasonable. The groups would work separately—Kerling's in New York State and Pennsylvania for the most part, and Dasch's in the Midwest—but would use their mail drops if either one needed additional men to handle a large job. But Kappe did not encourage ambitious projects. A string of small successes in safety was infinitely more valuable than large attempts which might fail and expose the men to capture.

This regard for them and their men was reassuring to Dasch and Kerling. Yet Kerling was not altogether satisfied. He was not as convinced about the quality of the men he and Dasch were leading as Kappe seemed to be. He said so to Kappe, as he had done once before at Quenz Lake. At that time his complaints had been directed at Burger, because he had been a Gestapo prisoner; at Neubauer—even though he was an old friend—because he had "splinters on top of his brain"; at Herbert Haupt, because "he couldn't see a woman without running after her." If anything, Kerling felt more strongly now, especially about Dasch's group. He knew that Heinck was irresponsible when he drank and that Dasch and Quirin had made a pact to cover up for him and to try to keep him out of bars. Kappe paid no attention to Kerling's complaints; all the men had shown their ability in classroom, laboratory and the field, he said; if they presented personal problems in the United States, these were part of the responsibilities of leadership which Dasch and Kerling now had. Kerling did not raise the matter again.

On Tuesday morning, all nine met at Kappe's office. Kappe outlined a busy schedule for the rest of the week—a detailed tour of German installations of the kind which would be their targets in the United States. They started that afternoon, despite a heavy rain, to inspect a canal system. Reinhold Barth, Dasch's cousin by marriage, who because of his nine years' experience with the Long Island Rail Road had been promoted from Army interpreter to work with Kappe, explained the moving parts which were most susceptible to a charge of dynamite. It was also suggested that the men watch for boat traffic, especially barges carrying cement. Sinking a cement boat would bring traffic to an effective halt, although it would not, of course, have as serious an effect as smashing a lock. An official from the inland waterways office supplemented Barth's remarks from time to time and eagerly answered questions. Kappe had told him that the men were part of an antisabotage group on its way to Russia, which impressed the official considerably.

Early Wednesday, they started on a day's tour of the railroad yards in Berlin. Although the chief engineer of the yards guided them—he had been told the same story of antisabotage in Russia—he soon bowed to Barth's superior skill.

At Quenz Lake, Barth had given the men a thorough exposition of the physical condition of American rolling stock, identifying lines whose equipment was old and neglected and those with fairly new cars and engines. He described the various types of engines and their average speed when hauling freight cars, the major terminal points in the United States and how they operated. Now he pointed out the vulnerable spots—bearings, oil systems, brakes, engines, signals and switches. Finally, although none of the men could see any practical benefits to this, he gave each one a short lesson in how to operate a train engine. It seemed more to the point when Barth explained that sand, emery dust or some other abrasive thrown into the bearings or the oil filter would effectively damage a locomotive, and that one of their pieces of dynamite disguised as coal and dropped into the tender would sooner or later blow up a valuable engine. In the evening the men gathered in Kappe's office once more for a final review of rail sabotage. Barth listed the important points of the day's tour and repeated his earlier instructions; he wanted no errors in his own specialty.

The next two days had been set aside for visits to the major aluminum and magnesium plants in Germany, including one that was still under construction. In view of the emphasis Kappe had put on the sabotage of American light metals industries, the time was not disproportionate. The men had already been indoctrinated in the location of the main aluminum factories in the United States, including those under construction and planned, and Barth had listed the railroads which carried their raw materials. Now, starting at 6:00 A.M. Thursday, when they boarded a train for the I.G. Farben aluminum plants in Bitterfeld, they were actually to see the counterparts of what they were to destroy. No pretense was made at Bitterfeld, and later at Aachen, that they were students of antisabotage; the Farben officials who led the tour knew exactly what this visit was about, and helped to make it profitable.

Burger, on whom the lessons made a lasting impression, remembered it clearly. "We were shown the various bottlenecks existing in each plant," he recalled, "the destruction of which would totally disable the operation . . . for a certain length of time. . . . The high-tension poles carrying the power into the plant would be the first and most vulnerable point of attack. . . . [They] are easy to damage, which, of course, would tear down the entire power line. . . . We were instructed that any damage planned to an aluminum plant should be carried out by a group of not less than four persons, inasmuch as there were too many spots which had to be destroyed at one time to permit less. . . . It was pointed out that if we were able to disrupt the power input for eight hours, it would destroy all the stoves and baths in which the aluminum is manufactured." They were also told how to damage transformers with dynamite or high-powered rifles and, conversely, of a number of simple methods of sabotage —here a hammer blow against a porcelain insulator, there a small charge of dynamite in the instrument room.

Studies at I. G. Farben were broken by a lunch in the executives' dining room which Dasch remembered as "the swellest dinner I ever had in Germany. Cigars and bottles of wine, we were treated like kings." After lunch they visited the newest installation and studied new equipment of the kind recently built plants in America might have. In the evening they reviewed until there was no doubt that each of the nine men knew the best ways of halting aluminum production. They spent the night at Bitterfeld and took the train the next morning to Dessau, where a bus took them to the aluminum and magnesium plants at Aachen.

The men were thoroughly exhausted when they arrived in Berlin at 2:00 A.M. Saturday. It had been a grueling four days, and they looked forward to the week end off, which Kappe had promised.

On Monday they started their last week in Berlin, and it passed more quickly and decidedly more informally than the one before. There were no more tours or lectures, but individual sessions with Kappe. By Thursday, he had issued each of them American social security and selective service registration cards and they had all been through a final drill on their new identities. They should have known them by then, even though each story had undergone some changes since Kappe first started rehearsing them in the early days at Quenz Lake. The stories were kept simple, often being no more than slight departures from each man's actual life, but filling with American jobs and residences the time each one had been in Germany. Kappe himself supplied a fictitious name, in each case retaining the initials of the man's actual name, and a suggested biography, but nearly everyone made some contribution to his own or someone else's life story before a final decision was reached. It became a game for one man to unexpectedly ask another where he was born, what his occupation was and where in the United States he had lived.

Dasch became Davis, retained his Christian name, and made his birthplace San Francisco before the earthquake and fire, thus obviating the need for proof if it were ever required. Kerling, whom Dasch once described as looking like an Irish bartender, became Edward J. Kelly. Five years were added to his age, so he could also be born in San Francisco before the earthquake. Dasch was irritated at being asked to look up the exact date of the earthquake, but it was the kind of detail Kappe insisted on checking. Werner Thiel's resemblance to a Pole at first brought him the role of a Polish immigrant named Bill Thomas. Burger thought he looked like an American Indian, but did not suggest that he pose as one. Finally, because it seemed easier to assume false native births than false immigrations, Thiel was to say he was born in the coal-mining area of Pennsylvania, which has a large Polish population. This took care of his accent, which could have passed as Polish. Heinrich Heinck became Henry Kaynor, with a Polish mother and a German father, from Wilkes-Barre, which he had left at an early age. This was troublesome at first because Heinck did not know how to spell Wilkes-Barre, but he finally learned that and all of his cover story. Richard Quirin changed his name to Richard Quintas, born in Lisbon, but emigrating to the United States with his parents at the age of three. When his father left his mother he had lived in eastern New York, which Quirin could be fairly knowledgeable about because of his stay in Schenectady. Hermann Neubauer became Henry Nicholas, born in Lithuania and brought to Chicago as a small boy. Joseph Schmidt had a Scandinavian appearance and could affect a Swedish accent when he spoke English; he became Jerry Swenson.

The two men who had held American citizenship, Haupt and Burger, raised special problems. Dasch thought Burger looked like a Jew and should therefore pose as a refugee from Germany. Kappe enlarged on this, and for a while Burger rehearsed as a Czechoslovak refugee who had stowed away aboard a Spanish ship. Toward the end of the training period at Quenz Lake, Burger himself suggested that, since he had a naturalization certificate and honorable discharges from two National Guard units, he should return to the United States under his own name. His only pretense would be that he had never left the country. Kappe agreed and took Burger's certificate, which had the words "Passport Issued" and the 1933 date stamped on its back. When Kappe returned the document, the back was completely clean. Haupt too would keep his own identity. His only difficulty was that, though he was of draft age, he had not registered before he left home. He would have to register as soon as he got back to Chicago. Until then, he would need a false draft card, and he suggested that it be in the name of Lawrence Jordan, a young man his own age whom he had known in Chicago. It was considered a perfectly logical story for him to tell draft board officials that he had failed to register earlier because he had been on an extended stay in Mexico, and he was sure he could work out a way of getting deferred.

As the rehearsal of stories continued, Kappe was busy outfitting his men with uniforms for the trip and civilian clothes decent enough to wear until they could buy new ones. Fortunately, most of them still had the American-made clothes with which they had returned to Germany, and although none would have won fashion awards they were certainly adequate for the short time they would be needed. Burger, who had been away from the United States nine years, had no American clothes at all, but Kerling, who was about his size, gave him an extra suit, shirt and tie, and Heinck gave him an undershirt.

If none of them had had American clothes, Kappe had ways to supply them. Schmidt had appeared in his office the week before he was due at Quenz Lake, complaining that he did not have a decent suit and no ration card to buy one, and Kappe had taken him to a building in the northwestern section of Berlin. After Kappe identified himself to an officer in charge, he and Schmidt were shown into a vast warehouse with rack after rack of overcoats, raincoats, suits, shirts, shoes, hats and underwear. Every size was available, and though the clothes showed signs of use they had been cleaned and pressed. Schmidt's choice was from clothing bearing the labels of Czech, Polish, Norwegian, Dutch and French manufacturers. He was not likely to have been concerned about the implications of the labels or to have given thought to the thousands of dead men in conquered nations who had once worn these clothes; he merely selected what he needed, lingering over color and size, and left the warehouse pleased at his new attire. Some of these clothes had been made in America, presumably for Europeans with means, and Kappe was prepared to search them out for his men, if necessary.

Uniforms—or rather Navy work clothes—were even less trouble. Kappe took the men to a military supply depot and supervised their selection: khaki trousers and jacket, gray woolen socks, high black boots and a cap decorated with swastika and wings comprised the standard outfit. The men were instructed to put them away until they boarded the submarine, and to take them off only after they had arrived safely in the United States. Kappe made it clear that if they were caught while landing, the uniforms would assure their being held as prisoners of war. Once they were in civilian clothes, their status would change. By that time, Kappe assured them, they would be securely established, and protected by their knowledge of America and the stories they had so carefully rehearsed.

While Kappe was directing the final preparations, the Abwehr laboratory, on instructions from Schulz and Koenig, was getting ready the portable arsenal the men would carry to the United States. There were eight wooden crates, each protecting an inner container made of galvanized sheet steel, which was soldered to make a thoroughly waterproof container. Six of the boxes were filled with the laboratory's special dynamite, mostly in brick shape, each individual piece wrapped in heavy paper, but with a number of pieces already disguised as lumps of coal. The packing itself was so neatly done that when the boxes were sealed not a single rattle could be heard. Two boxes were packed with a variety of timing devices, coils of wire, incendiary pen-and-pencil sets and sulphuric acid fillers for them, and a number of small screws. Wood shavings kept these small, sensitive mechanisms from getting knocked around in handling. Each man was permitted a look at the contents of the boxes before they were sealed and marked—an X on the boxes of explosives and no marking on those with fuses and other devices. Each group was to get three X-marked boxes and one of the others.

There was little left to be done now, except for the signing of contracts to formulate the payments to the men in return for a pledge of secrecy. This should have been a perfunctory affair, but Kappe found that on matters of money his nine colleagues had strong feelings. The pay scale was not the same for all of them, and in a group so small and so intimately involved, that could not be kept secret. Neubauer and Burger, having come to Operation Pastorius as Army privates, were to be continued at their military rate of pay of one mark a day. Burger did not complain, and asked only that it be added to the monthly check his wife received as a military dependent. Neubauer, however, had heard that the others were being paid salaries comparable to their civilian income, and he insisted on being paid at a higher rate. Kappe was in no mood to sustain a quarrel, and finally agreed. Neubauer was to have deposited to his credit at a Berlin bank the sum of 200 marks each month and his wife would continue to receive her regular military stipend of 235 marks a month. In addition, if Neubauer died on duty, his widow would receive 170 marks a month until her remarriage or death. He drove a hard bargain, which Kappe resented. Burger had simply agreed that his wife be given an unspecified lump sum on his death; he had no doubt that she would remarry since there was official pressure on all soldiers' widows to do so. The others agreed to figures generally in the area of Neubauer's contract, although Dasch and Kerling were the best paid; they received 600 marks a month. In addition, all were promised jobs commensurate with their ability when they returned to Germany.

The penalty for revealing what they had learned or were about to do in the United States was death. The men were not surprised at this, in view of the nature of the assignment. They noted, but did not protest, that they were not permitted to read all the clauses in the contract, and that when they signed Kappe drew the paper back to cover signatures which had already been placed there; despite the vows of secrecy, there were obviously some things Kappe did not entirely trust them to know. The men never did understand what, if any, position they held in the Army. Kappe had told them they were part of the Vertrauensmänner Abteilung, the Confidential Agents Section, and were considered V-men for administrative purposes. They had even been given cryptic V-names—Stritch, the German word for dash, was an obvious pun applied to Dasch; Neubauer was called Koch for his profession as cook; Haupt was called Bingo—under which their records would be kept in Abwehr files. But whether this carried a military rank or left some of them as civilian employes, was never made clear.

On Wednesday, May 20, Kappe informed the men that they would be leaving Berlin in forty-eight hours, but that evening there was to be a dinner at Berlin's famous Tiergarten (Zoo) Restaurant. This was to be their official farewell, and he implied that some of Germany's highest ranking officials and military men would attend. This led some of the men to expect Hitler himself, as well as members of the High Command. As it turned out, the highest ranking officer was Lahousen, who, though chief of Abwehr II, was still a colonel. Nevertheless, the party was a great success and the men left filled with good food and drink, and a sense of high purpose. There were many speeches, the tenor of which was that the assignment the men were on was a major contribution to the war effort, fully as important as that being made by the brave German soldiers on the Russian front. In fact Lahousen said even more: that if the two groups were successful they would be as valuable as two divisions of fighting men, and could very likely help decide the outcome of the war. The speeches and brandy had a heady effect, and after dinner, when the Abwehr officers and the nine men in civilian dress sat around informally discussing their project, it would have been hard to persuade any of them that they did not have the courage or the ability which was so generously attributed to them. When the last "Heil Hitler" was pronounced well after midnight, Kappe's men were at exactly the peak of emotional well-being he had hoped to attain.

On Thursday the men were permitted to recuperate from the evening's festivities and to settle whatever personal affairs were left. It was to be their last day in Berlin. On Friday morning, Kappe would lead them on the next leg of their journey.

PART II
ENEMY TERRITORY

Chapter 5
Passage to America

The prospect of a holiday in Paris, if only for a week end, gave the departure from Berlin an unreality quite at odds with the serious sense of mission the nine men had carried away from the banquet at the Tiergarten Restaurant. It had been Kappe's decision to leave for Paris a few days earlier than necessary. Tension had been accumulating in Berlin. It did not surprise Kappe; in a group so small he had expected some antagonisms. Nevertheless, the cumulative effect was strong: Kerling's lack of confidence in some of his colleagues; Burger's and Schmidt's distrust of Dasch as a leader; the general apathy to Burger and Haupt, though for different reasons; Neubauer's fuss about money. Kappe was sure this would all evaporate once the men were on American soil, but he evidently believed in the salutary effects of vacations.

He was right. Paris, even darkened spiritually and physically by German occupation, held the promise of pleasure. As the men waited for the Paris Express on Friday morning, May 22, the banter about women, champagne and night clubs was vastly at odds with their luggage—sea bags crammed with boxes of explosives and fuses, Navy fatigue uniforms, shovels, and thousands of dollars in American money. Once in Paris, it was far easier to accept the city's immediate charms than to ponder the past, much less the future. They were met at the Gare de l'Est on Saturday morning by an officer from the Paris branch of Military Intelligence, who escorted them to the Hotel des Deux Mondes, a relic of *fin de siècle* elegance on the Rue de l'Opéra, which the Germans had taken over for government officials and military officers. The sea bags were taken away and put under guard, after which Kappe called the men to his hotel room, handed them packets of money and, in the time-worn phrase which leaders use to ingratiate themselves with their subordinates, told them to "go out and have a good time."

They did, and to such an extent that if Kappe had known, he might have worried more about their future. Once, while drinking at the bar of the Deux Mondes, Heinrich Heinck announced loudly that he was a secret agent. This caused Burger and Quirin, who were with him, some concern, but they realized that it was the kind of statement which, coming from a man so obviously drunk, merely amused those who heard it. Most of the men, who had never been to Paris before, raced from one famous landmark to another, as if they sensed that this might be their only chance to get this close to the Louvre, the Eiffel Tower, the Tuileries, the banks of the Seine. The grim pursuit of the charms of Paris continued into the evenings. The money Kappe had distributed vanished in a round of night clubs and restaurants and the exorbitant fees of wartime prostitution. Haupt, who either ran out of money early or believed that the women were some sort of *lagniappe* for potential German heroes, caused a disturbance at the Deux Mondes Sunday night when he refused to pay the prostitute who accompanied him to his room. Her screams, in French, which he did not understand, carried the message to his companions in neighboring rooms. Not until one of them paid her did she quiet down and leave—presumably to be henceforth on her guard against civilians in American clothing. By late Monday, when the holiday was over and the nine men met with Kappe again, they were thoroughly fatigued, but also seemingly relaxed for the next step in their journey westward. All except Schmidt, who was starting to show symptoms of gonorrhea.

That evening they boarded the overnight train for Lorient, a French naval base which the Germans had occupied since June of 1940, and were using as a port for their North Atlantic U-boat fleet. As on the train from Berlin to Paris, the men had two adjoining first-class compartments, with those on either side of them kept vacant. But where the trip to Paris had passed in songs and joking, this one fell into a sullen listlessness. It may have been the realization that the serious work was now to begin, or it may have been a collective hangover. Schmidt, who must have been suffering remorse as well as physical pain, broke the strained quiet to bait Dasch about his qualities of leadership, and Burger on his troubles with the Gestapo. Neither was in a mood to respond to him, and he soon tired of the game. But Schmidt's querulous mood affected the others. Peevish quarrels flared suddenly as one or another found a real or fancied excuse to turn on a companion. By the time they reached Lorient at noon Tuesday, the good spirits aroused in Paris had been dissipated. The tension was somewhat relieved when Schmidt announced to Kappe that he did not think he should go aboard a submarine in his condition and Kappe, angrily agreeing, sent him to the local naval hospital for treatment. Schmidt was in good humor when he said his goodbyes and promised to meet them all in the United States. By then most of them felt that Schmidt had purposely courted venereal disease to avoid serving with Dasch and that he was gambling on being made a group leader on a future mission. None of the remaining eight men showed any regret at his departure.

The hotel to which the men were brought was called Jour de Rêve, but that day was far from dreamy for any of them. Dasch had the most trouble. On the ride from Paris he had put his pipe, tobacco pouch and wallet containing his false social security and draft cards in the netting above his berth. In the excitement of leaving the train and supervising the removal of the sea bags, he forgot them. When he discovered the loss toward noon, he panicked. He excused himself from lunch and raced to the railroad station. In his excited efforts to retrieve his wallet and yet not explain its contents, he made the soldier in charge suspicious. Dasch did not have proper German identification papers—Kappe had not considered that important as long as the men were traveling in a group under his guidance—but it was important to a pompous noncommissioned officer, and he immediately sent for his captain. Confronted by such authority, Dasch became insistent; he alluded to his lost papers as "hot" and said they were printed in English. The captain's response terrified Dasch; it was a matter for the Gestapo, and if Dasch had no identification he would have to be held in custody.

There was no way now for Dasch to keep his loss from Kappe. He asked the captain to have Kappe called at the hotel. The captain did so, but he telephoned the Gestapo as well. Kappe and a Gestapo agent arrived at the railroad station at the same time. Kappe was furious at Dasch's blundering, especially since it had provoked interference from the

Gestapo. He calmed down long enough, however, to prevail on the Gestapo agent to ask the others to leave the room so he could explain matters. Kappe then showed his authority from the High Command, and reluctantly gave some indication of the mission he was supervising. Dasch was released in his custody, but not before receiving a loud lecture from the Gestapo agent on carelessness in wartime. It was nothing compared to the speech Kappe made on the way back to the Jour de Rêve.

The next day the eight men were exposed to an error of Kappe's which was infinitely more dangerous to their security than Dasch's had been. The mistake was revealed when Kerling gathered his group to distribute money belts and pocket money. Kappe joined them to add some last-minute advice. The fifty-dollar bills, he said, should not be changed at banks nor deposited in savings accounts, nor should more than one bill be spent at a time. Although the money was not counterfeit, he assured them, many of the notes were numbered consecutively, part of a series which had reached Germany legitimately some years earlier. It was possible that the numbers were known in the United States. When the bills were changed, preferably in the course of buying something, the men could then open small bank accounts.

Kappe's attention to detail impressed the men—but only for a few minutes. Haupt looked at one of the bills closely, and made a chilling discovery. It was a gold certificate of the kind which had been withdrawn from circulation since 1933, when the United States went off the gold standard. The money was worse than useless; it was certain to cause an investigation the first time a bill reached a bank.

The men were frantic. Each started at once to claw through his money belt, throwing out the gold certificates as they turned up. Soon the flutter of discarded bills made a small mound on the bed in front of Kappe. Kappe, as alarmed as his men, explained that he had accepted the money in good faith from an intelligence officer in charge of such matters. The men found that most of their money was valid after all, and were ready to exonerate Kappe until he tried to dismiss the whole problem. "Don't worry about a little thing like that," he said as the men were repacking their money belts.

He had picked the wrong time to be frivolous. "It made the entire group dissatisfied with his careless manner and attitude," one of them said. Some even doubted the usefulness of any of the money. A few saw danger in the consecutively numbered fifties and wanted to get rid of them too. But this would have left practically no money and would have caused delay until more could be sent from Berlin. At last Kappe managed to convince them that the rest of the money was safe and, if cautiously spent, would not bring trouble. But when the meeting was adjourned, some of the men still had misgivings.

Kerling and his group did not have much time to do anything about their doubts. Since the Florida trip would take longer, they were scheduled to leave first. Their submarine was waiting, and they were to sail that evening. Immediately after the money crisis, Kappe prodded Kerling, Haupt, Neubauer and Thiel to change to Navy fatigues. Their civilian clothes, three canvas bags, the four crates of explosives and fuses, and the shovel were put in a large sea bag, which, with the money belts around their waists, represented their total luggage for re-entry to America. By the time they had finished packing the sea bag, Kappe was waiting in front of the hotel in a Navy car. There was no pause for farewells to the others. The car drove to the dock, and the men stepped aboard submarine *U-584*. Kappe introduced them to Lieutenant Commander Deeke, stayed long enough for a drink on board, and returned to the hotel. Four of his eight men were on their way, and he could take some pride in that, but he was also tired and irritable. What with Dasch's trouble at the station the day before and the argument about money today, Lorient had given him a trying time.

It was not over. That evening, he and Dasch argued violently. It was not a significant quarrel, but was carried on more as if each needed to win just to save something of these two days which had gone so badly for each of them. Dasch had dropped into Kerling's room while the argument about gold certificates was going on. He did not stay long enough to get involved beyond a casual observation that the bills looked perfectly legal to him, but retired to his room to examine his own money supply. He found no gold certificates, but of the small denominations which he was to distribute as pocket money, he found several dollar bills with what appeared to be Oriental block letters stamped on the backs. He guessed that they had come to Germany by way of Japan, and he certainly had no use for them. He had found more than a hundred, so that now each member of his group would receive $419 for immediate use instead of the $450 which had been planned. When Kappe returned from seeing Kerling's group off, Dasch confronted him with the marked bills. "This money I don't want," he said angrily. "You should be ashamed of having supplied us with money like that." Kappe had had enough of financial problems and was not disposed to argue; he wearily pocketed the marked bills.

In the face of this, Dasch did not pursue the matter but changed the subject, quietly enough, by seeking confirmation that his group would not engage in sabotage for three or four months after arrival in the United States. Kappe had, of course, first suggested such a delay. Now he disagreed, and strongly. He had no objection to waiting for major sabotage efforts, he said, but he did think that smaller diversionary efforts should be made. He was fond of his idea that occasional bombs be planted in department stores owned by Jews, and in bus and railroad station lockers. Dasch saw no merit in this approach, but finally agreed. Score one for Kappe. Then Kappe suggested that in the United States Dasch and Quirin should remain together as one pair, Burger and Heinck as the other. It was apparent that he felt Burger's stability would be a balance for Heinck's obvious nervousness. Dasch insisted that Quirin go with Heinck since they were such close friends. Besides, he wanted Burger with him, he said, because he did not yet trust the man who had had so much trouble with the Gestapo. Kappe argued for Burger's reliability, but eventually gave in. Score one for Dasch. Both men went to bed after midnight feeling better.

Wednesday should have been a day of quiet preparation for the second departure. Instead, Kappe was told that submarine *U-202* was not yet out of drydock, and there would be a twenty-four-hour delay. There was nothing to do in Lorient but eat, drink and wait. And argue. On Thursday the petty bickering broke into a full-scale quarrel which so exasperated Kappe that he nearly pulled Dasch off the assignment. It started when Heinck asked Kappe the advisability of seeking help from a friend on Long Island if necessary. Kappe not only thought it would be helpful in an emergency, but urged Heinck to bring the man into the sabotage work. "If Heinck visits this fellow he will have to do it over my dead body," said Dasch. He added that Colonel Lahousen himself had told him at the farewell banquet in Berlin that it would be dangerous to trust anyone in the United States, even former Bundists. There was no way of knowing how their political feelings had changed since the United States entered the war, and further, there was a good chance that they were being watched by the F.B.I. Kappe dismissed Dasch's argument out of hand. It reflected on his experience in the Bund. "You have no confidence in our people in Amercia who have been in the Bund," he said. "Heinck and I have been in America," he added, as if to show once and for all that his years in the United States were of more use to Germany than Dasch's.

Heinck, thus supported, showed spirit for the first time, or at least the first time sober. "Why, you dirty bastard," he shouted at Dasch, "we in the Bund had to fight people like you." He had hit Dasch in a sensitive spot; with Schmidt gone, Dasch and Haupt were the only ones of the eight without a certified prewar record of loyalty to the Bund or the Nazi Party, and Haupt could be excused because of his youth. But this was a race which went to the loud, and Dasch shouted right back. "I'll kill you if you call me a bad German again," he said. Kappe restored order by outshouting both. In the embarassed quiet which followed, Heinck spoke again, quietly, insisting that his friend could be trusted and would provide him with a hiding place if one were ever needed. His was the precaution of a frightened man, but Dasch had to get the last word. With the false social security and draft registration cards, he said, Heinck could move about as freely as he wanted without seeking help from outsiders. "If you have to have help," he told Heinck, "then you are no good." Neither Quirin, who had come to resent Dasch's arrogance, nor Burger, who was worried about Heinck's ability, took part in the dispute. It ended in a compromise that was actually a victory for Dasch. Dasch would take the address of Heinck's friend and it was to be used only if Dasch thought it necessary.

Word that their submarine was ready to sail that evening stopped further recrimination, but Heinck's distaste for Dasch had been intensified, and Dasch rarely spoke of Heinck thereafter without calling him "that little coward."

At six P.M., Dasch, Burger, Quirin and Heinck, accompanied by Kappe, squeezed into a command car and drove to Lorient's docks. Submarine *U-202* was anchored behind a freighter so that it could not be seen by anyone on shore;

despite the thoroughness with which the Nazis policed the town, extraordinary precautions were always taken when a submarine was about to depart. The men entered the *U-202* by boarding the freighter, crossing its deck, and then walking a precarious gangplank which connected the two vessels. In their fatigues and lugging the heavy sea bag, they looked like four sailors and an officer joining their ship, a common sight in Lorient. To Kappe the procedure must have been like a movie he had already seen. As he had done with Kerling's group, he made the proper introduction, stayed long enough for a few drinks, wished the men luck, and departed.

Submarine *U-202* had been commissioned a year earlier at the Krupp works in Kiel, and immediately joined the growing wolf pack fleet with which the German Navy was so successfully harrassing Allied shipping. Lieutenant Commander Lindner and his crew were relaxed veterans by now. Lindner permitted himself the luxury of a well-trimmed mustache and beard and his men the nonregulation pleasure of a symbolic ship's mascot. A multicolored porcupine, its quills bristling, was painted on the *202*'s conning tower. As a sign of their feelings for the animal, each of the forty-five officers and men wore on his cap a miniature metal porcupine which the chief machinist had stamped out. Lindner, who was never seen without his cap, wore one too, and the token linked the men and their commander in a bond of esteem and affection.

Soon after the *U-202* was guided out of Lorient harbor, Lindner made a brief announcement over the submarine's loudspeakers. The four strangers on board, he said, were being transported to the United States on a secret mission. They were to be treated as guests, but none of the crew was to ask them questions. On the submarine's return to Lorient no mention was to be made of their having been aboard. Violation of this last order would be punished by death. The crew responded to the announcement as if a trip to the United States was a normal activity for the *U-202*, even though she had never before gone more than a safe distance from the submarine supply ships which the German Navy had stationed in the North Atlantic. The fifteen days it took to cross the Atlantic passed peaceably, the major excitement being caused by a sailor with acute appendicitis. The *U-202* ran on the surface at night, and below during the day. Lindner ordered a practice alarm every day, during which the submarine crash-dived deep into the water as each man raced to his station. When the *U-202* reached the mid-Atlantic and the warm waters of the Gulf Stream, she surfaced by day to permit the crew to grease the deck guns and test them in the open sea. Until the *U-202* was actually within sight of the North American coast no special precautions were taken, and Lindner never permitted his men to feel that there was any special risk attached to this voyage.

Dasch and his partners did not enjoy this trip at all. For the first week they were almost continuously seasick. The crowded conditions, the strange sounds and smells, the tossing and pitching on the surface and the sudden descents were nerve-racking experiences. Yet they also found the submarine a friendly place. They were among men their own age, and found pleasure in small talk. Dasch and Burger were given bunks in the noncommissioned officers' quarters, and Quirin and Heinck with the enlisted men. Except for the radio and torpedo rooms being off limits, the men had freedom of movement, or as much freedom of movement as a submarine permits. Burger found a former Storm Trooper with whom he exchanged reminiscences about the good old days of the Nazi Party. Dasch cultivated Lindner and followed the *U-202*'s progress across the Atlantic on a large map in the control room. Quirin and Heinck kept to themselves, wishing the trip would end.

The last few days were a particular strain for all four. They knew they were approaching the American coast and were eager to get ashore. While surfacing in the Gulf Stream, they had tested the pneumatic rubber raft which would take them from the submarine to the beach. Now, as they approached the Newfoundland Banks, they checked their belongings nervously. From time to time they took their civilian clothes out of the sea bag, hung them up to get the wrinkles out and then promptly put them back to get more wrinkles. They discussed endlessly how they would pack the rubber raft with the four wooden cases, the sea bag and Dasch's money-filled canvas bag. When Lindner had to slow down his surface speed because of heavy fog, they chafed. More time was lost when Lindner received word from another submarine that a twenty-thousand-ton Allied ship was somewhere between Halifax and Boston and decided, against orders, to chase her. None but Dasch was aware of the short diversion, though, and when Lindner realized that his safest top speed in the fog was not fast enough to catch the ship, he returned to his original course.

As the submarine worked her way down from Nova Scotia, underwater most of the way because of the heavy fogs and the ever present danger of American patrol ships, the crew, too, became tense. They had never been this close to American shores. The fog cut their visibility and they moved south slowly. Lindner had predicted he would land the men by Thursday night, but that day they were just east of Cape Cod, about a hundred and twenty miles from their goal of East Hampton, and the fog had closed in tighter than before. Dasch had received Lindner's permission to enter the radio room during these last days, and he now spent most of his time listening to American news broadcasts. Even with the *202*'s slow progress, Dasch knew that they were not many hours from being put ashore. On Thursday he called the men together for the distribution of their money belts and cash. The scene reminded them of the other group's quarrel over gold certificates, but Dasch assured them that he had examined the bills, and they left to check their gear once more.

Friday, June 12, started with as heavy a fog as the day before. But by afternoon it cleared, and Lindner was able to shoot the sun to chart his position. At eight o'clock, when the fog returned, Lindner was certain he was opposite East Hampton. He told Dasch to bring his men to the mess room; they were to be landed that night.

Despite the anxious minutes it took to travel from the submarine to shore, Dasch was on the whole pleased at the efficiency of the landing. The fog had been a blessing; he was sure they had not been seen. It was 12:30 A.M. when Dasch turned from thanking the sailors, a little more than half an hour since he had said goodbye to Lieutenant Commander Lindner. Quirin, Heinck and Burger were up in the dunes, changing to civilian clothes. Burger would be down soon with the duffel bag stuffed with the uniforms to be returned to the submarine. In a few minutes Dasch would join his men, and they would bury the boxes and shovels and make their way toward town and the first train to New York. As he walked from the boat, he glanced casually down the fog-shrouded beach to his left, and froze in fright.

A man was walking toward them.

He was still some twenty or thirty feet away, a tall, eerie shape indistinct in the fog, at that moment no more than a dark silhouette formed by the hazy beams of a swinging flashlight. Dasch knew at once this was not one of his own men, and simultaneously he sensed from the man's slow, almost casual, pace that neither he nor his companions had yet been seen. Quietly but firmly, he told the two sailors to return to the submarine at once. It is unlikely they were conscious of danger on the beach. If they saw him at all, the approaching man could have been one of the landing party or someone meeting it. As the rubber boat was pulled away, Dasch sucked in his breath and walked carefully to the stranger.

Dasch's immediate reaction was sheer horror. But as he stepped toward the light, the fear was wiped out by a flash of clarity. Whoever this man was, Dasch knew he had to be kept from the others. The boxes of explosives and the German uniforms were still above ground and would be impossible to explain. But not until he entered the hazy circle of light formed by the man's flashlight did Dasch fully comprehend the extent of the danger. The man was wearing the uniform of the United States Coast Guard.

"Who are you?" the Coast Guardsman asked. The voice carried concern and still remained completely official, a manner of speaking bred into even the newest recruits of a service with a long tradition of finding, and saving, men in trouble. Dasch may not have heard. As if hoping for a denial, he asked, "Coast Guard?" The answer was prompt and proud. "Yes, sir." And again, insistently now, "Who are you?"

Dasch took a chance. He counted on Lindner's estimate that they had landed at East Hampton and on his own knowledge of the South Shore of Long Island. "We're fishermen from Southampton and ran ashore here," he said.

The Coast Guardsman accepted the explanation. "What do you intend to do about it?" he asked.

"Stay here until sunrise and then we'll be all right," Dasch replied.

The Coast Guardsman explained that there were four more hours of darkness and invited Dasch and his friends to spend them at the Coast Guard Station, less than half a mile away. This was how Dasch learned that he had come ashore at Amagansett. He was relieved; his first response to the Coast Guardsman could not have been a better one. On a night like this, people foolish enough to leave Southampton to fish could well have gone aground six miles east. His luck gave him a boldness he had not had a few minutes earlier. He agreed to go to the Coast Guard Station—and then just as quickly disagreed. Deception by flashlight on a foggy beach was possible; he might not carry it off under the bright lights of a Coast Guard office. He took a few steps with the young man, and then abruptly said, "I'm not going with you."

"Why?" asked the Coast Guardsman with the honest surprise of a man who could not conceive of such a response on a night like this. Dasch explained that he had no identification papers or fishing permit. The Coast Guardsman became the proper official. Dasch had to accompany him, he said, and took him by the arm. Dasch shook off the hand. He had to make his stand at once. "Now, wait a minute," he said. "You don't know what this is all about."

At that instant both men became aware of a shadowy figure coming toward them from the dunes. It was Burger, stripped to the swimming trunks he had worn under his Navy clothes, dragging the duffel bag toward the water. He assumed Dasch was talking to one of the sailors, and called to them in German. Dasch reacted violently. "Shut up, you damn fool," he shouted in English. "Everything is all right. Go back to the boys and stay with them." Completely taken aback, Burger turned without a word, pulling the duffel bag behind him. Heinck and Quirin were by the four boxes, also in their swimming trunks, and finding ease in the small bottle of German brandy which Heinck had managed to keep against Dasch's orders. They could not see Dasch from where they were, but Burger ordered them to keep their heads down, and whispered that Dasch had run into an American sailor. Heinck was too terrified to move; Quirin wanted to run to Dasch, overpower the intruder and send him out to the submarine on the rubber boat, but Burger, the soldier, had responded to Dasch's command, and managed to convince Quirin to remain quiet. Tensely, uncertainly, with only a few swallows of brandy left to comfort them, the three men waited.

At Burger's interruption, the Coast Guardsman showed nervousness for the first time. The foreign language, which he could not identify, made him suspicious and he had no way of knowing from Dasch's use of "the boys" how many men were hidden in the fog. He himself was unarmed; somehow he had to get away and report this. "How old are you?" Dasch asked abruptly. "Twenty-one," the Coast Guardsman said. "Do you have a father?" Dasch asked. The answer was yes. "Do you have a mother?" Another yes. "Well, I wouldn't want to have to kill you," Dasch said. There was a pause; the implications of what he had said may have affected Dasch as much as the Coast Guardsman. They walked about five feet. Dasch suddenly stopped and spoke again, the threat gone from his voice.

"Forget about this," he said, "and I'll give you some money and you can have a good time." Dasch held out two fifty-dollar bills. The Coast Guardsman refused to take it. Dasch reached for more money. "Here's three hundred dollars," he said. "Take this." The Coast Guardsman took the money. Dasch was relieved. "Count it," he said. Awkwardly holding his flashlight, the Coast Guardsman started to count the bills, then shoved them in his pocket. "No, it's all right," he said, and tried to leave. Dasch held him. "Wait a minute," he said, taking off his hat. "Take a good look at me." The Coast Guardsman turned the flashlight on Dasch's face. "Look in my eyes," Dasch said. "Look in my eyes," he said again, and then a third time. The Coast Guardsman was held in Dasch's stare, the fear of being hypnotized gripping him as hard as Dasch's hand on his arm.

Finally Dasch put on his hat and said, "You'll be meeting me in East Hampton sometime. Do you know me?"

"No, sir," said the Coast Guardsman. "I never saw you before in my life."

"My name is George John Davis," said Dasch. "What's yours?"

"Frank Collins," said the Coast Guardsman, backing away slowly. Then, suddenly turning, he ran into the fog.

Dasch found his way to the dunes and his three nervous colleagues, now in their wrinkled civilian clothes. He was smug about his achievement; he had averted danger by using superior intelligence. "I had him buffaloed," he was to say later of the meeting with the Coast Guardsman. He had become increasingly contemptuous of the other men on this assignment as their distaste for him had grown; now his arrogance was unrestrained. With curt commands, he tried to bully them out of their fears of being caught. "Do exactly what I tell you," he ordered. "Each of you get a box and follow me." He led them a few feet over the dunes until he came to a low-lying stretch of sand. He stopped and ordered them to dig a trench. When it was long and deep enough, he placed the boxes in it, and then had the others refill it and search for seaweed to cover the spot.

By this time Dasch was ready to change from the military trousers he was still wearing, and was furious to discover that "the bunch of bums" had not brought his clothes. He and Quirin left Burger and Heinck "shivering like kids," and returned to the previous resting place. He was in such a hurry that he wore his wet trunks under his civilian trousers and pulled on socks and canvas shoes, and was not aware until later that his socks did not match. He ordered a hole dug for the duffel bag and shovels, and after each of the men looked hurriedly around to make sure nothing had been left in the open, he led them inland. Dasch walked slowly, carrying his money-filled canvas bag and a pair of shoes, which had somehow remained dry. A few yards from a road, he called for a rest until there was more light. They were still not very far from where they had landed, but they were relieved to be off the beach itself. They were vaguely aware of houses on either side of them, but the fog here was as heavy as on the beach and they could not be sure. As they had since leaving the submarine, they found the fog as protective as it was threatening.

The sense of relief did not last long. They were by the side of the road less than an hour, long enough for the beginnings of daylight to clear some of the fog, long enough for the fears of being caught to return. The headlights of occasional cars on the road sent them flat on their stomachs. Once a military truck carrying uniformed men speeded by heading west, in the direction, Dasch alone knew, of the Coast Guard Station. Overhead they could make out revolving beacon lights; the beacon had been unable to penetrate the night fog, but now its brightness was a menace. Heinck's contribution to group morale was a single phrase, repeated as if by rote, "We're surrounded, boys." Even Dasch admitted that he was frightened. Quirin made nervous attempts at conversation, consisting mainly of asking each man to see whether he had accidentally carried anything of German origin from the beach. No conversation was sustained; each man was trying to keep up his own courage in his own way. During one of the intervals of silence they heard faintly, as from a great distance behind them, the sound of an engine. It was a familiar one; submarine *U-202* had switched from its electric motors to Diesel. It was four o'clock, and as the engine's sound faded the four men knew with chilling finality that they were now completely cut off on enemy soil.

Suddenly, in the silence which followed the submarine's departure, a telephone bell rang shrilly. The shock of the incongruous sound stiffened them; they held their breaths and stared at each other. A moment or two later, the ringing ceased and a light went on in a house some fifty yards to their left. They could hear a man talking, but could not make out his words. He stopped talking, walked to his door, went back to the telephone and spoke again. Then the light went out. The four men exhaled in unison, and in unspoken agreement stood up together and walked away.

Dasch led the way again, down a dirt road, seeking the Montauk Highway, the main east-west road on eastern Long Island's South Shore. He wanted to reach Amagansett, which he knew had train service to New York City. No one in the group had a compass, and when they reached the highway, Dasch was confused, but could not concede it, of course, and without hesitation turned right. It was a mistake; that direction was away from the town, away from New York City. The others followed, single file through deep grass and brush on the side of the road. They had no choice but to trust Dasch's judgment; he had insisted all along that he knew the area well. Their trust was shaken in less than a mile. They had not come to the town, which should have been opposite the beach, and the road still stretched ahead. Dasch sensed his error, turned left on the first dirt road he saw—and led the group directly to a trailer camp. A few of the trailers and cars showed lights, or Dasch would have walked into the camp itself. Instead he managed to cross to the opposite side of the road. As he led the others slowly past the camp, in fascinated terror they saw lights go on in one trailer then another, and heard the muted sounds of early risers. The effect was more devastating than the telephone ring in the dark; now they were watching the awakening of an entire community, and one which greatly outnumbered them. Dasch thought, "Jesus Christ, I am falling right into a trap." Wordlessly they inched past the camp, expecting at any moment the bright glare of an automobile headlight to be turned directly on them.

Beyond the trailer camp they found railroad tracks. Fortunately for Dasch, they were at a point where two sets of rails merged into one. Dasch remembered that the Long Island Rail Road became a single track east of Amagansett, and at least realized he had been going toward Montauk Point. He turned west on the tracks and followed them to the Amagansett station. It was 5:00 A.M.; they were dirty, their clothes were damp and stained by grass and dirt; and they were exhausted from fear and fatigue. New York was still three hours away by train. But no train was in sight, the tiny station was locked, and no time table was posted.

Daylight had by now all but cleared the fog. The realization that they were in public for the first time brought a flurry of useless activity. They nervously brushed and dusted each other's clothes. Dasch, uncomfortably damp in his swimming trunks and wet sneakers, went behind some bushes to remove the trunks and to put on the shoes he had carried from the beach. He carefully hid the trunks and sneakers behind a hedge and returned to the other men, who were pacing impatiently on the station platform. Dasch began cheerfully to make plans for the rest of the day, to suggest hotels and safe meeting places in New York. But no one really listened; they wanted to hear the sound of a train. At six o'clock Dasch maliciously suggested the possibility of no Saturday service from Montauk Point to New York. It was a thought which could well have destroyed whatever vestige of courage remained, but Dasch had made the cheerless joke when he saw smoke coming from the station-house chimney. There was train service, after all.

Inside the station house, Ira Baker, ticket agent for the Long Island Rail Road, was tidying up for the morning. It was Saturday, normally a slow day for traffic out of Amagansett. Although wartime restrictions on automobile travel had increased train traffic, not many people would be leaving town at the start of the week end.

At six-thirty Baker unlocked the station-house door and raised his ticket window for the day's business. He was surprised, but not so much that it made a deep impression on him, when a stranger, as dirty and rumpled as all other city fishermen, checked the time table tacked on the bulletin board and asked for four one-way tickets to Jamaica. New Yorkers on a fishing party, he guessed as he stamped the tickets. As if he divined Baker's thoughts, Dasch mentioned that fishing had been pretty bad lately. Baker nodded his agreement, collected twenty dollars and forty cents, and pushed over the tickets.

Dasch left the station with the tickets and the exhilarating information that the express to Jamaica would leave at six fifty-seven. In his excitement at what he by now considered a personal triumph of his intelligence and courage, he did not see a nail protruding from a bench, and ripped a large hole in his trousers.

The train conductor must have been as used to fishermen in torn and disheveled clothing as the ticket agent. He took the tickets without giving the men more than a conductor's normal unseeing look. Dasch bought four newspapers from a stack on a seat at the front of the car and distributed one to each man. The headlines proclaimed the first important American victory in the Pacific, the Battle of the Coral Sea, where, by these early accounts, fifteen Japanese warships had been destroyed at the cost of one aircraft carrier, the *U.S.S. Lexington*. But in Libya, Field Marshal Erwin Rommel of the German Afrika Korps was striking north after occupying Bir Hacheim; in Washington, President Roosevelt had called on everyone to dig into attics, cellars, barns and garages for old rubber as a contribution to the war effort; and in Alaska, a War Department communique said, the Japanese had landed small forces on the western tip of the Aleutian Islands. For whatever comfort it gave the four men that morning, it was apparent that the United States was in deep trouble. And for whatever amusement they may have derived from it, the papers carried reviews of a motion picture which had opened at the Rialto in New York the day before, entitled *Nazi Agent*, in which Conrad Veidt played German twins, one a loyal naturalized American, the other a German consul; not surprisingly, the American Veidt killed the German Veidt in the last reel.

With the newspapers to their faces, Dasch, Burger, Quirin and Heinck rode to Jamaica in silence. On the Long Island Rail Road there could not have been better immunity to suspicion.

The business area of Jamaica, the main terminal and transfer point of the Long Island Rail Road, is like dozens of others in Greater New York, in that anonymity is practically guaranteed. The four men were pleasantly reminded of this aspect of city life when they arrived there shortly after nine-thirty, and decided to buy fresh clothes before going into Manhattan. Like women who avoid reflections on their housekeeping by cleaning house before the charwoman arrives, the men needed presentable clothes at once in order to shop for better ones later. Dasch and Quirin agreed that they would break up into the previously arranged pairs— Heinck with Quirin, Burger with Dasch—all four to meet at three that afternoon in the Automat Restaurant at Eighth Avenue and Thirty-fourth Street. For the first time since they left the submarine, the pressure of time was off them.

Heinck and Quirin entered the haberdashery nearest the station and bought underwear, cheap trousers and sport shirts. They changed in the store's dressing room, bundled up their old clothes, dropped them into a trash can and, after having their shoes shined, felt quite presentable. After breakfast, they took the subway to the Thirty-fourth Street stop, beneath Macy's department store. There they bought suitcases, sport jackets, toilet articles, underwear, shirts and socks. By the time they had finished they were due at the Automat down the street.

Dasch and Burger were less modest in their purchases in Jamaica, and took longer to complete them. After checking Dasch's canvas bag in a railroad station locker, they bought trousers. Unfortunately, they were of a high enough quality so that the cuffs were unfinished. The haberdasher did not have the facilities to make them, and a tailor across the street could not do the job right away. Dasch and Burger put their first purchases in the locker and bought others, with cuffs, for $1.69. Dasch preferred the higher-priced clothing, but anything was an improvement over the clothes he had worn to Jamaica, and which he happily left behind in the store's makeshift dressing room. At a nearby shoe store they bought shoes and socks and changed into them at once, carrying their old ones in a package under their arms. Across the street two boys were shining shoes. The purchases so easily made, the money accepted without question, gave Dasch a resurgence of the smugness that had been shaken on the road from the beach to Amagansett station. New shoes or not, he wanted them shined, and he was going to pay with a flourish.

"I asked the little nigger boy, 'Boy, could you use a pair of shoes size 8½?' He said, 'Yes sir, man.' And I said, 'Here they are.' And I told Pete to give the other boy his shoes."

It was the kind of gesture that established one's superiority over one's fellows, and whether Dasch needed the assurance or not, his good humor was at once restored. He pulled Burger along on the shopping tour with the air of a *bon vivant* on a spree. At a haberdashery they bought shirts, trousers, underwear, ties and handkerchiefs. At an inexpensive clothier's they bought summer-weight suits. Alterations could be made on the spot, and while they waited they changed into the new underwear and shirts. Earlier, Dasch had tossed his hat on top of the bank of station lockers and because of the heat had left his red sweater in the washroom of a restaurant. With suit boxes in hand, the process of changing from old to new was complete. By this time it was after one. The two men had shopped with such singlemindedness they had forgotten to eat.

Nor did they take the time to do so in Jamaica. Instead, they took a Long Island train into the city. There would be time enough to eat when they met Heinck and Quirin at the Automat. On leaving Pennsylvania Station, the Long Island's terminus in New York, they saw the large sign of the Hotel Governor Clinton. It was a typical busy New York hotel, and therefore ideal for their immediate needs. Dasch registered as George John Davis of St. Louis, Missouri, and Burger used his own name, as planned. They were given nearby rooms, 1414 and 1421. This accomplished, Dasch suggested more shopping, but it was two-thirty, nearly time to meet the others, and for the first time that day they were both hungry.

Dasch was still enjoying himself. At the Automat he bought two kinds of salad—"my weakness, especially in the summertime"—followed by coconut pie and a glass of milk. Promptly at three Heinck and Quirin appeared, to Dasch's dismay in loud, striped jackets, sport shirts open at the collar and cheap slacks. He complimented them sardonically for looking so neat, but he was in too much of a rush to complete his own wardrobe to waste time on them. He told them to find a hotel nearby, suggesting the Chesterfield, and reminded them to buy suitcases first. They would all meet again the next day, Sunday, he said, at the Swiss Chalet, a small restaurant on West Fifty-second Street. If for any reason they failed to meet there at one o'clock, they would meet at six at Grant's Tomb, high on Riverside Drive, overlooking the Hudson River. Heinck and Quirin left Burger and Dasch, disregarding Dasch's recommendation of the Hotel Chesterfield, and registered instead at the Martinique, on West Forty-ninth Street. Heinck signed the register as Henry Kaynor and Quirin as Richard Quintas. Their masquerade had begun.

None of the four men were aware of it, since they did not leave the West Side all day, but just east of them, millions of New Yorkers were lining Fifth Avenue to watch the "New York at War Parade." That day, June 13, some 500,000 men and women representing labor and management, air raid wardens and all branches of the armed forces, as well as hundreds of tanks, guns and military vehicles, marched from Washington Square to Seventy-third Street, in a patriotic display that lasted eleven hours.

While Dasch and his colleagues were getting used to their new identities, and becoming familiar again with New York, subdued by the war and nighttime dimouts since they had seen it last, their fellow alumni of the school at Quenz Lake were still unhappily confined in submarine *U-584*, slowly approaching the Florida coast. Although Kerling's group had left Lorient on May 26, two nights before the others, they did not land until four days later. Lieutenant Commander Deeke of the *U-584* had chosen to reach his destination by the longer, but presumably less hazardous, South Atlantic route.

Deeke did not have to contend with the fogs that delayed Lindner and the *U-202*, but he ran into other delays which stretched his trip to three weeks. The morning after *U-584* was clear of Lorient she surfaced and was promptly sighted by a British airplane. Bombs began dropping about the submarine as Deeke ordered a crash dive. His four passengers were thoroughly frightened as the submarine rocked from the effect of the misses, but she was well underwater when the last of eight bombs struck the surface. *U-584* had escaped injury, but Deeke was forced to proceed at slow underwater speeds for longer than he would have liked. More time was lost when the *U-584* sighted another German submarine on the surface and made the inevitable halt for the exchange of courtesies and information. Still later, Deeke was tempted by an Allied freighter whose twenty thousand tons made a tantalizing target. He ordered a chase, but the freighter's speed and zigzag course kept the *U-584* from getting close enough to release a torpedo. By the time Deeke returned to his original route, another day had been added to the voyage.

Although the comparatively enemy-free South Atlantic permitted the *U-584* to travel many miles on the surface, especially at night, the confinement of submarine life was irksome. Haupt, Thiel and Neubauer settled into the dull routine with a lethargy which must have alarmed Kerling, but he was aware of its reasons and could do nothing about it. These four men found each other's company more congenial than did those in Dasch's group, which may have been due to Kerling's having qualities of leadership which Dasch, for all his bravado, lacked.

Kerling remained close to Commander Deeke throughout the trip, noting the slow progress with impatience. He passed his thirty-third birthday on June 12 quietly, not even mentioning it to his friends. One thing did mar the trip, and that originated in the United States, not aboard the submarine. Like Dasch, Kerling had started to listen to American news broadcasts as soon as the submarine was within domestic radio range. One announcement gave him pause: the Office of Price Administration had instituted gasoline rationing on the East Coast; pleasure driving was to be all but eliminated. Kerling had intended to bury the explosives in the Florida sand and return for them by car after he found a hiding place in Ohio or Pennsylvania; now he would have to think of ways to get around the new regulations. Kerling did not discuss this with his colleagues; he was aware that they were under enough strain just getting ready to land. No alternate plan occurred to him, and he was still concerned about it a few days later, when Deeke told him they were close enough to shore to make final preparations for landing.

But a faultless landing, and the four boxes safely buried on the beach at Ponte Vedra, put him in excellent spirits over dinner in Jacksonville that Wednesday evening, June 17. Kerling turned to immediate plans; Haupt and Neubauer would go to Chicago separately, he and Thiel to New York. Kerling knew they should stay apart as much as possible until he and Dasch made their sabotage plans on July 4. After that, he would figure out how to get them all East to begin work. As for himself, he would use the time to deal with his personal problems and at the same time try to find a way to get the explosives off the beach.

Almost at once, while still fresh with wonder that they were really able to move freely in the United States, the eight men sought to attain a deeper sense of security than their initial success had given them. The search brought one to his family, another to his mistress, a few to old and trusted friends, one even to strangers. The need for personal ties seems to have outweighed their pledges of secrecy and even the potential danger to themselves. Most of the men sought these ties immediately, while waiting for Dasch and Kerling to meet in Cincinnati on July 4, when Operation Pastorius itself would provide the security of action.

Herbert Haupt was by far the most ambitious in employing this interlude. He had been ordered to use his American identity, but he wanted nothing less than to pick up his entire life in Chicago where he had left off more than a year earlier. Not even the delicate question of Gerda Stuckmann Melind, who had started him on his feckless odyssey, deterred him. He was returning considerably more affluent than when he left, now that he had a money belt stuffed with fifty-dollar bills, and he had great faith in the power of wealth. Haupt's freedom with money had shocked his more conservative colleagues before, in Paris and even back at Quenz Lake. If this was attributed to youthful exuberance, as it often was, it was nevertheless a cause for concern. Burger thought "that if Haupt got a chance to double-cross the group . . . he might do so purely for money," and Haupt's purchase in Jacksonville of a gold wrist watch with a flexible gold band seemed excessive to the other members of his unit, who had limited themselves to the immediate necessities of clothes and suitcases. In spite of this, Kerling gave Haupt one of the three canvas money bags to take with him to Chicago. This seems rash, but Kerling's rationalization was sound; he believed it safer for Haupt to have a reserve if by any chance he spent the nearly $4,000 in his money belt;

Kerling also intended to retrieve the bag as soon as possible after July 4.

Kerling did not entirely share the general prejudice against Haupt, which, aside from his looseness with money, seemed to stem from an older generation's lack of sympathy with the younger. Burger had objected to Haupt's greasing his hair with "smelly brilliantine" and referred to him as a "playboy type"; Dasch had dismissed him as "a typical drug-store cowboy." Yet, as Walter Kappe had done, Kerling saw assets in his youth and his physical strength. Nor could any of his colleagues deny that Haupt had shrewdness and cunning, as separate from intelligence. Furthermore, as the man most recently in the United States, with, as far as anyone knew, no record of having gone beyond Mexico, Haupt was expected to resume American life with a minimum of difficulty. His usefulness obviously outweighed his shortcomings.

Kerling recognized this when he sent Haupt to Chicago to wait for further instructions. Communication with Haupt was to be made through his uncle, Walter Froehling, whose address was written invisibly on Kerling's handkerchief. Froehling was known to have been an ardent Nazi sympathizer; in case his views had changed, Haupt was to remind him that his brother Otto was in a concentration camp in Germany, where his chances of release depended on Froehling's cooperation.

Haupt arrived in Chicago Friday afternoon carrying, besides money, the self-imposed aura of a hero home in triumph. He knew that in the pro-Nazi community of his friends and relatives few things would be as impressive as an actual assignment from the German Government. He was pledged to secrecy, of course, but he could contemplate the exact degree of insinuation which would tell everything while telling nothing. In the light of his new role, it was not likely that much would be made of the shame attendant on his departure. Chicago was to see a new Herbert Haupt.

Haupt started at the railroad station by taking a taxi, a gesture at once gratifying in itself and a public announcement of his new wealth and position. He went to his uncle's first in order to reduce his mother's shock at his return. His uncle, aunt and two young cousins greeted him warmly, then Froehling telephoned Haupt's mother to come over. Haupt hid while his uncle prepared his mother for the surprise. When at last the reunion was accomplished she was, in her own words, "nearly paralyzed seeing him, and still I was happy to see him." While waiting for his father to finish work, Haupt gave the family a short account of his adventures. Not until he went into details about his grandparents in Stettin did they really believe that he had actually been in Germany. After that, they even accepted the unlikely story that he had returned to the United States on a German submarine.

When his father arrived, and he had repeated the story of his experiences, Haupt opened his new suitcase and elaborately removed Kerling's canvas bag. He carefully explained what it was, false bottom and all, and that its contents was evidence of Germany's faith in him. With his family's promise of secrecy, Haupt asked his uncle to hide the bag. "Don't give it to anybody, no matter what they say," he said with just the right note of drama. Then, still the hero cloaked in mystery, he displayed his money belt, which he had removed earlier because it was pressing against his stomach. Before leaving, he told his uncle there were three other people on the mission and that he was expecting a telephone call at the Froehling apartment on Sunday.

The Haupts took their son back to their apartment at eleven that night. If they were not quite clear about what he was up to and found his behavior somewhat strange, they did have his assurances that he was in no danger—"I was schooled," he kept telling them—and that he was involved in matters of major importance. They could take pride in that. As for Herbert Haupt, he slept soundly. He could not doubt that he would continue to play his part well and that Abwehr II and Walter Kappe would be proud of him.

One problem marred the homecoming. His mother told him that in December the F.B.I. had questioned her about his failure to register for the draft. She had told them he was out of the country and, with complete innocence, had shown the agents a cable he had sent from Japan. Haupt had been convinced that nothing could disprove his story of spending a year in Mexico, so, buoyed by the ease with which he had come through his first tests in the United States, he refused to be troubled. On Monday he would register for the draft and then report to the F.B.I. with a story to cover his mother's error. This problem was more than balanced by the good news that Gerda Melind had had a miscarriage soon after he left for Mexico. He could now look forward to seeing her with pleasure rather than trepidation.

Haupt loafed on Saturday. Toward midnight, he and his parents called on Mr. and Mrs. Otto Wergin, his friend Wolfgang's parents. Otto Wergin did not get home until three o'clock that morning because he was a drummer in the band at Haus Vaterland, a German-American social center. When he arrived, Haupt told his own story and gave a detailed report of Wolfgang's travels, which gave Wergin the impression that his own son would one day return to America on a German submarine too. Wergin was so carried away by Haupt's words that at one point he said, "Don't tell me, I know you're an Intelligence man." Haupt did not deny it. With an older man's sense of time passing him by, Wergin recalled that he had done some intelligence work for Germany in Egypt during World War I, and added, "If you ever need a good man to help you, I'm your man."

Haupt was moved by indications that the Wergins were not doing well financially. When he found himself alone in the kitchen with Mrs. Wergin, he gave her a fifty-dollar bill, saying that it was from Wolfgang. His manner told her that it was his gift, not her son's, and Haupt enjoyed her knowledge of that. He was most pleased, though, because until she looked at the money she thought it was a dollar bill. She had never seen a fifty in her life.

Haupt went from the Wergins' to sleep at the Froehlings' because he had told Hermann Neubauer to telephone him there on Sunday. He woke at noon to a scene of comic-strip confusion. His uncle and a friend were painting chairs while his aunt was trying to keep her two children from the paint, the wet chairs and the studio couch where Haupt slept. When the telephone rang at noon, his ten-year-old cousin answered it, understood nothing and handed the phone to her mother, who then passed it to Froehling, who at last realized it was the call Haupt was expecting. Neubauer had just arrived from Cincinnati and was eager to see Haupt. They arranged to meet at the Chicago Theatre. Once there, they decided to see the movie. It would have been hard to resist; the film was called *The Invaders,* with Laurence Olivier, Leslie Howard, Raymond Massey and Eric Portman. It had been made in Canada and England under the title of *The Forty-ninth Parallel* and was the story of six survivors of a bombed German submarine making their way across Canada. Afterward, neither ever recalled more than the title and the bare outline of the story.

After the movie they talked briefly at a restaurant next to the theater. Haupt was optimistic; Neubauer was worried, and said he thought Kerling and Thiel were upset as well. He reported that they had covered the telephone while speaking to each other in the hotel room in Jacksonville and that they had refrained from taking taxis. Haupt considered these normal precautions for men using false identities, and tried to get Neubauer to accept his interpretation. More pertinent was Neubauer's message from Kerling, whom he had met again, briefly, in Cincinnati on his way to Chicago. Kerling now planned to arrange with Dasch to hold a meeting in Chicago on July 6. After Haupt made a few more efforts to cheer his colleague, the two men parted with an agreement to meet at the same theater on Wednesday.

Monday morning, Haupt set out to overcome the major barrier to his security in Chicago. He reported to Local Draft Board No. 66, explained his absence in Mexico, and without any difficulty was registered. With a perfectly legal draft card in his pocket, he was supremely confident as he took a taxi to the local office of the F.B.I. Boldly he told an agent that he understood there had been inquiries about his absence from the United States. He was there, he said, to explain what had happened, and thus clarify his status. His explanations had been carefully thought out and, while not entirely true, contained enough truth for Haupt to believe they would be plausible. He had gone to Mexico, he said, not to evade the draft, but because he had been wrongfully accused of causing the pregnancy of a woman who was a habitual drunkard and who had slept with some ten or twelve men. Because of her reputation he did not want to marry her, and so did what any normal young man would have done under the circumstances: he left town. In Mexico he had spent most of the year living with Indians in the hills, prospecting for gold. On a visit to Mexico City he had met some men who said they were going to Tokyo. It seemed a good idea at the time to give them ten or fifteen pesos to send his mother a cable from Japan with his signature. He learned when he came home that such a cable had been sent. He was sorry for the misunderstanding it had caused, especially since he had never left Mexico. Now that he was back and had his draft card, he assumed the F.B.I. was no longer interested in him. The F.B.I. agent listened without comment, and when Haupt was finished, gravely asked him if he would fight for the United States if called to military service. That day at least, Haupt knew when to underplay his part. He would rather not fight against the German people, he said, but if called he would go. The agent accepted this answer calmly, and informed Haupt that, with his registration, the F.B.I. had no further questions. Haupt left the office with complete self-confidence. It had been remarkably easy.

When Haupt walked out of the building, an F.B.I. agent followed, and remained a discreet distance behind him.

Back home, Haupt burned the false draft card Kappe had given him in Berlin in the name of Lawrence Jordan. As if, somehow, the burning was not enough expiation for the trouble it could have caused his acquaintance, Haupt abruptly decided to visit Jordan's parents. It was not the kind of gesture Haupt was used to making, and he spent an uncomfortable ten minutes with Mr. and Mrs. Jordan, trying to make proper conversation. It was a painful visit for them, too. Lawrence Jordan had been reported missing in the Philippines and his parents were living with more grief than hope. They talked of their son and passed his photograph from hand to hand. Haupt mentioned briefly that he had been in Mexico for the past year, and got up to leave. Then, as if to impress on them that his own patriotism, if not equal to their son's was at least undeniable, he blurted out that he had registered for the draft that day. Later, the Jordans barely remembered the conversation.

That evening Haupt and his parents visited Andreas Grunau, a family friend who was decidedly pro-Nazi, an opinion which he managed to hide in public; he was also superintendent of the Simpson Optical Company, where Haupt had worked. The firm was now operating overtime to meet government contracts for bomb-sight lenses and other military instruments. Grunau welcomed Haupt's interest in coming back to work, and Haupt promised to start Thursday. It seemed a good place to be until Kerling made definite plans.

On Tuesday Haupt proceeded to attend to other important matters. Foremost was Gerda Melind. He recruited his mother as intermediary, and the two women lunched while Haupt went to the movies. When he returned, his mother told him Gerda was eager to see him. He called her and made an engagement for the same evening, and then went out with his father to buy an automobile. Kerling had specifically told him not to do this until so instructed, but Kerling was less persuasive than a nearly new Pontiac convertible coupe. Haupt justified the purchase by asking that the papers be made out in his father's name.

That evening he proposed marriage to Gerda Melind. He certified his intentions by giving her ten dollars to pay for the blood test necessary under Illinois law before a marriage license can be issued. Haupt did not tell her any more than that he had been to Mexico. It must have been with great restraint that he omitted the hints of his new grandeur which he had thrown so freely at his parents, the Froehlings and the Wergins. She seems to have been sincerely confused. "I couldn't understand why he wanted to marry me all of a sudden, after not hearing from him a whole year," she said later. "So I thought, well, I would agree to have [the test] taken, and maybe by that time he would tell me a little more why he wanted to marry me all of a sudden, what the reason was." She had the caution of a lady once burned, but Haupt's gesture may well have been, by his own lights, the gentlemanly thing to do after running away.

On Wednesday, Haupt took possession of the Pontiac. He intended to use the money from his belt for the down payment, but his mother withdrew a hundred and fifty dollars from her own savings account to replace three of Haupt's fifty-dollar bills. She had read in the papers that the government was watching for large bills coming into the United States from Axis countries. Haupt also met Neubauer that day, called Gerda, lied to her about having taken a blood test himself, and then embarked on what he considered the most important activity of all—draft dodging.

The job at Simpson's might bring a temporary deferment because of the company's military contracts, but that was not the kind of assurance Haupt wanted. To solve his problem, he turned to William Wernecke, a young, bitterly fanatic anti-Semite who was a volunteer worker for some of the isolationist societies in Chicago whose efforts on behalf of Germany during the war came close to actual treason. Wernecke himself had ambitions to be a Storm Trooper when the inevitable German conquest of the United States brought him his reward. He had hidden in a farmhouse a small armory of rifles, shotguns, 2100 rounds of ammunition, a collection of dueling pistols and two cans of blasting powder. Before Haupt left for Mexico the two men had practiced their marksmanship on the farm dressed in black trousers, brown shirts, dark ties and black leather puttees. Now Haupt found Wernccke distraught, in fear of the F.B.I. because of his illegal activities and uncertain that they were recognized in Nazi Germany. Haupt did not trust Wernecke, but he needed him. He brightened Wernecke considerably by telling him that the German Consul in Mexico was familiar with his good work. The lie was effective. Wernecke energetically set out to solve Haupt's draft problem.

Draft dodging had become Wernecke's specialty since the start of selective service, and he was expert at it. Beginning early Thursday, he exposed Haupt to a side of his home town most Chicagoans had never seen. He started at the office of a doctor to whom he regularly brought bundles of pro-Nazi literature from the presses of the organizations he represented. Haupt was advised to tell the doctor that he had "coronary thrombosis, rheumatic pains, swelling of my ankles, pain in my upper left arm, dizzy spells now and then, headaches every week, indigestion, pains in my chest and pains in my back." The doctor found Haupt's blood pressure high—"probably due to nervousness," he said. He also thought Haupt's heart was not all it should be and Haupt suggested fever in Mexico and bad effects from quinine as the likely cause. They agreed that a cardiogram was warranted, and the doctor wrote a note, which Haupt could show at Simpson's, requesting that he be kept from undue physical exertion until a definite diagnosis was made. There was no charge for the examination; it was the doctor's own small contribution to the German war effort.

Wernecke's medical expertise was mainly in heart ailments. Three one-one-hundredth-gram pills of nitroglycerin taken just before an examination would cause heart palpitations, he said, and was the method he had used to manage his own draft deferment. At a downtown pharmacy the next day, Haupt asked for six such pills, and was amazed that they could be purchased only in quantities of a hundred or more. But at thirty-nine cents a hundred they seemed a bargain. The two young men then went to the hospital where the doctor had arranged for Haupt's examination. Fifteen minutes before he was to be called, Haupt swallowed three pills. While Haupt was being examined, Wernecke from behind a door coached him with gestures to hold his breath and beat his chest so as to further disturb the cardiograph. A watchful nurse kept Haupt from following all the instructions, but he did manage to hold his breath. He paid for the examination and made arrangements to pick up the results on Saturday.

Medical problems in hand, Wernecke then undertook to examine religious possibilities for deferment. He had told Haupt that he was a member of a group called the Christian Mobilizers, which made him a bona-fide Bible student and a conscientious objector in case the medical deferment should be canceled. Very little was necessary to become a minister, he explained, if one's ambitions were in that direction. One method was simply to start a religion. This sounded like a lot of effort to Haupt, and he decided to stay within the existing order. Whereupon Wernecke left Haupt for a while and came back saying he had been to his church. "He told me," Haupt recalled, "that he had spoken to the head man about my case, and the head man told him that the Administration was against God, but he was for God, and he would help any man to stay out of the Army to keep from fighting against God. For $100 this man would register me as a Bible student dating back to 1941, and would ordain me as an assistant minister." It was not as cheap as nitroglycerin pills, but obviously an investment worth thinking about. Haupt took an application form from Wernecke for membership in the Christian Mobilizers.

In the evening Haupt met some friends, men he had known at Simpson's, and relaxed in a way he knew best—drinks, dinner, and more drinks. He deserved a night off, and took it with pleasure.

Early the next morning he got into his new car and headed for the hospital to pick up the cardiogram. It was Saturday, June 27. He had been back in Chicago a week, and had performed without any flaw that he could see. His accomplishments were formidable by any standard—draft, job, Gerda, car, family and friends were all in order. He had money to enjoy himself, and was on the way to arranging his draft deferment.

He drove to the Loop and turned into Webster Avenue.

Behind him, another car made the same turn . . .

Chicago had nothing at all to offer Hermann Neubauer, and his experience there was, in contrast to Haupt's, almost completely unsatisfactory. He had not been in the city since the World's Fair in the thirties, had no friends there—unless

Haupt could be called a friend—and did not want to see the parents of his American-born wife. He had known loneliness in battle and in hospitals, but it was nothing to the loneliness of hotel rooms. He changed hotels three times, as much from wanting something to do as from nervousness. He moved from the LaSalle to the Sherman to the Sheridan Plaza and still was not satisfied; having worked among hotel and restaurant workers, he was afraid he would be recognized. He did not find release in drinking, and so passed up the companionship to be found in bars. He went to the movies frequently, chain-smoked cigars, and gloomily waited for Kerling to come to Chicago.

Seeing Haupt on Sunday helped, but after Haupt's departure, the loneliness returned. The next day was intolerable. Neubauer was so depressed that he could not remember a week or so later whether it was Monday night or Tuesday night that he decided to call on Harry and Emma Jaques, people he had never seen before. Neubauer had met Mrs. Jaques' sister in Germany, and "they were friends of my wife, and I knew they were Germans and did not believe they would give me away." These were slender supports for a relationship, but by that time Neubauer would have acted on less.

At ten in the evening, Neubauer called the Jaques apartment. He introduced himself as Henry Nicholas and, after being assured there were no visitors, asked if he could drop by. Possibly intrigued, and despite the hour, the Jaqueses agreed. "I guess it looks kind of funny for me, a stranger, to drop in on you," he said when he arrived. "You don't know me." He told them that he was Alma Wolf's husband. Mrs. Jaques, who had been in correspondence with her sister in Germany before the United States entered the war, asked him to show his wound and name the hospital he had been in. He pointed to the scars on his right cheek and his left calf and said that it was the hospital in Stuttgart where Mrs. Jaques' sister and brother-in-law had visited him. "Then you must be Hermann Neubauer," Mrs. Jaques said, and he felt that he had found friends at last.

The three talked at length about mutual friends in the United States and Germany, until Mrs. Jaques went to the kitchen to make coffee and sandwiches. Neubauer then nervously told Jaques that he had arrived in America on a German submarine and that he was on a special assignment from the

German Government. Giving even this much away was against orders, but he might have told even more. Jaques, however, with the wisdom accumulated through guarding his own illegal status in the United States—he had jumped ship years earlier—did not want to hear any more. A number of Germans, he said, had already been picked up by the F.B.I. and were in American concentration camps. Before Mrs. Jaques came back, Neubauer did manage to show Jaques his false draft card on which his name appeared as Henry Nicholas. He was registered under that name at the Hotel LaSalle, he said, in case Jaques wanted to reach him.

In Mrs. Jaques' presence the conversation reverted to Neubauer's war experience, conditions in Germany, and old friends. Mrs. Jaques mentioned casually that she had received a letter from her friend Mrs. Kerling in New York. Neubauer, surprised at this coincidence, could not resist saying that Kerling had returned to the United States with him. He stopped at that, respecting Jaques' desire to be kept in ignorance. But before he left he asked the couple to hold some money for him. It was an imposition on comparative strangers, he knew, but he did not want to carry the money with him, so he had no other choice. He had gotten rid of the money belt and was now carrying the fifty-dollar bills in two LaSalle Hotel envelopes. His original $4,000 had been reduced to $3,800 when he returned the gold certificates to Kappe. He showed the money to the Jaqueses, told them that it had been received from the German Government, and gave them all but $200 of it. When he left at 2:00 A.M. the Jaqueses put the money in a five-pound coffee can, which they set on a shelf in the pantry, and went to bed.

On Wednesday, Neubauer met Haupt in the Chicago Theatre again and told him he planned to change hotels. On Thursday he did so and went to the movies again. He went back to visit the Jaqueses Friday evening. They did not raise the subject of his presence in the United States, but talked comfortably once more of the old country. When the Jaqueses mentioned rumors in the radio news that Germans were being landed in the United States by submarine, Neubauer dismissed this casually. That sort of story had been in the papers before, he said. When he said goodbye after midnight, he told them he was now at the Sheridan Plaza. Jaques asked him if he wanted any of the money. "No, I don't need any at this time," Neubauer said, and left with a promise that he would call on them again the following week.

He liked Harry and Emma Jaques. They were as congenial as his wife had told him they were. But he did not want to wear out his welcome. With them, occasional visits with Haupt, and the movies, perhaps Chicago would not be so lonely in the ten days that remained before Kerling was due. Neubauer spent the night at the Sheridan Plaza, and the next afternoon went out to still another movie. As he returned to the hotel that evening, Saturday, June 27, he decided it would be safer to move again . . .

Edward Kerling took seriously the responsibilities of leadership which Kappe had placed on him; although he would have preferred to have his old friend Neubauer as a traveling companion, he realized the extent of Thiel's dependence on him. Werner Thiel, who was born to follow, could never have made decisions on his own, and Kerling did not leave him on his own for very long. Thiel left Jacksonville for Cincinnati on Friday, the day after they landed, and Kerling met him and Neubauer there at noon Saturday.

Kerling had purposely chosen to go to New York by way of Cincinnati because he was under the impression that passenger lists were checked on trains traveling along the shorter East Coast route. He was confident now that he had come so far, and was pleased at how easily he adapted to American customs. He had not even been outraged when a hotel bellboy in Jacksonville overcharged him for a pint of whiskey—"I quoted my price," the boy said later. Kerling did, however, insist on normal precautions. When he bought two tickets for New York, he gave one to Thiel and they boarded the train separately. In New York, he relented and took a double room at the Hotel Commodore. He knew Thiel's need for his presence, and he also felt secure at the Commodore. It was convenient to subway and bus lines, could be entered directly from Grand Central Terminal if necessary, and was a large, busy hotel.

Kerling and Thiel slept until late Sunday afternoon. Around six o'clock, after a brief meal, Kerling began to set his house—or in his case, houses—in order. He was sure he could manage this without endangering the mission. He went to visit Helmut Leiner, a friend who was so trustworthy that his name had been put on Dasch's handkerchief as one of the reliable sources of help. Kerling meant to reach both his wife and his mistress through Leiner. Since Thiel had met Leiner in the Bund, Kerling allowed him to go along. When they got to Astoria, Long Island, after the long subway ride, they found Leiner's porch crowded with visitors. Kerling decided his appearance would require explanations, and sent Thiel to the house instead. Thiel managed the situation quite well. He greeted Leiner, was introduced to the visiting relatives, chatted briefly, and then suggested that Leiner walk down the street with him. Kerling was waiting for them at the corner. Leiner was genuinely surprised; the last he had seen of Kerling was before he returned to Germany. He readily accepted an invitation to dinner, said goodbye to his family, and went with Kerling and Thiel to the Blue Ribbon, a German restaurant just off Times Square.

Kerling knew and trusted Leiner enough to tell him briefly how he had come and what his purpose was in America. Leiner, for his part, was prepared to help Kerling in his dealings with the two women in his life. Mrs. Kerling, Leiner said, was working as a cook in a fashionable New York apartment; Hedwig Engemann was helping out at her family's grocery store in Yorkville. Leiner would arrange for Kerling to meet each of them. After dinner the three men moved a few doors east to a bar and talked over drinks for three hours. Here, Thiel decided that Leiner could help him as well. Before the evening was over, Leiner had agreed to get a message to Anthony Cramer, Thiel's closest friend in the United States.

Thiel's message for Cramer was in the best undercover tradition. Leiner was to tell Cramer that "Franz from Detroit" wanted to meet him Monday evening at nine at the Grand Central Terminal Information Desk, possibly New York's most popular meeting place. Leiner did well. Cramer was at the appointed place, from which he and Thiel walked a few blocks to a bar at Forty-fourth Street and Lexington Avenue for an evening of catching up on old times and old friends. Thiel was uncertain as to how deeply he wanted to get his friend involved, and was circumspect during this first meeting, although he said later that he thought Cramer had guessed his mission. He was even more convinced the next morning when he saw an item in a newspaper column normally devoted to Hollywood and Broadway chitchat that "F.B.I. agents are swarming through the Florida swamps because of stories that Nazi submarine crews in civilian clothes are at large in that state." That evening, Thiel did not hesitate. He met Cramer at the same bar and asked him to take his money belt. Cramer agreed, and Thiel went to the men's toilet, removed the belt and gave it to his friend. About this time, Kerling, on his way to meet his wife and his mistress, joined the two men for a drink.

Not long after Kerling left them, Thiel and Cramer concluded their evening with pie and coffee at Thompson's Cafeteria, down the street from the Commodore Hotel, and made arrangements to meet again the next day. Cramer promised to bring with him a former sweetheart of Thiel's named Norma Kopp, who as far as he knew was then working as a domestic in Westport, Connecticut. Just before eleven-thirty they said their good nights. Now that he was rid of his money belt, Thiel was relaxed for the first time in the six days he had been back in the United States. Kerling had indicated that they would soon be leaving for Cincinnati and Chicago, and Thiel, despite his friendship for Cramer, was eager to move on. It was Tuesday, June 23. As he walked the short distance from Thomspon's to the Commodore, Werner Thiel hoped strongly that Kerling would straighten out his personal affairs in a hurry and make definite plans for departure . . .

When Kerling left Thiel and Cramer to meet his wife, he was satisfied that he could combine business and pleasure in the days ahead. He had done quite well already, in less than seventy-two hours in New York. He had met Hedy Engemann at Central Park on Monday afternoon for an hour. It was enough time to find out that her feelings for him were as strong as ever, and that she was ready to go with him to Cincinnati, Chicago and Florida. He had not been completely frank with her. He had told her he had come back by submarine, but not much more, and she had not questioned him closely. It seemed to be enough that her lover was back. When they met again Monday evening, Kerling gave her a few of the fifty-dollar bills to change, and promised to see her Tuesday. She knew that they would have to talk to his wife, but in this amazing triangle, Hedy Engemann and Marie Kerling had reached an agreement of their own not long after Kerling returned to Germany. Mrs. Kerling considered her relationship to Kerling to be more like that of a sister to a brother than that of a wife to a husband. She had told Hedy she was ready to divorce him. When Kerling left her Monday night, Hedy Engemann was making plans to go away with the man she loved.

Tuesday afternoon Kerling took a recess from personal affairs to seek help in arranging a hideout for the explosives, once he brought them north. He and Leiner went over to Newark, New Jersey, to locate a minister whose name was one of the two invisibly written on the handkerchief Kappe had given Kerling, but they couldn't find him. Kerling had read in the Cincinnati papers on Saturday that the F.B.I. had picked up a pro-Nazi minister in Philadelphia, and he assumed it was the man he sought. He was not altogether disappointed, though. He had come more and more to feel that he would have to carry the burden of the sabotage program by himself. What he had to do first was free himself of possible complications with his wife.

When he and Leiner returned to New York that evening, they walked from Pennsylvania Station to the Crossroads Inn at Times Square for dinner. From there Leiner called Mrs. Kerling and, without telling her Kerling was in New York, asked to meet her at the Engemann grocery store. They took a cab east to Lexington Avenue, where Leiner dropped Kerling for his meeting with Thiel and Cramer. That done, Kerling walked the five blocks north to meet his wife and Hedy Engemann.

His plans at that moment were simply to find the right hideout for himself and Hedy. Maybe a farm in Pennsylvania would be best; it would be close enough to the major sabotage objectives, yet isolated enough for safety. Before that, though, there was some catching up to do. He would go to the public library tomorrow and read the back issues of newspapers so that he would not be guilty of obvious ignorance of recent events. This was only Tuesday, June 23; he had until July 4 to get to Cincinnati for the meeting with Dasch, and then to Chicago to give instructions to Haupt and Neubauer. There was a great deal of work to be done, but first he would settle matters with his wife. He reached the corner and walked back and forth impatiently . . .

When Heinrich Heinck and Richard Quirin left Burger and Dasch at the Automat on Saturday, June 13, their first day in New York, they took a double room at the Hotel Martinique. The hours since the landing at Amagansett had been exhausting, and they went to sleep at once. They were to meet Burger and Dasch at the Swiss Chalet the next afternoon, and they hoped that Dasch would have plans for them all to leave the city soon. From the start Quirin felt vulnerable in New York, and had even convinced himself that five-fifty a day for their hotel room was too expensive; if they were not to leave right away he intended to look for a cheap rooming house where he and Heinck, at least, would be less exposed.

It was natural for Quirin to be making the plans for both. Heinck, by far the weaker of the two, had begun to lean on Quirin even more than he had during their training, as if to absorb some of his strength and assurance. Heinck was not considered very intelligent by his colleagues, but he had a reputation for absorbing and remembering his lessons better than any of them. He seemed, however, to be perpetually apprehensive, and to find solace only in liquor. When that was unavailable, Quirin gave him what support he could. For his own part, Quirin thrived on the responsibility and potential danger of the sabotage assignment, and he did not find Heinck a burden; although the man's drinking worried Quirin, himself a man who could hold large quantities without difficulty, he knew he could influence Heinck. Since Quenz Lake, Quirin had had a vague mistrust of Dasch and Burger, and perhaps required Heinck's dependence to confirm his own purposes and to keep him from a tendency toward impulsive actions. By now the barrier between him and Dasch and Burger had drawn him even closer to Heinck.

Heinck and Quirin waited at the Swiss Chalet for more than an hour on Sunday, but neither Burger nor Dasch appeared. It was a frustrating start for the day. The two men spent the hot, humid afternoon walking the nearly empty streets of New York. They were early for the second rendezvous, up at Grant's Tomb, and mingled with other sightseers as they waited impatiently. Finally, at six-twenty, just as Quirin was ready to give up in exasperation, Burger and Dasch arrived by taxi. In separate pairs, the four men walked toward Broadway and Columbia University. Quirin impatiently reminded Dasch that Kappe's instructions had been for them to establish themselves in Chicago as soon as possible. He felt it was unsafe to be in a hotel, exposed to the public, and he was irritated with Dasch's failure to keep the earlier appointment. He was on the verge of an open fight with Dasch, and his anger increased when Dasch cut him short by saying he had to attend an important meeting outside the city, and that they would all have to stay in New York until he returned. As for the hotel, Dasch told Quirin he could do as he pleased. Neither Burger nor Heinck intruded in the strained discussion but it was apparent where the loyalty of each belonged. When Dasch and Quirin had agreed to meet again on Tuesday at the Automat, Quirin and Heinck walked away without goodbyes.

Early Monday morning Quirin and Heinck packed their clothes and left the Hotel Martinique. They found two rooms in a nondescript rooming house at 149 West Seventy-sixth Street. Quirin was looking for security, and his instincts were exactly right. Thousands of New Yorkers lived on just such a street in just such a brownstone house; staying in the open in this neighborhood was the best way to hide in the city. Heinck had wanted to find rooms in the Bronx, where he had once lived and with which he was familiar, but he bowed, as he did in all things, to Quirin's decision. Heinck signed as Kaynor, as he had before, but Quirin, who had used Albany as his false address at the Martinique, now decided to use it as a name; a second alias added to his sense of security. The two men spent the rest of Monday shopping. Somehow, spending money seemed a safe and easy way to pass the time.

When Heinck and Quirin went to the Automat on Tuesday, only Burger met them. Dasch's absence infuriated Quirin, and he reiterated the argument he had made Sunday at Grant's Tomb about the urgency for leaving New York. Burger attributed Quirin's feelings to strained nerves and worked hard to calm him down. Dasch, he said, was making plans for their next move, and these took time. He was lonely with Dasch gone, he said, and he suggested that he join Quirin and Heinck on Wednesday. They agreed to meet at the Fifth Avenue entrance to the public library. From there they were just across the street from Rogers Peet, a men's clothing store, where they planned to buy suits. Burger had put the other two in a better mood. They were frank with him, and gave him their new address.

That afternoon Quirin accompanied Heinck to Astoria, where Heinck called on a friend named Hermann Faje. As Neubauer and Thiel were to do a week later, Heinck was disregarding the most elementary security precautions; he was also disobeying Kappe's direct orders to let only Dasch get in touch with this friend. Faje was not home, but Mrs. Faje invited Heinck and Quirin to return for dinner. That evening the two men could not resist telling their host and hostess that they had arrived in the United States by submarine, and Heinck gave Faje his money belt for safekeeping. To him, as to three of the others, getting rid of the money seemed imperative. Heinck also asked Faje to get a fifty-dollar bill changed for him; ironically, he was to buy a pen-and-pencil set.

On Wednesday, Burger surprised the two men by going to their room on West Seventy-sixth Street instead of waiting at the library. When he told them Dasch had spent the night playing pinochle, Quirin became abusive and threatened to take over the leadership of the group himself. Burger's calm words and even disposition were again effective. He said that Dasch now had definite plans for going to Chicago, and this mollified Quirin, at least long enough for them to go downtown to be fitted for clothes. Quirin did not give the salesman his correct address, and insisted that the three men would pick up the clothes on Saturday rather than have them delivered. With the improvement in Quirin's mood, Burger suggested that the three of them meet later at the Swing Club on Fifty-second Street, where he had already found the music, liquor and girls to his liking. It was the kind of evening that relaxed Quirin completely; his weakness for women and his capacity for liquor had been apparent in Paris. Heinck enjoyed the liquor, and until 3:00 A.M., at least, both men forgot their troubles with Dasch.

Thursday evening, Heinck visited Faje while Quirin and Burger made a round of the night clubs on Fifty-second Street, including the Swing Club once more, where they discovered a girl named Frankie, who, coincidentally enough, had two friends. A triple date was made for Friday evening. It was so late when this arduous day ended that Quirin took a room for the night near Burger's at the Governor Clinton.

Quirin was cheerful when he went to bed, but by morning, prodded by a hangover, he again became abusive about Dasch. What was more, he told Burger, he and Dasch were living more expensively than they should, and by staying in a popular hotel they were needlessly exposing themselves. He left abruptly. As soon as Burger was dressed, he followed Quirin to the rooming house. Once more, but with great difficulty this time, he managed to soothe Quirin, mostly with reminders of the evening's entertainment which lay ahead. The three men returned to Burger's room, where they called Frankie to confirm their engagement, and after dinner they taxied to the East Side address she gave them. It was so satisfactory an evening that none of them could remember the names of the girls, although Heinck recalled that the madam of the establishment was named Anna.

The three men met again on Saturday to pick up their suits. Quirin and Heinck had killed time before meeting Burger by attending the newsreel theater in Grand Central, where some newly released films of the attack on Pearl Harbor were being shown. With their clothes in hand, they dropped in at a bar and grill across the street from the clothing store. Quirin's irritation with Dasch's absence had lessened. It may have been the sense of security that a full week without trouble gave him, or Burger's strongly worded faith in their leader. Whichever it was, when he and Heinck rose to leave Burger, they talked about what they would do tomorrow, whether to go to the beach or to Palisades Park, an amusement area across the river in New Jersey. Quirin and Heinck were, on the whole, in a better mood when they caught their uptown bus. True, it had been an unsatisfactory week in terms of Dasch's infuriating absence and the lack of any positive action. But Burger had turned out to be a decent fellow after all, and they were secure on West Seventy-sixth Street. And Quirin was prepared to move on his own if Dasch did not come back soon. In what direction he was not quite sure.

He did know that on this Saturday evening, June 20, there was not much he could do about anything. He and Heinck were both tired, perhaps they should have a nap when they got back to their room. They left the bus at Seventy-second Street and Broadway and walked to Amsterdam Avenue. Quirin walked ahead toward a tailor shop, while Heinck stopped to make some purchases at a drug store and a delicatessen. He would catch up with Quirin in a few minutes, he said, as he dropped behind . . .

The partnership of Peter Burger and George Dasch was as lacking in passion as a marriage of convenience. Burger had resented Dasch almost from the beginning. For one thing, his feelings were those of a well-disciplined soldier who, having done his duty, watches special privileges going to one who has not. As far as Burger could see, Dasch paid no attention to the instructions at Quenz Lake, sat listlessly through the classes to which he invariably arrived late, wore civilian clothes while the others wore the black-dyed Czechoslovakian uniforms they had been issued, and rarely participated in the sports program. This struck Burger as all the more distressing in one who had been given the responsibilities of leadership. Worst of all, Dasch's behavior had Kappe's acceptance, if not approval. "Kappe did whatever Dasch wanted," Burger recalled, "and Dasch could do anything he wanted at school." Dasch's loss of his wallet and papers on the train at Lorient helped confirm Burger's doubts about Dasch's sense of responsibility.

Dasch's feelings about Burger are less easy to determine. He was so self-centered, and so ambitious after the years of unfulfillment in the United States, that it is hard to believe he could feel deeply about any other human being; he was the kind of person who had acquaintances but no friends. When his group was formed at Quenz Lake, it included Schmidt, who resented him, and Quirin and Heinck, who had formed their own partnership, which became stronger in Berlin, Paris, Lorient and on the submarine. This left only Burger. Dasch's references to their relationship never reflected any of the emotions normally associated with equals but were rather those of an employer discussing a diligent employe.

Yet despite their feelings toward one another, they had no choice but to remain together. By the Saturday morning of their landing, Burger and Dasch were fully committed to an alliance of their own, however uneasy. And within twenty-four hours after their arrival in New York, their relationship took on a new meaning. The uneasiness remained for Burger, the smug self-assurance of a boss toward a worker remained with Dasch. Still, and in the absence of complete trust, they made a commitment whose implications neither was ever to understand fully but whose immediate results were unmistakable. Dasch was going to betray Operation Pastorius, and Burger was going to help him.

The circumstances under which this remarkable pact was made will probably never be known. We have only the accounts of the two men, and, while it would be easy enough to accept their nearly identical versions of what took place, the very similarity also suggests that they spent as much time preparing their stories as they did in deciding how to go about turning in the plans, explosives and the other six men. What is clear is that some time between his recruitment for Operation Pastorius and his arrival in New York City, Dasch had decided to wreck the mission. If the decision was made as early as Berlin or Quenz Lake, as he said, he had carried on a superb masquerade which fooled not only Kappe and the top officers of Abwehr II, but the men with whom he lived for nearly two months. Though it seems unlikely, this is possible, and whether his motive was deep-seated anti-Nazi convictions, as he claimed, or the prospect of reward in America, is not as important as his having played a difficult role so convincingly. If the decision came on the beach at Amagansett, it is easier to understand; he may have realized that bribing a Coast Guardsman was no guarantee of safety, and that there was less personal danger in giving up voluntarily than in being caught. His face had been seen by flashlight; he was the only one who could be identified; his danger was greater than that of the others. Given those conditions, it may not have taken much further thought to reach the decision he did at the Hotel Governor Clinton.

Whatever Dasch's motivation, he required an accomplice, if only to support the story he meant to tell. He had no choice but to confide in Burger, and Burger, either voluntarily, under threat, or from fear, said he would go along. Considering that Burger always mistrusted Dasch, and that he had a history of remarkable survival, self-preservation seems the most likely reason. If this was his motive, he was now embarked on a cynical and dangerous game. If Dasch did turn in the others, Burger had to appear to the authorities as if he, too, had been eager to do so. If Dasch merely disappeared with his money-filled suitcase, Burger had to continue to appear to Heinck and Quirin, and later to Kerling and his group, as the loyal Nazi and saboteur.

The story Burger and Dasch told of their decision to reveal the sabotage plans and bring about the capture of the others had its own logic. The decision itself, they said, ended a period of anguish that had, for each of them, begun long before the courses at Quenz Lake. Each was essentially anti-Nazi, they said, Burger as a result of the treatment he suffered at the hands of the Gestapo, Dasch because of what he saw of conditions in Germany almost immediately after he arrived there in 1941. Each had independently decided, they said, that Operation Pastorius was a ready means by which to return to America and join the fight against Hitler. Each, without confiding in the other, had understood at Quenz Lake that they were not at all like the others in the training program.

The first night in America, they said, this wordless communication suddenly found expression, as they had dinner in the Coral Room of the Governor Clinton. "We discussed the various jobs which we had been instructed to do in the United States," Burger recalled, "and the political situation in Germany, and George also expressed to me some of the difficulties and hardships which his relatives were going through in Germany. I told Dasch of the difficulties I had experienced, . . . and finally George declared he had a plan, which if followed out, would keep us out of difficulty over here, and avoid all trouble and help our people back in Germany. George also said he believed his plan would help out the people in Germany with the same political beliefs that we had.

"This convinced me that George was against the present regime, as I was, and that he did not wish to carry out the orders we had received. Then he told me he would have to put me through different tests before he explained what he wanted to do. At the moment, I told him right to his face that I knew exactly what he wanted to do. His answer was that if I knew that, I would have to kill him. At that I smiled and told him that I was quite sure that our intentions were very similar. After this the restaurant became crowded and we left."

They did not go back to their rooms, but joined the Saturday night strollers along Fifth Avenue—more than usual this evening because of the parade during the day. They paused at Rockefeller Center, crowded with sightseers, and walked by the gardens, now a vegetable patch to symbolize the wartime need for food instead of flowers. Dasch enjoyed the role of guide, and led Burger to the murals of José Maria Sert, which, he explained, "illustrated the history of mankind from early days of slavery to the present." Dasch's motives in exposing Burger to the paintings were subtle in the extreme; he wanted, he said later, to keep Burger in the proper mood to accept the idea of deserting the sabotage plans.

Yet because of fatigue—the two men had not had much sleep since Thursday, their last night on the submarine— or of wariness, the two men talked no more that evening about plans for betrayal. Burger said later that he remembered Kappe's saying in Germany that there would be no reprisals against any member of the sabotage team who killed another attempting to expose the plan. If he were being led into a trap, there was no point in rushing it. Dasch may have been slow in revealing all his plans to Burger, but he could not resist playing the mysterious hero to old acquaintances. The walk back from Rockefeller Center was a strange performance. The two men walked west on Forty-eighth Street, until they came to a coffee house which served as a club for waiters in the midtown area. Dasch left Burger standing outside and walked in to a warm welcome from old friends. He stayed long enough to joke about being back, made allusions to having been in Russia, and then announced that he was going to Washington to hit Hitler "where it counts." "You'll be reading all about it in the papers pretty soon," he said. On this dramatic note, he returned to Burger on the street.

When they came to a restaurant on Broadway where Dasch had once worked, he again asked Burger to wait while he went to greet his former boss. Without much prodding Dasch said that he had just returned from Germany, where things were horrible, and that he was going to give Hitler a taste of his own medicine. It would soon be in the papers, he said, and left.

Sunday morning the two men had breakfast in Dasch's room. A night's rest seems to have engendered a degree of trust, and by lunchtime each had told the other his life story. Dasch, who was unable to omit the dramatics, especially where his own role called for heroic gestures, recalled the start of the day in terms of a Grade B movie. "After I pushed the breakfast cart into the hall," he said later, "I locked it outside, tossed the key into the bathtub, and closed the bathroom door. Then I threw open the windows and looked down on the street, ten or eleven floors below [it was actually thirteen]. Burger was watching a little apprehensively, waiting for an explanation of this odd behavior. I told him we were going to have a talk and if we didn't agree with each other, only one of us would leave the room alive." Either Burger was totally unimpressed by this performance or it never took place. In his own account of this meeting he simply said, "I met George in his room, where we had breakfast. We resumed our conversation of the night before."

However the day started, the men were in agreement by noon. About that time they realized that they were to meet Heinck and Quirin at the Swiss Chalet. They decided to cancel that and continue talking instead. But when they called the Hotel Chesterfield and found that Heinck and Quirin were not registered there, they had their first indication that these two might be difficult to control. Burger and Dasch were still talking at five-thirty when they saw that they would be late for the second rendezvous. They decided they could not neglect this meeting, and ran for a taxi to take them to Grant's Tomb.

Quirin's antagonism made the meeting far from satisfactory, but another one was scheduled for the next day. It was obvious that if they were going to achieve anything out of revealing the sabotage plot—and Dasch, at least, had by this time convinced himself he would be rewarded by the United States Government—they had to keep the other men available.

On the way downtown from Grant's Tomb, Burger and Dasch stopped at a hotel and found the telephone number of the F.B.I.'s New York office. Dasch went into a phone booth while Burger waited nervously outside. Both were still inclined to believe—or at least not disbelieve—stories that Kappe had told in Germany of Gestapo infiltration of the F.B.I., and as he dialed, Dasch was conscious of running a risk. He decided that the call would be in the nature of a commitment to himself and to Burger to go through with their plans, but that it was not necessarily the time to reveal himself. That he would do in Washington, where, in the fantasy he had now created, he would be welcomed by J. Edgar Hoover and members of his staff, invited to tell all, and be suitably repaid with a position of influence and power.

The realities of wartime never permitted the dream to move beyond the telephone booth he was standing in. The F.B.I. agent he reached—Dean F. McWhorter—listened politely to Dasch's statement. It was short and simple enough. Dasch said that he had arrived in New York from Germany the day before, that his name was Franz Daniel Pastorius, that he had information suitable only for J. Edgar Hoover, and that McWhorter should inform Washington that this information would be given on Thursday or Friday. McWhorter, like other agents of the F.B.I. and the police departments of various cities, had in the seven months since Pearl Harbor received his share of crackpot calls. Dasch's breathless message and the insistence that only Hoover could be trusted with it were so much like the fruitless ones that had gone before that McWhorter could do no more than insist that his caller come to the F.B.I. office and deliver his information in person. Dasch refused, and repeated that it was a matter for Washington only. He hung up and reported the gist of the conversation to Burger. Both men seemed satisfied that they had made progress. It was, as Dasch said later, "check and recheck."

Agent McWhorter's written report of the conversation made it clear that he did not attach much significance to the telephone call. Far from being "check" or "recheck," it was simply marked: "Re: F. D. Postorius, Memorandum for the file." "Please be advised," McWhorter wrote, "that at 7:51 P.M. on this date, Frank Daniel Postorius called this office by telephone, and advised the writer that he had made the call for the purpose of having a record of it, in this office. Postorius advised that he had arrived in New York City two days ago from Germany. He would not reveal his present address in the city, and remained uncommunicative concerning any information that he might be able to furnish this office. He stated that he was going to Washington, D.C., on Thursday or Friday of this week, and would talk to Mr. Hoover or his secretary. He refused to come to this office and report his information and said that he had to see a certain person in Washington first, but he wanted this office to make a record of his call and to notify our Washington office that he was coming there. This memo is being prepared only for the purpose of recording the call made by Postorius." The memo did not go to Washington.

Despite his strong feeling that he ought to get to the capital as soon as possible, Dasch remained in New York four days more. The reasons for this delay have not been made clear, least of all by Dasch. Chances are that fatigue and the emotional impact of the decision he had reached made him incapable of immediate action. Certainly his activities during his last days in New York support this view. On Monday he and Burger talked from time to time, shopped briefly, but for the most part remained in their rooms until evening. Dasch had made it clear that he did not wish to face Heinck and Quirin again; presumably he did not feel up to another quarrel with anyone as strong-minded as Quirin. After a smorgasbord dinner, Burger returned to the hotel and bed, while Dasch embarked on a minor adventure of his own.

He returned to the waiters' club. This time he made no teasing references to his forthcoming role against Hitler. Instead he sat down and played two-handed pinochle with a waiter he knew only as Fritz. For Dasch this was no ordinary time-killing activity. It became a compulsive method of escape from the anxieties which had accumulated. An inveterate bridge or poker player would find his performance understandable: he played all night Monday, all day Tuesday, and through Tuesday night until seven o'clock Wednesday morning. Besides purging his emotions, the nearly thirty-six consecutive hours of playing permitted him to ingratiate himself once more with men whose company he seemed to enjoy. "During [the playing] time," he said, "a lot of the other members of the club came over to me and greeted me and asked me questions which I did not answer directly. I merely said, 'Boys, don't ask me nothing. I cannot tell you the truth anyway.' In that game there were all kinds of fellows betting on the side of my opponent, the waiter Fritz. At the end of the game the conclusion was reached that I must have won about $250. That morning in order to rectify myself, to rectify the winnings I took away from the poor sucker, I paid all the bills of everyone in the house. I paid all their bills. Outside of that I gave a Polish boy I know under the name of John . . . ten dollars because the boy was busted. Another Jewish boy who made a touch I gave five dollars. Then I went and took a taxi and went to the hotel. I was dead tired." He was not aware that during his playing hours he was overheard to mutter, "If I talk it means death" and "Thank God, I don't have to work as a waiter any more," among other cryptic expressions. But the hours at cards had their effect; Dasch awoke at noon Wednesday refreshed and eager to leave for Washington.

By the time Dasch had breakfast and was ready to shop for items he considered necessary for the trip, Burger had returned from his most unsatisfactory session yet with Heinck and Quirin. He did not think they could be kept under control long, he told Dasch, even though he had lied to them about going to Chicago soon. This information seemed to undo the relaxed mood which Dasch had brought from the pinochle game. He paced the floor, insisting that he did not want to see either of the two men. Burger managed to calm him with a reminder of how well things had been going so far and that it would only be a matter of days now before he saw the F.B.I. The words cheered Dasch. After dinner that night—Dasch was proud of his ability to select restaurants for quality and variety, and chose Dinty Moore's, which specialized in corned beef and cabbage, in contrast to the Kungsholm of Monday evening—Burger met Heinck and Quirin at the Swing Club while Dasch went to bed.

On Thursday morning Dasch and Burger had their last meal together. Dasch could not wait any longer; he was going to Washington that afternoon. His final instructions to Burger were to stay at the Governor Clinton, to keep Heinck and Quirin placated and, of course, not to let them know he was in Washington. As Burger departed to carry out his part of the plan, Dasch moved on his own. He was troubled by the large amount of cash he held. His first thought was a safe-deposit box in a bank, but the only ones available were too small to hold all his bills. It then occurred to him that he ought to carry the money with him, and for thirty-seven dollars he bought a fine leather brief case. At a stationer's he purchased three manila envelopes and rubber bands.

Back in the hotel, he asked the manager to make reservations for him in Washington and went to his room to pack. He carefully removed the fifty-dollar bills from the still damp bag in which they had been carried since Berlin, and divided them into envelopes around which he put rubber bands. Then he wrote a note, "Content $82,350. Money from German Government for their purpose but to be used to fight them Nazis. George J. Dasch, alias George J. Davis, alias Franz Pastorius," and put it with the envelopes in the brief case. Packing his clothes took less time; by then he was informed that he had a reservation at the Hotel Mayflower in Washington. Dasch paid his bill, and Burger's as well. He also wrote a short note to Burger. "Dear Pete," he said. "Sorry for not have been able to see you before I left. I came to the realization to go to Washington and finish that which we have started so far. I'm leaving you, believing that you take good care of yourself and also of the other boys. You may rest assured that I shall try to straighten everything out to the very best possibility. My bag and clothes I'll put into your room. Your hotel bill is paid by me, including this day. If anything extra ordinary should happen, I'll get in touch with you directly. Until later, I'm your sincere friend, George." He left the note and the receipted bill in Burger's box. At two-thirty that Thursday afternoon, about the time Kerling was organizing the dispersal of his group from Jacksonville, Dasch caught the Washington train from Pennsylvania Station. He had been in the United States six days . . .

When Burger returned to the hotel he read the note and knew that, however it turned out, his commitment to Dasch was now irrevocable.

On Friday evening, Heinck and Quirin came to his room in preparation for their evening with the girls whom Frankie, the enterprising young lady from the Swing Club, had arranged for them to meet. "While I was in the bathroom," Burger said, "I noticed Henry open up the drawer of my writing desk and take out the letter which George had written. . . . I observed this through the mirror. Henry then appeared to read the letter and he handed it to Richard. They then returned the letter to the drawer. I also observed that Henry took the paid bill of the Hotel Governor Clinton from the right desk drawer and looked at it. . . . In order to prevent any possible bodily harm to myself and in order to prevent Richard and Henry from asking me questions, I hurriedly dressed and we all left the hotel."

The prospects of female companionship may have been stronger than the urge to know the meaning of Dasch's note. Neither Heinck nor Quirin mentioned it to Burger that evening, nor, for that matter, when the three men met again on Saturday. It is likely that Heinck and Quirin wanted to discuss it privately before they confronted Burger with their knowledge of it. What with the long night Friday and sleeping late Saturday they could not have had a chance to do more than wonder out loud about it before meeting Burger.

When they left him Saturday afternoon, Heinck and Quirin gave Burger the impression that they suspected nothing. The conversation about a day of pleasure at Palisades Park was certainly not the talk of men about to make a drastic move. Burger returned to his hotel room, tried on his new clothes, observed their effect in a mirror, liked it, and sat down to read the afternoon paper. He felt that he had Heinck and Quirin under control, but the old doubts about Dasch recurred, his unstable temperament, his unreliability, his towering ego which could just as easily prompt him to change all plans and leave Burger adrift. It seemed strange that he had not sent any word. It was now June 20, a little more than forty-eight hours since Dasch had gone to Washington. Certainly no government agency, however bureaucratic, could take this long to act on what Dasch had to tell. Shortly before five, Burger checked his door to make sure it was not locked, and went back to his newspaper . . .

Chapter 7
Counteraction

The young man who called himself Frank Collins and accepted George Dasch's money on the fog-bound beach at Amagansett was John C. Cullen, twenty-two, seaman second class, United States Coast Guard. It had taken him about twenty minutes to walk the half-mile from the Amagansett Coast Guard Station to where he was confronted by Dasch in the early morning of June 13. It took him less than eight minutes to get back. As he quickly told his story to the boatswain's mate who was acting officer in charge of the station, the events he had just participated in seemed no more real than the action on a motion-picture screen. A stranger in a fog joined by another, words spoken in a foreign language, a bribe, an implied threat on his life, his own instinctive response of a false name—these were indeed movie material. Yet the Coast Guard's Beach Patrol— "beach pounders," as they called themselves—had been established for just such a possibility. The boatswain's mate telephoned Warren Barnes, chief of the station, and immediately distributed arms and ammunition to Cullen and three other beach pounders on duty. The five men raced to where Dasch had been seen. Even with the help of powerful flashlights, nothing was visible in the dense fog. By Cullen's reckoning, it had been between fifteen and twenty minutes since he was last on this spot.

As the men searched fruitlessly for evidence of Cullen's

meeting, there came from the sea the distinct sound of a motor starting. The Coast Guardsmen strained to see through the stubborn fog. Cullen was the first to perceive a slow-moving, long, dark object on the water. He could not identify it beyond that, but now a breeze brought the smell of oil. Long after the object faded from sight and the sound receded, the smell remained on the beach.

About this time Barnes arrived at the Coast Guard Station. He telephoned Coast Guard Headquarters in New York to seek guidance and to suggest that the matter be forwarded to Intelligence. Then he joined the other men on the beach looking for something to support Cullen's story. Properly enough, Cullen was the first to discover a package of German cigarettes half buried in the sand. He gave these to Barnes and soon afterward was recalled to the station; Coast Guard Intelligence officers were on their way from New York to question him. As he left, Barnes and the others started to work their way up the dunes toward the road.

Understandably enough, Barnes reacted as if this were an invasion attempt, however minor. As more Coast Guardsmen reported, he deployed them along the beach and on the dunes. Then he, too, caught the odor of fuel oil in the air. Visibility had improved somewhat and he could discern the outlines of a vessel about a hundred and fifty feet out in the water. Even so, he could not be sure that he saw a submarine. The superstructure appeared to resemble "the pilot house on one of those old rum boats they used to have in the bootlegging days," he said. Barnes was a Coast Guard veteran who had returned to service after retirement; his memories were linked to Prohibition. As he tried to make sense of the vision, regretting he did not have field glasses, the sound of the *U-202*'s motors grew louder. At this Barnes started to run toward the station while keeping his eyes on the moving vessel. Outside the station he shouted to a Coast Guardsman in the lookout tower to ask if the boat were still visible from that position. It was moving east, came the response. Barnes was taking no chances. "What way are you facing?" he called. "Are you facing the ocean?" "Yes," said the lookout. "Which hand is it on?" asked Barnes. "On my left hand," said the lookout, annoyed at the doubt cast on his intelligence. "She's going east." Barnes was satisfied.

As Coast Guardsmen made their way along the beach, not knowing what they were looking for, and not finding it, either, Barnes suddenly remembered that two dories lay unguarded at Yamico Beach, about a mile away. He sent two men to guard them, and another to a nearby Army post to say that help was needed. By then it was 4:15 A.M., and it was apparent to Barnes that they would have to wait until daylight to find anything more. He returned once more to the station, where Cullen was eagerly waiting to get rid of the bribe money. He and Barnes counted it; the $300 that Dasch said he had given him turned out to be $260—two fifties, five twenties and six tens.

At daylight Barnes returned to the beach. Now the search was for marks made by a duffel bag dragged in the sand— Cullen had recalled that specific action. Amazingly enough, despite the number of men walking in the sand that morning and the natural action of wind and mist, the marks were found. It was not one complete trail, but broken, as if the object had been carried from time to time. Yet it was quite distinct. Barnes, racing ahead of the two men in his party, followed the trail up a small ridge which led to the sand dunes beyond. From there he looked down on the signs of a recently filled hole.

The men dug excitedly with their bare hands. They did not have far to go. Less than a foot beneath the surface were two boxes, below them two more, by then thoroughly sticky, sandy and damp. Barnes ordered one of the men to return to the station for a truck while he and the others continued the search. About a hundred and fifty feet northeast of the first hole, they found another. In this they found the dirty gray duffel bag loaded with damp and wrinkled uniforms. Under it were two trench shovels. Nearby were a raincoat, a pair of bathing trunks and a single white canvas shoe.

By the time Barnes had satisfied himself that there was nothing else around, the truck had arrived from the Coast Guard Station to pick up his find. At the station, Barnes found Lieutenants F. W. Nirschel and Sydney K. Franken of Coast Guard Intelligence questioning Cullen. Their instructions from Captain John S. Bayliss, their commanding officer and captain of the Port of New York, had been to drive out to Amagansett and "don't drag anchor." The two men must have broken all the speed laws; they made the three-hour trip in little more than two. When Barnes returned with the truck, the officers left Cullen to examine the boxes and clothes in the station garage. Nirschel and Franken opened only one of the four boxes, and removed just a few small items from it. It did not take them long to be aware of the significance of their discovery. Nor did they have to be trained experts to recognize the insignia of the German Navy on the buttons of the work uniforms.

Nirschel and Franken loaded their station wagon with everything Barnes had found and drove into New York City. They arrived at the Barge Office on the Battery, which served as Bayliss' headquarters, at ten twenty-three, and opened the other three boxes. Bayliss acted swiftly. The Coast Guard had done its duty; now this was a matter for the F.B.I. At eleven he called the agency's New York office. By noon, agents Charles F. Lanman, Thomas J. Donegan and Elmer F. Emrich had seen the results of the Coast Guard's morning activities. It was less than twelve hours since Dasch and his group had gone ashore at Amagansett, and nearly everything they had brought with them except the clothes they wore and the money they carried had been found.

The boxes, clothes, duffel bag and shovels were moved to the F.B.I. office and methodically examined item by item. Spencer J. Drayton, chief of the New York office, called headquarters in Washington to ask for the immediate assignment of an explosives expert. He got more than that; J. Edgar Hoover named Assistant Director Earl J. Connelley to direct the investigation. Connelley arrived in New York that evening with D. J. Parsons, a chemist who for eight and a half years had examined explosives, incendiaries and other tools of sabotage for the F.B.I. Few people in the country knew more about these weapons than he. While waiting for the Washington men to arrive, Drayton tagged each piece found in the four boxes, the boxes themselves, the wet and damp duffel bag and each item of clothing it contained. By eight o'clock that night, in the shooting range of the basement of the Federal Court Building in downtown New York, Parsons had a complete inventory before him and was ready to start testing the explosives, incendiaries and fuses.

Even before Parsons fired bullets into the innocent-looking yellow blocks and checked time fuses against a stop watch, F.B.I. agents were at work on eastern Long Island. Men were assigned to watch the area where the boxes had been buried, ready to seize anyone who gave the appearance of returning to dig them up. Agents were posted not only on the beach itself but in the Coast Guard tower and in a nearby cottage. As men took on this watch, other agents questioned every Coast Guardsman who had been on duty the night before, and Cullen most intensively. A description of Dasch was given to agents who then went from door to door in Amagansett in the hopes of finding someone else who had seen him. Several men who met Dasch's description were questioned by the F.B.I. while Cullen, hidden by a one-way window, observed them unseen.

The $260 which Dasch had given Cullen was turned over to the F.B.I. laboratory for fingerprints. None of any value was found. The money led to inquiries at every bank on the South Shore of Long Island from Riverhead, the county seat, to Montauk Point, the Island's eastern tip. There had been no unusual transactions, no withdrawals or deposits that could be connected with the bills. The Federal Reserve Bank in New York City was brought into the investigation, but its officials could offer no theory which would help trace the money. The only article of clothing worth checking was the raincoat bearing the label of Crawford Clothes. The results were as fruitless as tracing the money. The coat, the management of Crawford Clothes told the F.B.I., was one of a lot purchased from a New York manufacturer and carried no identification to indicate which of the many Crawford stores had sold it.

The possibility that a resident of Long Island had helped the men who came ashore could not be overlooked. Agents checked F.B.I. records for known Nazi sympathizers in the vicinity, and a number were questioned. Nothing tangible came from any of the hours of legwork until Ira Baker, the Amagansett station agent, remembered the sale of four tickets to Jamaica early Saturday morning. Even this was not a great step forward since Baker had not really observed the purchaser. Nor were the conductor and the ticket collector on the early morning train any more help. Later in the week, Baker did find stuffed in the hedge by the station a pair of swimming trunks, a shirt, a single tennis shoe, a pair of white socks and two which were not mates. By that time the F.B.I. had accepted the grim logic that the men it was seeking were somewhere in New York, and that, short of some unexpected break, what lay ahead was the painstaking and tedious investigation of every possible lead, however outlandish.

Shortly after 7:00 P.M. on Thursday, June 18, Dasch arrived at Washington's Union Station and went immediately to his hotel. Rooms were at a premium in wartime Washington, and especially so in a hotel as popular as the Mayflower, the residence of many Congressmen and government officials. Dasch was assigned Room 351 with the understanding that he would leave by Monday evening. He had no choice in the matter, but he didn't see how his business could take any longer than that, anyway.

Despite his having called the F.B.I. the previous Sunday in New York, Dasch was now confused as to where to start. It occurred to him that perhaps the Army's G-2, which was, after all, the counterpart of German Military Intelligence, might be a more logical place than the F.B.I. But there was not much he could do about it at night, he decided, and he went out for dinner. A streetcar brought him to F Street, Washington's main thoroughfare, where he wandered aimlessly looking for a restaurant.

At last he walked into one, without much thought to its name or location. When he sat down to order, he found— almost inevitably for a man who had spent so many years in his profession—that his waiter recognized him. It does not seem to have frightened Dasch as much as it offended him. He had so thrust himself into his new role that he did not want to believe anyone could penetrate the disguise he mentally wore. "I just wanted to find out how far I could go until I could be a different person," he said of this evening. For most of the meal he ignored the waiter's obvious desire to renew old acquaintance, but Dasch could not restrain himself for long, and the desire to play the hero won out before dessert. "I could see the boy thought I was a conceited brat," Dasch said. "I called him over and I said, 'Boy, you are correct in identifying the fellow you thought I was.'" There is no telling how the young waiter reacted to this rather mysterious statement, but he accepted Dasch's invitation to drinks after work. Over Scotch and soda Dasch told the comparative stranger what he intended to do, and asked for advice on the proper authorities to whom to present his story. The waiter, who did not believe a word of Dasch's story, suggested the Attorney General of the United States, and Dasch conscientiously made a note of the name.

The next morning, though, the Attorney General did not have as much appeal for Dasch as he had had over drinks.

Like thousands of visitors to Washington, Dasch called the United States Government Information Service. He asked the difference between the F.B.I. and the Secret Service, and the properly trained young woman asked Dasch the nature of his business. He readily explained that he had a statement to make of military as well as political value. It is not likely that the Information Service got that kind of request very often, but in a manner indicating that it was as common an event in Washington as a trip to the Pentagon, the girl suggested that he call Colonel H. F. Kramer of the Army's General Staff Corps.

Kramer was out of his office, and Dasch left a message that George John Davis be called back as soon as possible. Then he dialed the F.B.I. number. Now, at last, he found an audience for his story. The agent who answered was Duane L. Traynor, who was naturally called "Pie" out of deference to Pie Traynor, baseball's greatest third baseman. (It was the kind of Americanism which appealed to Dasch, and thereafter he referred to Traynor by his nickname.) Traynor listened patiently to Dasch's quick summation: he was George Davis, he was the leader of a group of eight men who had just come over from Germany, and he wanted to talk to someone about sabotage. It sounded like a crackpot call. Dasch's previous call had sounded that way to McWhorter in New York, who was not aware of the discovery at Amagansett. Traynor was. He knew of the investigation which had continued for nearly a week now, and insane as this call might seem, it had to be checked. He told Dasch he would have him picked up in half an hour.

While Dasch was waiting, Colonel Kramer telephoned. Dasch told him substantially what he had told Traynor, but added that the F.B.I. was on its way. Kramer did not pursue the matter but made a note for his own files. Dasch then showered and wrote an optimistic note to Burger. "My Dear Friend Pete," he said. "Got savely into town last night and contacted the resonsibly parties. At present I'm waiting to be brought over to the right man by one of his agents. I had a good night rest, feel fine for phisical as well as mentally and believe that I will accomplish the part of our participation. It will take lots of time and talking but please don't worry, have faith and courage. I try hard to do the right thing. In the meantime take good care of yourself and of the boys. Please don't go all over town. Keep silent to everybody. I promise you to keep you posted on the future developments. Before I left you, I begged the mgr. of your hotel, Mr. Weil, to take good care of you, for you are a Jewish refugee, so please act accordingly. Best regards and Wishes Geo. J. Dasch. I'll forward to you my address where you reach me, via mail or phone, soon."

Dasch sealed the note and gave it to the floor waiter who came to clear his breakfast dishes. F.B.I. agents arrived soon afterward, as Dasch was finishing dressing.

A guard was posted on Dasch's room and he was brought to Traynor's office in the Justice Department Building. Dasch faced Traynor almost submissively. He had gone through considerable mental strain and hardship for several months, he said; now he had a long story to tell and he wanted to tell it from the beginning in his own way, and he wanted to tell it only to Mr. Hoover.

Dasch did not see Hoover, but for a while, at least, he was permitted to tell his story his own way. Inevitably, he was interrupted by pertinent questions, especially since his discourse had a tendency to go far afield, with more emphasis on his own essential good will than on where the other seven men might be found. His own notion of what would constitute help for the F.B.I. was that he be permitted to meet his three colleagues in New York, and then proceed to the July 4 meeting with Kerling, as if he were still a participant in Operation Pastorious. In that way, he said, he would lead F.B.I. agents to each of the men; he would be the finger man, the role he knew Sebold had played in the arrest of the German spies more than a year earlier.

This was not quite what the F.B.I. had in mind. Rounding up seven potential saboteurs required trained professionals who knew how to find evidence as well as men, and Dasch was placed in protective custody for questioning. In the course of five days, the F.B.I. obtained from Dasch the basis for instructions to its agents in New York and Chicago. What Dasch had to say in the period filled 254 typewritten pages, much of it irrelevant to the immediate job at hand. Before he finished talking the F.B.I. had arrested five of the men and were on the trail of the other two.

Dasch's reluctance to permit the F.B.I. to make the arrests without him was finally broken down at eleven-thirty Friday evening, thirteen hours after he arrived at the Justice Department. Then he told where Burger was staying. Connelley, still directing the investigation in New York, was immediately notified, and agents went to the Hotel Governor Clinton in the early morning. Their watch was unrewarding until 2:00 P.M. Saturday, when Burger left his room to keep his appointment with Quirin and Heinck to pick up their suits at the Rogers Peet clothing store.

The F.B.I. wanted to arrest each man separately, to keep from each the knowledge that any of his colleagues had been caught. The hour that Burger, Quirin and Heinck spent in the store and the forty-five minutes they remained in the bar across the street dragged for the F.B.I. agents posted on the short block of Forty-first Street and its exits at Fifth and Madison Avenues. At last the three men emerged, and walked to Fortieth Street and over to Broadway. When Quirin and Heinck boarded a northbound bus, two F.B.I. agents got on at the same time, and two F.B.I. cars remained close behind. Connelley, accompanied by four agents, followed Burger back to his hotel.

A few minutes after five, while Burger was still reading the afternoon paper, the F.B.I. men came to his room. He offered no resistance, and was immediately put under arrest. His room was searched and his personal effects taken from him. Besides $83 in his pocket, $3,550 in his money belt, the false social security and selective service cards, and the legitimate naturalization certificate and honorable discharges from the Michigan and Wisconsin National Guards, Burger had one inconsequential, but rather ironic, item in his wallet. It was a card he had carried a long time; the inscription read, "Bucyrus Erie Company Safety Contest, 1930," and below that, in bold letters, "Please Be Careful."

The agents following Quirin and Heinck had to be even more patient than those at the Governor Clinton. When the two men left the bus at Seventy-second Street and Broadway, they showed no immediate disposition to separate, but walked slowly to Seventy-fourth Street and Amsterdam Avenue. Not until they had walked these three long blocks did Quirin and Heinck part. Heinck entered a drug store, while Quirin walked two blocks north to a tailor shop. On signal, the F.B.I. agents split into two groups. Those who remained with Quirin had a ten-minute wait before he returned to the street. When he did so, they arrested him. Those who watched Heinck permitted him to leave the drug store and walk another block. He stretched their patience a few minutes longer; he entered a delicatessen. When he left this shop they arrested him at once.

Neither Heinck nor Quirin attempted to make their lies stick. Quirin made a brief effort to use the cover story he had so patiently rehearsed, and to insist that he was really Richard Quintas with a draft registration and social security card to prove it. This claim could not, of course, stand up under the F.B.I's knowledge of his identity, and he soon made a straightforward confession. Heinck tried to save his friend Hermann Faje; he told the F.B.I. agents that he had given his money belt to Dasch. He could not maintain the lie through long questioning, however, and within a day of Heinck's arrest the F.B.I. had the money belt from the Fajes, as well as the change from the fifty dollars he had given them.

The roundup of the Long Island group was complete a week after the landing at Amagansett. Yet Connelley and his agents knew that the comparative ease with which this was accomplished would not necessarily hold true for the Florida group. Dasch's information about Kerling's whereabouts was vague to the point of uselessness; he did not know, of course, that they had landed only two days before he went to Washington, or that Kerling and Thiel had reached New York the day after his questioning began. The F.B.I. did not want to wait for the July 4 meeting in Cincinnati. Despite Dasch's assurances that no sabotage was to take place until then, the F.B.I. could not be sure that Kerling and his men might not indulge themselves in at least some of the nuisance bombings Dasch had described. Connelley's job was to find the men who had landed in Florida before that could happen.

Dasch could tell his questioners Kerling's name and could even give them the handkerchief which carried the names and addresses of contacts in the United States, but he could not remember the chemical fumes which made the writing visible. "If I had known you boys were going to ask all these questions about it," he said at one point, "I would have learned it all good, so I could tell it to you." At about the time he finally recalled that the writing would appear if the handkerchief were exposed to ammonia, the F.B.I. laboratory had made the same discovery. The handkerchief revealed, among other things, the address of Helmut Leiner. Agents were assigned to watch it. F.B.I. records on Kerling, filed at the time of the *Lekala* incident, showed that he was married. On the assumption that he would seek his wife, agents were also sent to watch Marie Kerling.

It was not until Tuesday, June 23, that the F.B.I. had the information from the handkerchief, and by this time some help from Burger as well, on which to base fresh action. The agents assigned to Leiner were almost immediately rewarded. He left his home that morning for Pennsylvania Station and met a man whom the agents recognized from Burger's accurate description as Kerling. The trail of the two men led to New Jersey and back to New York, to dinner at the Crossroads Inn, and finally to their separation. A few agents followed Leiner; others watched Kerling join Thiel and Anthony Cramer for a drink. Some remained with Thiel and Cramer and the rest followed Kerling as he walked to Fortyninth Street and Lexington Avenue, where he paced impatiently, a man obviously waiting for someone who was late for an appointment. The agents permitted him to pace for fifteen minutes. There was no doubt he was their man, and at 10:00 P.M., he was taken.

The agents with Leiner watched him enter Hedy Engemann's grocery store and wait until ten-thirty, when Marie Kerling showed up, followed by the agents assigned to her. The three then proceeded to the rendezvous with Kerling. They chatted nervously on the street corner from eleven to midnight, and then parted, upset and uncertain. The two women were not to see Kerling again until they faced him some weeks later in a courtroom; Leiner was not to see him at all. Agents watched Leiner closely for another week, by which time it was apparent that he would not provide any new leads. Then he too was arrested.

The agents who remained with Thiel and Cramer recognized Thiel from Burger's description. They stayed close to him and Cramer at the bar, and behind them as they walked to Forty-second Street for their farewell pie and coffee. At eleven-thirty, when Thiel walked alone to the Commodore Hotel, the agents picked him up. A watch was maintained on Cramer, and two days later, when he was seen leaving a bank in the Yorkville area, he was arrested. In the safe-deposit vaults of the bank, the agents found seventy fifty-dollar bills, the contents of Thiel's money belt.

Now the trail of the remaining two men led to Chicago. Because Dasch's information was so slow in coming, the agents did not find Herbert Haupt until Monday morning, June 22, when he appeared at the F.B.I. office to report his compliance with the draft regulations. As a result they missed his meeting with Neubauer on Sunday. The delay was to cause the chase to last nearly a week longer than it otherwise might have. But from the moment Haupt left the F.B.I. office, secure in his mind that he had outwitted the agent who questioned him, he was under constant watch. Dasch's handkerchief had provided the name and address of Haupt's aunt and uncle, the Froehlings, and agents were sent there as well.

Their young quarry led the agents through many streets and to many houses in Chicago and the vicinity, but not to Neubauer. They watched him and Wernecke, the draft-dodging expert, go from doctor's office to drug store to hospital; they were with him when he bought his car, and when he took Gerda Melind to a tavern; they watched him visit the Jordans, and former fellow employes at Simpson's; they were nearby as he tested a number of bars and attended many motion pictures. Inexplicably, they did not follow him into the Chicago Theatre on Wednesday when he did sit with Neubauer. Saturday, June 27, the F.B.I. decided that Haupt should be picked up; perhaps he knew where Neubauer was, even if there were no indications that he had seen him. That morning Haupt left his house a little after nine o'clock and drove his newly purchased car to the Loop. As he passed the elevated railroad station at Webster and Sheffield Avenues, the car behind him, carrying F.B.I. agents, forced him to the curb. He was arrested as he got out of his car to protest the other driver's outrageous conduct.

The F.B.I. had not depended entirely on Haupt to bring its agents to Neubauer. It had posted men outside the home of his wife's parents, and throughout the week hotels were painstakingly checked. The results were completely negative. Not until Haupt was arrested did agents have the knowledge they needed. They went to the Sheridan Plaza, where Neubauer had registered the day before. Their wait lasted until six forty-five, when Neubauer came back from his lonely movie. A few minutes after he entered his room on the twelfth floor, he was taken. Neubauer, who knew least how to pass his free time, had had more of it than any of the other seven men in Operation Pastorius.

While waiting for the arrests of Haupt and Neubauer, the F.B.I. still had to recover the explosives on the beach at Ponte Vedra, and to continue questioning the six men they had apprehended. Kerling, the tough Nazi, who had his doubts about some of his colleagues but not about his mission, was a realist in defeat. He accompanied agents to Jacksonville and led them to the three palm stumps which marked the spot where he had directed the burial of the four boxes. An agent who was with him reported no expression of emotion on Kerling's part until they reached that spot. And all he said then was that he was pleased that nobody else had found the explosives and got hurt by digging them up. Kerling was back in his New York cell on Friday, June 26.

The day before, Dasch had been brought from Washington to New York, where his status was at last changed from protective custody to formal arrest. While in Washington he had been taken back to his room at the Mayflower each night to sleep while guarded by F.B.I. agents. The move to New York bewildered and upset Dasch; the F.B.I. had not seemed to accept at face value his claims of deep-rooted anti-Nazism or his offers to help find the other men. Now for the first time he realized that he was not a heroic figure, as he had assumed Sebold to have been and as he expected to be, but merely another prisoner. In the face of this he had one request to make: that he be jailed with the others so they would not know that he had been the turncoat. The F.B.I. was more than pleased to comply. It had no intention of letting Germany know the means by which its sabotage plot against the United States had been broken.

PART III
SECRET TRIAL

Chapter 8
Room 5235,
Department of Justice

The story of the saboteurs and their capture, or as much of it as the F.B.I. felt it could release in wartime, was made public on the evening of June 27, 1942. A few hours after Connelley was notified that Neubauer had been arrested, the press was summoned to the New York office of the F.B.I. in the Federal Court House in New York. J. Edgar Hoover had come from Washington to make the announcement and answer questions, of which there were surprisingly few. The account released that night was sparse; the names, photographs and brief biographies of the eight men, a description of their weapons, a list of their objectives, where and how they landed, and very little else. After Hoover's brief announcement, nearly every detail of what one newspaper called "the Nazi plot that failed" was kept secret.

Yet the little that was told was enough to make headlines of a size that had hitherto been reserved for the war's major battles. The capture of the eight men represented a kind of victory, comparable perhaps to the Doolittle raid over Tokyo which some months earlier had made an important contribution to American morale. To a nation starved for good news, the frustration of the sabotage plans had aspects of a military triumph as well as a good detective story. In many newspapers the Hoover announcement was given greater prominence than the fierce battle then being fought around Kharkov or the Anglo-American promise of a second front in Europe. Most of the news from the Pacific had been bad; in Europe, the Russians were being pushed back by the Panzer divisions; and England was under constant bombardment from the Luftwaffe. Now, as relief from the grim reports from all war fronts, there was a palpable success at home. With no information about how the success had been achieved, the public took the news as undeniable proof that Nazi fiendishness was no match for American G-men. The arrests delighted President Roosevelt, who heard of them by telephone at his Hyde Park home from Attorney General Biddle, as much as it did the rest of the nation.

Aside from the headlines, most newspapers handled the story with restraint. There seemed to be a realization that, if this were a victory, it was essentially a negative one; the enemy had been checked, but no advance had been made by our side. Full credit was given to the F.B.I.—Senator James M. Mead of New York proposed that a special medal be struck in honor of Hoover—and for a while, at least, there was a general acceptance of the need for secrecy. Hoover had implied that other sabotage attempts were a real possibility, and he was not disposed to discuss how the eight saboteurs were caught.

In the absence of fresh details, newspapers found space for the trivial interviews, rumors and half-truths which so often turn up in the wake of extraordinary news stories. Since Haupt was the youngest of the eight captured men, the only one whose friends and relatives were mentioned in the announcement, and an American citizen, interest centered on him at the start. A reporter for one press association interviewed Gerda Melind and found that she had had premonitions. Under these circumstances, women with premonitions make good newspaper copy even if their recollections are not verifiable. "He called me Wednesday, Thursday and Friday," she told the reporter, "but I wouldn't see him. I had a hunch there was something wrong, they'd have him by then. He had mentioned marriage Tuesday, and we agreed to be married this week. After this I'll follow my hunches." Despite her sense of impending tragedy, Mrs. Melind admitted that she was "shocked to learn about his arrest. I never suspected him of any activity of that kind. He always appeared to be a gentleman. . . . Now I am ashamed of him and don't want anything more to do with him."

Haupt's story included not only a woman's outraged innocence, but also parents betrayed. This element was supplied by another press association whose report, including an error in Haupt's Christian name, was coupled by many newspapers with the Gerda Melind interview. "A man and his wife sat embraced tonight in a modest North Side Chicago home vainly trying to comfort each other," the account began. "The tear-stained faces were those of Mr. and Mrs. Hans Haupt, father ahd mother of Herman W. Haupt, whom F.B.I. agents seized last night. . . . 'This is the greatest disgrace we have ever faced,' murmured the distraught father. 'We cannot believe that our boy would turn against the country we taught him to love. I have no use for Hitlerism, the bunds or any other person or organization which is un-American. I am an American!' The thought never entered his head the boy was actually a spy. 'Why,' he said, 'Herman was actually plotting against mama and me.' " Unfortunately for "mama and me," they were arrested within a few days. The Justice Department took so jaundiced a view of the Haupts' distress that it planned to prosecute them on charges of treason for knowingly helping their son prepare to commit sabotage.

Some newspapers had to seek solace in so-called "local angles." California reporters found waiters and others who "remembered" Dasch. One concluded that Dasch had acted "as a German spy" in San Francisco from 1928 to 1940, and that he had used forged union cards to obtain employment as a "sleek, super-efficient waiter in prominent hotels in San Francisco and Sacramento and nearly half a dozen night clubs in the North Beach area." A woman who claimed to be one of Dasch's former employers got her name in the papers with a forthright opinion. "He was a trouble maker," she recalled. "He constantly talked to the other waiters about the wonders of Germany and the rottenness of America. I fired him so fast that he didn't know what hit him."

The excitement over the thwarted plot was intensified when there were indications that the United States was uncertain how to prosecute the eight men. Hoover told the press that this was a problem for Attorney General Biddle, but implied that there were some questions as to what legal steps would actually be taken. "We've been working at top speed," he was quoted by reporters, "and didn't have time to look into the legal aspects of the situation." Nobody doubted that the death penalty would be sought; it was merely a matter of finding what law best fitted the case. Although newspapers generally used the words "spy" and "saboteur" interchangeably, legal proceedings could not be worded that loosely. The only comment from Biddle was that the Justice Department "will proceed swiftly and thoroughly" to prosecute the men. The indecisive posture of the government was summed up by Clifford Berryman, political cartoonist for the *Washington Evening Star*, who portrayed Hoover firmly guarding the eight prisoners while a hopeful Francis Biddle stood on a ladder in front of a shelf of law books. "You hold on to them, Edgar," Biddle was saying, "and I'll find something here that we can punish them under."

If there was doubt in the Justice Department, there was none among politicians, the press and most of the public. Representative Carl Vinson, chairman of the House Naval Affairs Committee, said simply, "They ought to be shot, since they are clearly spies." Senator George Norris was more judicious. He said, "These men should be punished to the fullest extent. If death is the penalty they should be executed." Biddle's delay in announcing legal steps raised some fears that the men might escape punishment altogether. Senator Tom Connally, chairman of the Senate Foreign Relations Committee, said, "The severest penalty should be inflicted on these men, and they should be promptly tried." This order of penalty first and trial second—if at all, in the view of the many—became the prevailing attitude. Lewis Wood, a Washington correspondent for the *New York Times*, reported on the basis of public-opinion polls and dispatches from *Times* correspondents around the country that "Americans everywhere were demanding [the death penalty] for the audacious criminals. Americans wanted to hear the roar of rifles in the hands of a firing squad." *Life* magazine headlined its account of the capture: THE EIGHT NAZI SABOTEURS SHOULD BE PUT TO DEATH. At the end of a brief account of the sabotage plans, full-length pictures of the prisoners and closeups of pen and pencil incendiaries, electric matches and timing devices, there was a picture of eight men in American Legion uniforms, their rifles at the ready, aimed directly at the photographer. The text said, "Nothing less than the death penalty will satisfy patriotic Americans—among whom are members of the Raymond Henry American Legion Post of Olyphant, Pa., who volunteered their services free as a firing squad."

Sometimes the demand for vengeance took bizarre forms. A columnist for the Orlando, Florida, *Sentinel Star* showed ingenuity in his proposal for the demise of the eight men. "We are in full accordance," he wrote, "with the universal desire for summary dealing with vermin of this type—after they have been squeezed, wrung, twisted, hammered and pounded completely dry of every speck of information which might lead to the apprehension of others of their ilk. . . . And as to the method of the ultimate disposal of these would-be murderers, what could be more appropriate than to dispatch them with the same instruments of destruction with which they planned to blast hundreds of Americans into oblivion? When one of these back-stabbing chaps is discovered pouring acid on the controls of one of our war planes or otherwise preparing it for an inevitable crackup, think how soul-satisfying it would be to rig him out in a cheesecloth parachute, shove him into a plane, take him up around 20,000 feet and shove him out to flop around with the rest of the buzzards." Obviously pleased with his own imagination, the writer concluded: "If Uncle Sam will just organize . . . an OSR (Office of Saboteur Retribution) we would gladly accept the post of office boy or janitor for our board and keep for the privilege of offering just one technical suggestion a week."

While Americans were expressing themselves quietly or openly, depending on their access to the printed page, the Justice Department realized that neither secrecy nor the death penalty could be guaranteed in a civil trial. Biddle conferred with representatives of the War Department on the practicability of a military trial. Together, Justice and War reached a solution which President Roosevelt approved and immediately put into effect. The men, though captured as civilians, would be tried by a military commission, under the rules of courts-martial for military personnel. There was precedent for such a procedure, although it went back seventy-seven years to one of the darkest events in American history. The last civilians to be tried by a military commission in the United States had been the seven men and one woman who were charged with conspiring with John Wilkes Booth to assassinate Abraham Lincoln.

President Roosevelt's announcement was made on July 2, less than a week after the men had been caught. There was no denying its intent: the death penalty for all eight prisoners. Legal questions on the propriety of trying civilians by a military court were not immediately raised, although President Roosevelt seems to have been sensitive to them. "This does not suspend the writ of *habeas corpus*," he told William

D. Hassett, a confidential secretary, who was with him when he signed the proclamation. "But it does deny access to the civil courts of certain described persons."

The President's proclamation was, by custom, formally phrased and precise: "Whereas, the safety of the United States demands that all enemies who have entered upon the territory of the United States as part of an invasion or predatory incursion . . . should be promptly tried in accordance with the Law of War; now, therefore, I, Franklin D. Roosevelt, . . . do hereby proclaim that all persons who are subjects, citizens or residents of any nation at war with the United States or who give obedience to or act under the direction of any such nation, and who during time of war enter or attempt to enter the United States or any territory or possession thereof, through coastal or boundary defenses, and are charged with committing or attempting or preparing to commit sabotage, espionage, hostile or warlike acts, or violations of the law of war, shall be subject to the law of war and to the jurisdiction of military tribunals; and that such persons shall not be privileged to seek any remedy or maintain any proceeding, directly or indirectly, or to have any such remedy or proceeding sought on their behalf, in the courts of the United States. . . ."

Given the national mood, there was need for the President to show speed as well as determination. Simultaneously with the proclamation, Roosevelt issued an order which established a military commission to meet on July 8, "or as soon thereafter as is practicable, to try for offenses against the Law of War and the Articles of War" the eight prisoners held by the Justice Department. The order named the seven members of the commission, three major generals and three brigadier generals under the presidency of Major General Frank R. McCoy; the prosecution, Attorney General Biddle and the Army's Judge Advocate General, Major General Myron Cramer; and the defense counsel, Colonel Cassius M. Dowell, a Regular Army officer, and Colonel Kenneth C. Royall, a temporary officer. General McCoy had been on the board which investigated the events at Pearl Harbor prior to the Japanese attack and a member of the court-martial which in 1925 tried Brigadier General William Mitchell, the outspoken advocate of air power.

Under the terms of the President's order, the commission would have the right to admit evidence which in the opinion of McCoy had "probative value to a reasonable man." This was a legal device, most often used in government agency hearings, to permit the commission to accept testimony which might not be admitted by civil courts under the rules and traditions which Anglo-Saxon law has developed to protect the accused.

The President himself, as Commander in Chief of the Army and Navy, would make the final decision on the sentence after the trial record was sent to him with the commission's recommendations. There would be no appeal.

The press and the public considered the President's action both bold and proper. Most editorials favored a military trial over a civil trial. "There should be no quibbling or fine-spun devotion to the nicer technicalities of the law in dealing with these Nazi Criminals," and the military will provide "more justice than they really deserve" were some of the phrases which reflected press opinion. Not until the trial was actually under way was there any criticism, and that, understandably, came from Washington correspondents and their publishers, and was directed at the secrecy of the proceedings.

By the time the commission met, the conflict over secrecy tended to overshadow the trial itself. Elmer Davis, a highly respected radio commentator, who three weeks earlier had been appointed director of the government's new Office of War Information, sided with the press. Except for withholding information which would aid the enemy, Davis had pledged "to give the people a clear, complete and accurate picture" of what he called the "people's war." It was obvious from the efforts he made to open the trial to the press that he did not intend the enemy to be aided, especially since he was willing to compromise for limited coverage by either a member of his staff or a single representative of the press, and to submit to military censorship. His position, however, was contrary to that of Secretary of War Henry L. Stimson, who felt that the secrecy was in the national interest. When a reporter asked Stimson whether Davis would supervise Army communiqués, he answered, "in some heat," according to those present, "Is Mr. Davis an educated military officer?" The reporter said he did not know, but facetiously suggested that Davis might be a "civilian general." To which Stimson replied, "There are many of them." The spectacle of a public feud among high officials was abruptly ended by President Roosevelt, who called Davis and Stimson to the White House.

The White House agreement was that the trial would be closed to the press, which was a victory for the military; there would be daily communiqués issued by McCoy, which was considered a triumph for freedom of the press—until the first communiqués were seen. They consisted of the hours at which the commission convened and adjourned; occasionally they mentioned that witnesses, never identified, were examined. Other concessions were made to Davis, but they were as hollow a triumph as the communiqués. One was to permit twelve reporters to visit the trial chamber and write uncensored accounts of what they saw. However, proceedings were suspended while the reporters were marched into the trial chamber, and they were allowed less than fifteen minutes to make their observations of the room, judges, prisoners, lawyers, witnesses and exhibits. Another concession was to allow the Army Signal Corps to take photographs and silent motion pictures of the trial and the principals, and these were duly distributed.

The last concession was that more informative bulletins would be released by the commission. This was undertaken with all seriousness, but the first of these was very nearly the last. "George Washington, an attorney on the staff of Assistant Solicitor General Oscar Cox, of the Department of Justice," it solemnly announced, "is the first President's nearest living collateral descendant."

Neither this release nor the other concessions placated the members of the press, and most continued to be critical of the secret proceedings. Official secrecy, when the need for it is made clear, has rarely been questioned by reputable newspapermen; war correspondents were told in advance the probable date of the D-Day invasion, among other major military secrets, and were as reliable as any military man. But from the time of Hoover's announcement of the capture of the eight men, until President Roosevelt's verdict was announced, a number of reporters and publishers were not convinced that every detail of it would harm national security.

As the trial continued, the competition became intense among Washington correspondents for "inside" or "exclusive" stories, with journalistic ingenuity trying to make up for the lack of official news. Probably the most enterprising of the reporters assigned to the story was Jack Vincent, a member of the staff of what was then the International News Service. His sources of information were so reliable that he managed to come up with accurate accounts almost daily—about defense and prosecution moves, commission decisions and the verdict itself—which were confirmed at the time or which have been proved true in the years since. The most dramatic of the early unauthorized stories was provided by Thomas F. Reynolds of the *Chicago Sun*. Reynolds had seen a short published report from New York which hinted at the Coast Guard's presence on the beach at Amagansett at the time Dasch and his group landed, and he assumed that, if the Coast Guard did have a role in the capture, there would be people in Washington irritated at the service's failure to receive credit, and eager to speak out. On July 3, the day after the President announced the date and method of trial, Reynolds had a complete account of Cullen's meeting with Dasch and the subsequent events of the morning of June 13.

It was by far the best story since the capture announcement itself, and it had the further effect of giving the nation a young hero. The Coast Guard did not officially confirm the story until two weeks later, and when it did, the press release was a paraphrase of Reynolds' account.

If the public was told very little, the eight prisoners, now under heavy guard in the District of Columbia Jail, in separate cells and with no means of communication, had been told even less. They had been brought in secret from New York to Washington in the early hours of Saturday, July 4, the same day Dasch and Kerling were to have met at the Hotel Gibson in Cincinnati. Later that morning, Brigadier General Albert L. Cox, Provost Marshal of the Military District of Washington, officially took over their "control and custody" from the F.B.I. The F.B.I. had done its job thoroughly; each of the eight had been rigorously questioned, always separately, and had signed confessions which, except for lapses of memory and a few ineffectual attempts at lying, coincided. It would have been difficult, once Dasch and Burger gave such complete accounts, for any of the others to hold out for long. Before the eight men were moved to the District Jail, their statements, which were so self-incriminating, had already become the basis for the formal charges to be made against them.

The initial interviews between defense attorneys Royall and Dowell and their clients were frustrating to the two lawyers, who knew the thankless task they had been given. None of the prisoners felt that an active defense would be made; they were suspicious of Royall and Dowell, and considered them part of the machinery established to convict them. The two lawyers worked patiently to attain the men's confidence, but did not really get it until they requested that Dasch be defended separately. It was apparent to the lawyers that Dasch's testimony could be most damaging to the others, and that .there was a good chance he would become a government witness in order to win a lighter sentence. By this time the others knew of Dasch's role, and their bitterness against him would have made their difficult defense even harder. When the trial started, Colonel Carl L. Ristine, a lawyer in the Army's Inspector-General's office, had been appointed counsel for Dasch alone, although Dasch would be tried with the others.

Dowell and Royall had not sought their assignment to defend these men; both had been ordered to do so. Dowell had an unblemished military career now nearing its end; he was a forty-year man who had accomplished the rare feat of rising from private to commissioned rank in the pre-World War I Army. He had been wounded in World War I, had studied law between the wars, had taught it to other officers and had handled a multitude of legal affairs for the Army. He was not a trial lawyer, as Royall was, although he was thoroughly at home with the Courts-Martial Manual and military law procedure. Despite the fact that he was senior in both rank and age, he requested that Royall assume active direction of the case.

Royall, who had also served overseas in World War I, had just been appointed by Secretary Stimson to head the legal section of the Army's division charged with financial supervision of military contracts. He had graduated from Harvard Law School in 1917, where he was an editor of the *Law Review*, and had had a brilliant career in his native North Carolina. He had served a term as president of the state bar association and later became an influential member of the State Senate. Royall was tall and energetic, with a soft voice bearing traces of a Southern accent, and gave the appearance of a young man—he had to be reminded of his forty-eighth birthday on July 24, when the trial had been on for two weeks. He had been in Washington on his new job less than a month, so that his assignment to defend the prisoners came as an unpleasant surprise. Royall suggested that civilian, instead of military, lawyers handle the defense. His proposal was rejected, and having always prided himself on his skill as a trial lawyer, Royall immediately took over leadership of the defense with a vigor that alarmed the higher echelons of the War Department.

Royall and Dowell both took literally the words of the Courts-Martial Manual on the duties of defense counsel: "He will guard the interests of the accused by all honorable and legitimate means known to law." This is, of course, to act in the finest traditions of the legal profession, yet it is often misunderstood.

Before the trial was under way, Royall and Dowell gave warning of their intentions. On Monday, July 6, they wrote President Roosevelt—necessarily in secret, although they sent copies of the letter to McCoy, the prosecution attorneys and Secretary of War Stimson. They raised specifically the question of civil rights for the prisoners which the President's proclamation had so firmly denied. "Our investigation convinces us," Royall and Dowell said, "that there is a serious legal doubt as to the constitutionality and validity of the Proclamation and . . . of the Order [setting up the military commission]. It is our opinion that [the accused] should have an opportunity to institute appropriate proceedings to test the constitutionality and validity of the Proclamation and of the Order. In view of the fact that our appointment is made on the same Order which appoints the Military Commission, the question arises as to whether we are authorized to institute the proceeding suggested above. We respectfully suggest that you issue to us or to someone else appropriate authority to that end."

They did not hear directly from the President. Instead, Marvin McIntyre, Roosevelt's secretary, telephoned the next day. His answer for the President was simply that the two men would have to make their own decision as to their duties and authority. Royall and Dowell replied at once, and in a way which left no doubt as to where they stood. "We . . . are of the opinion," they wrote, "that we are authorized, and our duty requires us, first, to try to arrange for civil counsel to institute the proceedings necessary . . . and, second, if such arrangements cannot be made, to institute such proceedings at the appropriate time. Unless ordered otherwise, we will act accordingly."

They were not ordered otherwise, and continued to feel duty-bound to "act accordingly." Meantime, they prepared to defend their clients, as ordered, behind the closed doors of the Justice Department.

On the fifth floor of the Justice Department Building, carpenters had erected barriers on either side of a long corridor which held two large assembly rooms, ordinarily used by the F.B.I. for lectures and motion pictures in its training programs. One of these, Assembly Hall No. 1, whose main entrance was Room 5235, was converted into a courtroom. The windows were covered with heavy black curtains which completely blocked daylight, and green velvet was draped over the motion-picture screen. At the head of the long, narrow room—about 100 by 20 feet—in front of the covered screen, three office tables were placed end to end. This was the bench for the seven military judges, McCoy in the center, three major generals on one side, three brigadier generals on the other. The tables were uncluttered except for paper pads, pencils, water carafes and glasses. Behind McCoy's chair an American flag hung loosely.

To the left of the generals was a standard dark mahogany government office chair for witnesses. Next to the chair was a smaller table for the court reporter. Longer tables were placed parallel to each other, at right angles to the bench and several feet away from it. The one to the left of the judges was used by Biddle and the half-dozen men helping with the prosecution. J. Edgar Hoover, who took no open part in the trial, and was not officially listed as present, sat at the prosecution table at nearly every session. The defense staff had the table on the right. Behind it, against the wall, were chairs for the prisoners, who were arranged in alphabetical order, separated by unarmed soldiers. To the rear of the room was another group of tables, on which would be placed, until called for by the prosecution, the clothing, explosives and boxes to be used in evidence. The air-conditioning and artificial light, the absence of spectators and the nearly complete use of the available space for a bare minimum of people and furniture, gave Room 5235 a cold, grim appearance.

Outside the trial room Army enlisted men patrolled the corridor. Not far away, Attorney General Biddle's suite of offices had been divided by a plywood wall to make space for the defense staff. Nearby was the Justice Department press room where the reporters assigned to the trial could conjecture at the comings and goings of witnesses. Thus when Gerda Melind arrived wearing a white dress suitable for the oppressive Washington heat, she was inevitably called "The Lady in White," and one headline asked: "Will she try to save the life of her former sweetheart? Or will she support the story of Nazi activities on the part of Haupt . . . ?" Events outside the courtroom necessarily received the reporters' close attention. One of these, repeated on each of the eighteen trial days, was the manner of bringing the prisoners from their prison cells to the trial chamber. Tom Reynolds described the scene on the first day. "The eight accused men were brought to the Justice Department Building from the District Jail in two covered black vans. A carload of F.B.I. men led the procession. Then came an Army scout car, with two mounted machine guns aimed at the vans. The guns were manned by steel-helmeted troops, and two other soldiers flourishing Tommy guns stood in the scout car behind the mounted machine guns. Behind the scout car came the vans, with an armed soldier standing on the rear platform of each. . . . This procession wound through the broad avenues of Washington as crowds were going to work shortly before 9 A.M. At one point the crowd stood for a few seconds in amazement. Finally the cry spread: 'There go the spies' and the crowd surged after the vans."

Neither the descriptions of such scenes, nor the rumors and unconfirmed reports which the press printed in lieu of news of the trial, were ever mentioned in Room 5235. There, starting Wednesday morning, July 8, events moved in an orderly—if not always militarily precise—manner, and in complete isolation from the world outside. The stringent secrecy was emphasized afresh each day as witnesses were called on to take, in addition to the standard oath to tell the truth, another one binding them not to divulge "the proceedings taken in this trial to anyone outside the court room until released from your obligation by proper authority." The secrecy was maintained not only throughout the trial, but for nearly eighteen years after. Except for a few excerpts released after the war, the trial transcript of three thousand pages of testimony and legal argument remained a classified government document until 1960.

The question of secrecy did not appear to bother Americans generally. As there had been since Hoover's announcement of the capture of the eight men twelve days before the trial started, there was a feeling that the legal procedure was a necessary and bothersome detail to justify the death sentence. The nearest people came to arguing about the case was whether hanging or shooting was the more appropriate method to get rid of Nazi saboteurs. Traditionally, hanging is the more ignominious death, whereas death by a firing squad has somehow attained honorable connotations. The question was one that privately bothered President Roosevelt, whose decision it would have to be. When the trial was in its fourth day he told Hassett that he hoped it would not be a long-drawn-out affair, and then asked, "What should be done with them? Should they be shot or hanged?" Hassett had no doubts; he was for hanging, and even wanted pictures distributed as had been done in the case of Lincoln's assassins. The President considered this response but did not return to his original question or offer an opinion of his own. Instead, he closed the discussion with, "Hope the findings will be unanimous." There was no doubt that he meant unanimously guilty, and in this he was expressing the hopes of nearly all his countrymen.

Chapter 9
Biddle for the Prosecution

Notwithstanding a general assumption that the eight men on trial before the military commission were guilty, and doomed, Attorney General Francis Biddle had the responsibility of proving the charges against them in a way that could not be denied by the commission or by history. His was to be a simple presentation, but its very simplicity required that he develop it with care. He did not believe this would take long, but he did not expect, as some did, that the case would be over in a week or less. He was too experienced a lawyer to underestimate opposing counsel. Nevertheless, as he prepared to build his case, he was confident of the results and of his own ability to shape those results.

As President Roosevelt's fourth Attorney General and

the sixty-first in the nation's history, Biddle had won many legal fights for the government. From the first Attorney General, Edmund Randolph, one of Biddle's distinguished ancestors, until the present, none had compiled as many successes before the Supreme Court. His legal skill was based on experience which went back to 1911, when he was graduated from Harvard Law School and became private secretary to Supreme Court Justice Oliver Wendell Holmes. After service in World War I and many years with a Philadelphia law firm, he was appointed judge of the Circuit Court of Appeals. He spent a year on the bench, was named Solicitor General, and was quickly promoted to Attorney General. He was a short, dapper man, with a thin, neatly trimmed mustache and fine clothes—during this midsummer trial he favored double-breasted white linen suits. Biddle had an incisive mind, an ability to grasp the essence of legal arguments and respond to them quickly.

Arguing before a military commission and under the rules of military law was a new experience for Biddle. He was not expected to prosecute the entire case himself, of course, and had by his side Major General Myron Cramer, the Judge Advocate General of the Army; several of Cramer's talented legal officers; and civilian lawyers from the Justice Department—but as a practical matter, Biddle would speak for the prosecution and handle the legal skirmishes with Royall.

The first came before the commission had properly organized itself, and before anyone except the court reporter had been sworn. When McCoy called the commission to order and announced it "open for the trial of such persons as may be brought before it," Royall struck at once, as he had told President Roosevelt he would, at the validity of the order creating the commission. Civil statutes covered the crimes that were charged, and civil courts were open to try the case, he said. Royall was brief; aware that what he said would not cause the commission to disband itself, he was simply getting his position on the record to, as Dowell added, "ward off any assumption that the defense accepts by participating in this proceeding the legality of the tribunal or its method of constitution." Biddle had seen Royall's correspondence with the President, but had not expected the fight over this question to come so soon. His quick response did not show his surprise. He dismissed Royall's argument out of hand: "[this] is a trial of the offenses of the law of war, which is not cognizable by the civil courts. It is the trial . . . of certain enemies who crossed our borders, crossed our boundaries . . . in disguise in enemy vessels and landed here. They are in exactly and precisely the same position as armed forces invading this country. I cannot think it conceivable that any commission would listen to an argument that armed forces entering this country should not be met by the resistance of the Army itself under the Commander-in-Chief or that they have any civil rights that you can listen to."

McCoy gave notice at the outset that he would preside firmly and in accordance with the President's order. He cut further debate between Biddle and Royall until the commission was formally sworn and the oath of secrecy administered to all present. Then, as anticipated, he overruled Royall's objection to the commission's jurisdiction; the trial would proceed as planned.

Immediately there followed that awful moment in capital trials, the readings of charges which carry the penalty of death. Those for whom the reading was most important had already heard them once; Royall and Dowell had told the prisoners the week before.

The first charge specified in the language of military law how the eight accused men were in "Violation of the Law of War." They were enemies of the United States, "acting for and on behalf of the German Reich," who had "secretly and covertly," while in civilian dress, passed through American military lines for the purpose of committing sabotage and other hostile acts in order "to destroy certain war industries, war utilities and war materials." The second, "Violation of the 81st Article of War," charged that they "relieved or attempted to relieve enemies of the United States with arms, munitions, supplies, money and other things, and knowingly harbored, protected and held correspondence and gave intelligence to enemies of the United States." The third charge was "Violation of the 82nd Article of War" which covers spying, and specified that the prisoners had been "lurking or acting as spies in or about the fortifications, posts and encampments of the armies of the United States." The fourth simply accused them of conspiracy to commit the previously listed crimes or, in the military phraseology, that they "did plot, plan and conspire with each other, with the German Reich, and with other enemies of the United

States, to commit each and every one of the above-enumerated charges and specifications."

Having read the charges, Colonel F. Granville Munson, the official accuser, had one more formality. "Are your clients ready to plead?" Munson asked defense counsel. Royall rose and stepped toward the commission's tables. He was expected to enter pleas of not guilty at this point, and allow the prosecution to get under way. Instead he moved to strike certain of the charges, because he did not see how it was "a violation of law for a German to aid the German Government, any more than it could be . . . for an American to aid the American Government." Furthermore, Dowell concluded for the defense, the charges were vague and did not properly inform the accused of the acts they were said to have committed; in military, as in civil, courts, the right of the accused to hear the precise charges against him is a sacred one. Like the previous objection to the commission's jurisdiction, the defense motion was an effort to get these objections into the record. Biddle seemed to sense this, and that the motion would not be upheld. When McCoy reminded him that he had only five minutes before the lunch recess, Biddle said he could confine his remarks to that time and did. Soon after the start of the afternoon session, McCoy announced that the defense motion was not sustained. No one was surprised.

Now Munson returned to his postponed duty, the pleas of the prisoners to each of the charges. Burger was first. "How do you plead to Specification 1 of Charge 1?" Munson asked. "Not guilty," Burger said. Despite the confessions which he and his fellow prisoners had made, this plea was the only hope of avoiding the death penalty. The dialogue was identical for each of the specifications and charges, as each prisoner rose in turn. There was no room for any variation in the questions, and only the slightest in the response. Each man offered a flat "not guilty," except Dasch and Kerling, who added "sir" to their answers, a gesture without meaning except perhaps to themselves. When Thiel sat down, the last "not guilty" recorded, Biddle could finally start. Quibbles over jurisdiction and the charges were out of the way. He would now develop his sequence and establish proof of guilt. From now until they were called as witnesses in their own defense, the eight prisoners would be spectators, not participants, of this trial.

Biddle opened slowly, almost pedantically, by reading War Department orders and documents which, he said, proved the east coast of the United States to be a zone of war. His last document was a confidential map of the coast of Long Island, showing the Coast Guard stations on active duty. This was a logical introduction to the events at Amagansett during the morning of June 13, as seen by the men from the Coast Guard Station there.

Thus Coast Guardsman second class John C. Cullen, the first man to spread the alarm of strangers on the American coast, became the first man to testify against them. There was no mistaking the terror of his experience. His brief answers conveyed the suspense of his patrol on the foggy beach and the sudden discovery of shadowy silhouettes. Nor did the presence of so many high-ranking officers force Cullen into stiff and artificial language. When he told of shouting to the vague figures at the waterline, "I hollered out," he said. And when he hollered, Cullen went on, "one of the men walked toward me." Biddle's questioning of Cullen up to that moment was preparation for the first of the dramatic confrontations to be made in this trial.

Biddle: *Do you recognize the man in the court who walked towards you?*

Cullen: *I think so, sir.*

Biddle: *Will you stand up and identify him, if you see him in the court? Stand up, please. Now, do you see the man?*

Cullen: *Yes, sir.*

Biddle: *Which is he?*

Cullen: *Right here (indicating), sir.*

Biddle: *Go and point to the man that you have in mind. It won't hurt you. Just go and point at him. Point at him. Which is he?*

Cullen: *Yes, sir. Right here (indicating).*

Biddle: *Will you stand up, please?*

  (One of the accused stood and approached the witness.)

Biddle: *Is that the man you remember seeing?*

Cullen: *Would he mind saying a few words?*

Biddle: *Do you want to identify him by his voice? Is that what you mean?*

Cullen: *Yes, sir.*

Biddle: *Do I have the commission's permission to permit the person whom the witness has identified to speak, so*

> *that he may be able to identify him by his voice?*
>
> Gen. McCoy: *If there is no objection on the part of the defense.*
>
> Col. Royall: *I do not represent him, sir.*
>
> Col. Ristine: *No objection.*
>
> The Accused: *What is your name?*
>
> Cullen: *Yes, sir.*
>
> Biddle: *What do you mean by "Yes, sir"?*
>
> Cullen: *That's the man.*
>
> Biddle: *That's the man you saw at that time?*
>
> Cullen: *Yes.*
>
> Biddle: *The record, I think, should show that the witness identified the defendant Dasch as the man whom he saw on the beach at that point.*

Cullen continued to respond forthrightly to Biddle's questions. After a long, uninterrupted period of testimony, Cullen described his first look at the boxes of explosives, which he called "this equipment they had dug up." Royall was on his feet at once. Such a statement, he said, was hearsay. Biddle had no alternative but to agree. McCoy, however, wanted "a little discussion about this." He alone would pass on the admissibility of evidence, he said, and "I take it, from the President's proclamation, that there is an unusual freedom for both sides in the term 'probative value for a reasonable man.' So I want to make it perfectly plain that the rulings will be to give full and free presentation of evidence that would fit into that statement." Biddle was in the strange position of siding with opposing counsel. "The objection was," he told McCoy, "that since [the witness] did not see the boxes dug up, he cannot testify with respect to their being dug up. We shall later show that they were dug up and put the witnesses on. I said I had no objection to its being stricken out." Almost reluctantly, McCoy accepted Royall's objection. It was the first time in the trial that the defense was sustained by McCoy.

Since Cullen's testimony was most damaging to Dasch, Ristine handled most of the cross-examination. His major effort was to show that Dasch attempted no violence on the beach and that he even sought to be identified. Under questioning, Cullen conceded that his use of a flashlight made it possible to identify Dasch, whereas he could not recognize any of the other men, even Burger, who had come as close as two or three feet. Biddle was apparently satisfied that the cursory cross-examination had not damaged Cullen's testimony. In requestioning Cullen, he tried only to weaken the point on the lack of violence. "You said that Dasch had made certain suggestions to you as to what might happen if you did not go away. What were these suggestions?" Biddle asked. "He said he would not want to have to kill me," Cullen said. "But you did not take that as violence?" Biddle asked. "No, sir," said Cullen. With Biddle's "That is all," and a reminder from Munson about the oath of secrecy, Cullen left the room.

Biddle proceeded from the men on the beach to the boxes they left there. Warren Barnes, the chief of the Amagansett Coast Guard Station, followed Cullen to the witness chair to describe his own part in the events of June 13, and identified the articles that were buried on the beach. One by one the duffel bag, a single white sneaker, the trench shovels, the broken package of cigarettes, the boxes of explosives themselves were brought before the witness and the seven generals. The collection arrayed on the mahogany table must have struck the prisoners with more force than the words that had been exchanged up to now. Except for the encounter with Cullen in which Dasch and Burger had participated, everything Cullen and Barnes had said was new to all eight men. For the four who landed at Amagansett, especially, the version they were hearing must have had an eerie, almost surrealistic effect, as of looking into a mirror by candlelight. Yet the objects before them were real. Not so long ago they had carried those boxes over a sandy beach, had dug with those shovels, worn those clothes. At that moment, just before the commission adjourned for the day and the prisoners were escorted back to their cells, the eight men must have realized with new horror the complete helplessness of their situation.

Before the second day's session was far along, the exceedingly fine care with which Biddle was developing his case became evident. He traced—with witnesses for every step—the movement of the articles found at Amagansett to the Coast Guard Office in New York, and from there to the F.B.I. He had the F.B.I. agents to certify that they had, indeed, been given the boxes, and he had the F.B.I. explosives expert, D. J. Parsons, to swear that he had tested each of the devices found in the boxes and that they were exactly as described—bombs, fuses, wires. There was nothing defense counsel could do but listen carefully for a flaw that could be exploited, an excessive claim that might be denied, a deviation from legal procedure that could be argued. There were no significant slips. Occasionally a witness would go beyond Biddle's carefully phrased questions and testify to something he had not himself seen or heard, and Royall would rise swiftly to object. Most of the time Biddle permitted the objection to stand. It hardly mattered; he had other witnesses who had seen or heard.

Parsons was in a modestly efficient way one of the most effective of Biddle's witnesses. In his quiet understatement, the potential dangers of the innocent-looking pen-and-pencil sets and the simulated pieces of coal achieved great force. As he described each device, Biddle handed either a photograph or the object itself to the commission members. The simple but effective tools of death, whose mechanisms Parsons explained in nonscientific detail, fascinated his audience. As he described one of the delayed-timing devices, he told what each wheel and pin did, and how the timer could be set for various periods of time.

"In an actual test which I ran," Parsons said, "the clock was set for a fourteen-day delay period, and actually went off in a period of fourteen days and three hours." It was obvious that Parsons had affection for a device which could operate within such a narrow margin of error. Now McCoy leaned forward, and for the first time a member of the commission asked a witness a question. "What do you call that in the profession?" he asked Parsons. There was no special name, Parsons said, it was simply a clockwork delay mechanism. "Is the operation audible?" asked one of the generals. "No, sir. It is very quiet," Parsons said. "The sound is no more than that of a fine watch. It must be held closely to the ear. That is now running, if you care to listen to it." The general listened. It was the kind of concrete evidence that military men understood.

With the contents of the duffel bag and the boxes in evidence, Biddle started to relate these physical goods to the men on trial. To do this he simply called the F.B.I. agents who had arrested and questioned the defendants. Burger, it developed, had signed a waiver permitting the F.B.I. agents to search his room at the Governor Clinton. He had signed it on June 22; the search had taken place during and after his arrest on June 20. Royall interposed to say that this made it an unlawful search. The Constitution of the United States, he said, does not permit search without legal warrant and the courts have held that evidence so obtained is not admissible. Biddle countered that Burger had not objected to the search. That made no difference to Royall; the constitutional requirement remained. Biddle was adamant. "I know of no constitutional right," he said, "which prevents a duly designated agent of the F.B.I. . . . from searching a defendant with the defendant's permission, after the description of what had taken place beforehand. . . . It would be like saying that when you arrested a man in the midst of his committing a crime, you could not search him afterward." Biddle's was the pragmatic point of view, and it carried.

This was a preliminary to the trial's major debate, in which Biddle's practical approach clashed with Royall's adherence to "due process." It got under way on Thursday afternoon, when F.B.I. agent Charles F. Lanman was in the witness chair identifying a series of photographs, each of which had been signed in his presence by Burger, who had written a brief note on each: "Spades used to bury boxes and sea sack on beach of Amagansett, L.I., June 13, 1942." "Shoes worn by myself." "One of shoes, which I believe worn by Quirin." "Shoes worn by Henry [Heinck]." "Socks worn by myself." "Time clocks and accessories similar to those landed by myself, Dasch, Quirin and Heinck at Amagansett. . . ." On the face of it, this was a simple, straightforward presentation, in keeping with Biddle's careful development of his case. Royall, seeing it quite differently, precipitated a legal discussion of the kind which is full of hair-splitting technicalities, but which often reaches the essence of a case, and of law itself.

Royall could not quarrel with the evidence now being shown by Biddle—insofar as it pertained to Burger. But under both civil and military law, he insisted, the evidence could not be admissible against his other clients. The Courts-Martial Manual was quite specific on this point: "The acts and statements of a conspirator . . . done or made after the common design is accomplished or abandoned, are not admissible against the others." As he developed his position, Royall injected a touch of humor. Chances are that most of those present did not think it funny at all, but it was the first of the rare attempts at lightness in the entire trial. For Burger's statements to be valid as testimony against the others, Royall said, they "must be made in furtherance of the conspiracy; and it is manifest, of course, that statements made to the F.B.I. could not be in furtherance of a conspiracy, unless it could be contended that the F.B.I. were going to participate therein, which I think we cannot assume."

There was no pause for laughter, and Biddle rose to support his own use of evidence. Royall's position was a technical one, Biddle said, and could not stand up against a key provision in the President's order establishing the commission: the right to admit evidence which had "probative value to a reasonable man." "Is not the very purpose and essence of that clause," he asked, "to disregard the highly technical and complicated rules of evidence and to consider whether or not when Burger freely and without duress says, 'I recognize these clothes as having been worn by one of the men that was with me,' it is convincing to a reasonable man?"

Royall was on his feet at once; the "reasonable man" provision was obviously going to cause him trouble throughout the trial unless he could weaken it at once. To use that provision as a guide for evidence, he said, "is to say, in effect, that all our courts and all our jurisdictions, the liberal as well as the strict, the English as well as the American, have been enforcing for generations a rule that has no reasonable basis. I say to this commission that this rule is fundamental; that no man can be convicted by what is purely hearsay evidence of what another man says. One thing we are proud of in this country—and I am not trying to get oratorical about it, but I think it is so essential that I want to make this point—is our system of administering justice. We are proud of it particularly in times like this, when it stands out in sharp contrast to other systems whch we are fighting. . . . When we deal with a fundamental principle of trying seven other men upon an unsworn, unexamined, and uninvestigated declaration of an eighth, we are encroaching . . . upon a fundamental element of our administration of justice. We sincerely trust that this court will rule this evidence to be incompetent as to all the defendants except the defendant Burger."

McCoy ordered a recess while he conferred for a few minutes with his fellow officers. But the commission was not yet ready to answer so basic a question, and McCoy announced that he would postpone a ruling on Royall's objection. The trial continued, as Biddle had Burger's confession read in its entirety. Although Royall did not know then whether it would eventually be used solely against Burger, or against his other clients as well, he did not object. On Monday, after a delay of three days, the commission decided against Royall. It looked as if the "reasonable man" provision was going to be Biddle's greatest strength in the case for the prosecution. Royall accepted the ruling, as, of course, he had to, but said he hoped that the commission would later reverse itself. He still intended to object to the admission of statements by one defendant against another and, no matter the nature of Biddle's questions, did not intend to cross-examine one man about another. He was so persistent in this that the commission in effect suspended its ruling once more, and did not make a definitive decision until the prosecution's case was all but made. Until that time, it was at least a tentative victory for Biddle, and he proceeded as if he had no doubt of the eventual outcome.

When it came to matters of military law as specifically described in the Courts-Martial Manual, the commission did not delay decisions. On Saturday, the trial's fourth day, Biddle was questioning F.B.I. agent Norval D. Wills about statements Dasch had made while he was in F.B.I. custody. During the lunch hour Dasch told Ristine something he had not known before—that Dasch had been promised, or at least thought he had been promised, leniency by the F.B.I. if he would plead guilty and not testify about his role in the capture of the other seven men. If Dasch's interpretation of the offer was true, it may have been made in expectation of a conventional public trial, in which his testimony would have revealed more than the F.B.I. wanted Germany to know. Such a promise invoked the rule, which applies in both civilian and military law, that statements induced "by hope of benefit or fear of punishment" are involuntary, and therefore inadmissible as evidence. The proposal was made to him, Dasch recalled, on June 27, two days after his long confession was signed. Thus, as far as Ristine was concerned, only Dasch's confession was valid evidence; anything he was reported to have said after June 27 was not.

Immediately after the commission reconvened for the afternoon session, and Wills had returned to the witness chair, Ristine was on his feet. "If the commission please," he said, "in view of some new facts . . . I should like to be permitted to ask a few additional questions of this witness with a view to making a motion respecting his testimony." Biddle at once objected. "This witness was put on and examined at great length," he said. "Now here, in the middle of the evidence, counsel again wishes to ask him questions. I have no objection if the commission thinks that is a proper procedure. I do not want to be technical about it, but I want to get on with my case." The commission decided to hear Ristine.

> Ristine: *Mr. Wills, were you present on Saturday, June 27, 1942, in the evening, with [agents] Donegan, Johnstone, and Traynor when a proposal was made that Dasch should plead guilty?*
>
> Wills: *I was.*
>
> Ristine: *And was it stated as part of that proposal that after his plea of guilty he should be sentenced and that during the trial he should not divulge anything with respect to the agreement that was made, and that after the case had died down and for about, say, three to six months, the F.B.I. would get a presidential pardon for him?*
>
> Wills: *That, in substance, is true.*
>
> Ristine: *And was the statement also made to Mr. Dasch that that would be the best procedure for him to follow in order to protect his father and mother in Germany?*

Before Wills could answer, Biddle objected. "Wait just a minute," he said. "I think the witness ought to be asked what took place, instead of having words put into his mouth, and then saying yes or no." Ristine took the interruption in stride. "I am perfectly willing to phrase the question the other way," he said. McCoy looked up from the commission's table and said, "Develop the question." Ristine turned back to Wills.

> Ristine: *Would you tell the commission what was said in favor of the proposal, if anything, respecting his father and mother?*
>
> Wills: *The proposal was given to protect the father and mother and relatives in Germany or in German-occupied countries.*
>
> Biddle: *To protect them from what?*
>
> Wills: *From harm.*

Ristine: *Following Dasch's statement that he would not go through with that proposal, did you, in company with Mr. Johnstone, make any efforts to persuade him to agree to go through with it?*
Wills: *Yes, sir.*

Ristine then turned to McCoy. "Now, if the commission please," he said, "in the light of what the witness has said, we submit that his testimony with respect to any conversation subsequent to that proposal . . . is not admissible or competent for any purpose. We not only object to his giving testimony further about the matter, but move to strike out the testimony already given." Biddle could not accept this without another attempt to regain his witness. He questioned Wills again to show that he had testified only on what Dasch had said prior to June 27. Thus, Biddle contended, even had there been an inducement, it was not pertinent. "There is no suggestion of any impropriety in the case at all," he said.

But Ristine was not ready to concede anything. He wanted Dasch's entire confession, all 254 pages of it, read into the record. The Courts-Martial Manual says, "Evidence of a confession or supposed confession cannot be restricted to evidence of only a part thereof." By now his original objection had been lost amid charges, countercharges and interruptions. Royall, who was not directly involved, was jogged into the need for clearing the air. "What we are really arguing," he said, "is whether we are going to put in this accurate, complete stenographic record [of Dasch's confession] or let the witness select what he testifies about. On that question there are only two considerations. One is . . . time, and that might be very important . . . in some cases. But in this case it should not be . . . when the charges are as serious as they are. . . . The only other possible motive—and I am not saying this with any reflection upon the eminent Attorney General or upon the F.B.I., because it would probably be correct trial practice—would be to bring out those things that are most damaging . . . leaving it for the cross-examination to go into the substance of the entire 254 pages. That might be a technical advantage for the prosecution, but if it is, it certainly does not commend itself to a sense of justice, it seems to me."

Although Royall's sense of justice was outraged, he was arguing for practical considerations as well. The confession, which he had not seen because he did not represent Dasch, could affect his clients as well. All that he wanted, and all that Ristine wanted, he said, was to put in evidence "what the man said and signed, and try this case just as you would any other case where a man's life is at stake." By this time Biddle could not restrain himself. As far as he was concerned, Dasch's was a "self-serving" statement. "Colonel Royall wants me to try my case according to the way he wants it done," he said. "He wants me to put in this long signed statement. I propose, with the commission's permission, to try the case in exactly the way I think it ought to be tried . . . and not as Colonel Royall or anyone except the commission suggests." This was the nearest the two men had come to personal acrimony. Now it was Royall's turn. "I am not trying to tell the Attorney General how to try his case," he said, "but that remark does not deter me from objecting to testimony that I think is clearly incompetent, and his desire to try the case as he wants does not give him blanket authority to violate the rules of evidence any more than it would give me the authority."

After conferring for fifteen minutes, the commission was still not clear as to what was at issue, which was not surprising in view of the various directions the argument had taken. Now, more calmly, McCoy sought the views of the three lawyers once again. It took the better part of an hour before McCoy finally ruled that Wills could talk only about what Dasch had said prior to June 27. Biddle started once more with Wills and, except for loss of time, was not really worse off than he had been; Dasch's full confession was not yet in the record. By the time the day's session had ended—McCoy let it run later than usual because of the delay—Biddle could take his turn at some mild humor. In cross-examining Wills, Ristine had referred to the fact that Dasch's address book contained the name of Francis Biddle as a possible source of help in Washington. A moment later, Ristine paused while standing near Biddle's chair, then walked toward Wills with a smile. "The Attorney General is interested in whether you know who recommended him," he said. With a straight face, Wills explained that it was the young waiter Dasch had met his first night in Washington.

The next day Biddle turned to the part of his presentation that featured secret writing and confessions of cloak-and-dagger activities. He called as a witness J. W. Magee, a chemist with the F.B.I.'s Technical Laboratory, and handed him the handkerchief which Dasch had turned over to Traynor. As far as anyone could see, it was an ordinary white handkerchief, and Magee explained that when examined under normal light in the laboratory there were not any visible pen marks on it. Then, he said, he exposed the handkerchief to ammonia fumes, and writing appeared. Biddle produced a container of ammonium hydroxide and Magee stretched the handkerchief on a frame and held the taut cloth over the ammonia. Immediately red letters formed on the handkerchief. Biddle, who was supervising the demonstration, was not quite sure its effect had reached the proper audience. "Can the commission see?" he asked McCoy. "The commission," McCoy assured him, "can see and smell."

Magee then read the names and addresses which had appeared on the handkerchief; this performance was perhaps even more striking than the earlier display of explosives, for this was, after all, the stuff of which spying is made. Even where Magee noted unintelligible words, he added to the aura of intrigue. By the time Ristine came to cross-examine Magee, there seemed to be nothing he could ask which would erase the effect of the smelly ammonia fumes on a common handkerchief. Nevertheless, he maintained a steady defense: Dasch had cooperated with the F.B.I., had given them the handkerchief, and had done all he could to decipher the writing on it, even though he had forgotten the name of the substance which would make the writing appear. But Magee had seen Dasch only once. Dasch did try to help deciper the words, he recalled, but the implication was strong that the help was not very significant.

Biddle had more than demonstrations to offer. Although he had been reluctant to introduce Dasch's statement, he had no hesitation in having Heinck's and Quirin's confessions in the record. They read like the straightforward confessions of men caught in a criminal act, including the quite normal attempts to distort the truth from time to time. From a prosecuting attorney's point of view, they were ideal material to convince a jury, or a military commission. When the F.B.I. agents who had questioned Heinck and Quirin finished reading the statements, Biddle produced the false social security and selective service cards and photographs of the clothes and other items which Heinck and Quirin had identified as their own. Each was placed in the record as a prosecution exhibit.

By July 15, the eighth day of the trial, Biddle had made his case against the four men who landed at Amagansett and was ready to proceed as carefully and thoroughly against the other four. But Ristine could no longer permit Dasch's statement to be ignored. He knew that coming back to it later, when he started his defense arguments, would make it appear a weaker document. On the ground that Biddle had presented part of the confession, he now insisted that all of it be placed in the record. When Dasch, sitting next to him, urged that it be not just inserted in the record, but actually read aloud, Ristine passed his request to the commission, and added with some feeling, "Who am I to suggest the contrary? I was appointed to represent Mr. Dasch. It is his freedom that is at stake, not mine." This simple declaration may have carried more weight with the commission than the legal arguments three days earlier. It took the members fifteen minutes to rule that "the paper concerned, the so-called confession of the defendant Dasch, will now be read." Relays of junior officers and F.B.I. agents required from midafternoon Wednesday to noon Friday to read it in its entirety; and then at such an unusually rapid pace that Royall later complained that it had been hard to follow even with the text before him.

With Dasch's statement recorded, Biddle at last started the case against the Florida group. His confidence by now was so great, and the design of his prosecution so well established, that for the first time since the case opened he did not take personal direction. Oscar Cox, the Assistant Solicitor General, took over briefly. As before, but faster, because this was necessarily repetitious, the articles associated with each defendant were shown and identified. For a while it looked as if the prosecution could complete its case against the last four defendants in less time than it had taken for just one of the previous four.

But a snag came during testimony against Kerling. The witness was Joseph G. Fellner, an F.B.I. agent who was on duty in the New York office at the time of Kerling's arrest. He answered some routine questions from Cox and then submitted to cross-examination by Royall. For the first time, Royall began to draw evidence which suggested that a confession was made under duress. It took lengthy questioning to get even the slightest concession from Fellner, but at last he agreed that "Kerling said that someone hit him in the face." Fellner made it clear that he did not do the hitting and was not present when any such event took place. All he knew was that when Agent Thomas J. Donegan asked Kerling about the incident, Kerling said, "Well, you brushed me lightly on the side of my face." Kerling had later retracted this, but it was never made clear in the testimony whether the retraction preceded or followed a private conversation between Kerling and Donegan. Later, Donegan denied he had ever struck Kerling or had even brushed his face lightly. Donegan conceded that he might have spoken roughly—"some rather strong language," he said, which he didn't think was fit to be put on the record—but as for physical violence, he insisted none had been used.

Leaving the point unsettled for the time being, Royall then sought to determine the amount of sleep Kerling was permitted the night he was arrested. According to Fellner, Kerling slept most of the time when he was with him, from 10:15 P.M. of June 23 to 8:50 the next morning. Actually, Fellner said, "I couldn't tell you if he was sleeping or not, but he certainly had his eyes closed and his head hung most of the time." Then, said Royall, "everytime he got his eyes a little closed, you would wake him up and insist on continuing his questioning, would you not?" "I would ask him questions, yes," said Fellner. All of which meant, said Royall in summation, that he had to object to the reading of Kerling's confession. The Courts-Martial Manual says that the prosecution has to prove that a confession was voluntarily made; under the circumstances, Royall insisted, this was clearly not done. Cox replied that Royall was drawing inferences from the witnesses and that Kerling's statement actually opened with a declaration that it was voluntary. "It is elementary, I think," said Royall, "that the mere fact that the witness says in the statement that it is voluntary is entitled to no appreciable weight . . . the statement . . . cannot pull itself up by its own bootstraps."

The commission disagreed. It considered Kerling's confession voluntary, and ordered it read. Then, without much discussion, those of Haupt, Neubauer and Thiel were heard as well. By Saturday evening, as the tenth session of the trial was about to adjourn, Biddle was able to say that he had completed the case for the prosecution. He preferred, however, not to make a formal close until Monday, in the event that Royall or Ristine had further cross-examination.

Cross-examination did not delay Biddle's closing; but one last fight—and the definitive decision—on the admission of evidence did. McCoy allowed Biddle and Royall to sum up their arguments on this basic issue. Royall could now cite an earlier remark of Biddle's in which he conceded that if the case were being tried under the rules of common law evidence, and not before a military commission, "the confession of one man is not evidence against another" except in a conspiracy. Royall insisted this had to be so in a military trial as well; otherwise hearsay would prevail.

To Biddle it was a simple issue which involved incontrovertible facts. To deny them because of a technicality in common law was preposterous. "Those men," he said, "not having an opportunity to confer or talk it over, on the whole made confessions entirely bearing out what each other said. Dasch supports Burger, Burger supports Kerling, and so on, right down the line. . . . The defendants say that in spite of that close interlocking of all those statements, all alike, all bearing the obvious marks of truthfulness, all comparable to each other, all showing this essential common intent . . . you must in some curious way take out of your minds with respect to some defendants the confessions of the others."

Biddle concluded by comparing the powers of the commission with those given to administrative tribunals such as the National Labor Relations Board and the Securities and Exchange Commission, which, he said, were not bound by the hearsay rule. "I cannot conceive," he concluded, "that you, as a body of reasonable men, would exclude this evidence on the ground that it does not carry weight. . . ." Biddle's reference to administrative boards gave Royall one last chance. "Am I to understand," he asked, "that the prosecution in this case says that a man's liberty is to be determined upon the same basis that businessmen would arbitrate a dollars-and-cents controversy? If that is the law, we are losing mighty near all of our vaunted system of criminal justice."

Royall's eloquence was wasted. What Biddle called the "practical way of arriving at the truth"—by evidence which would convince "reasonable men"—was accepted. The commission upheld Biddle just before noon on Monday, July

20; it would "admit the confessions and admissions for all purposes." It was a major victory for Biddle, as important in its way as the evidence he had presented. Shortly after lunch, he turned to the commission and quietly announced, "The prosecution rests its case." What with the legal arguments, it had taken eleven days, a good deal longer than he had anticipated, but as he prepared to watch the defense develop its case, it would have been hard to imagine—after the detailed evidence against each man, and the commission's ruling on the weight of that evidence—that the defense could produce anything which would in any way injure his case.

Chapter 10
Royall for the Defense

Under normal circumstances, defense attorneys have a slight advantage over the prosecution. In Anglo-Saxon legal tradition, people charged with committing a crime are presumed innocent until proven guilty; the burden of proof is on the prosecution, and the evidence it offers is accepted or rejected for reasons which have tended to give defendants the benefit of any doubt. In view of the military commission's decision on the admission of evidence and the literalness with which it was taking the "reasonable man" position in its charter, this advantage had vanished for Royall at precisely the moment he was to present his case for the defense. The burden of proof had shifted, and it was now up to him—and to Ristine on behalf of Dasch—to establish the innocence of the defendants so as to overcome a presumption of their guilt. It was not going to be easy, the defense counsel knew, and least helpful would be the defendants themselves. To seven tough-minded generals, none of the men except possibly Kerling and Burger seemed likely to make even an understandable case for themselves.

While preparing his case under these difficulties, Royall had also been working tirelessly for his clients in another direction. He wanted a civil court test of the President's proclamation and the jurisdiction of the military commission. If he was to do what "duty requires," as he had written President Roosevelt he would, he could not delay the moves that he hoped would lead to a Supreme Court hearing.

Royall's first efforts had been to seek assistance from civilian lawyers, especially experts on the Constitution. He was aware that the day-to-day activity before the military commission would severely limit what he himself could do. He did not want—nor did he have authority—to ask civilian lawyers to take over the civil test. Because of the limits on his time, he did want guidance from experts on constitutional law. He first called Zachariah Chafee, Jr., professor of law at Harvard and one of the country's outstanding authorities on constitutional law and civil liberties. Chafee was sympathetic but, not having actually practiced law for some years, did not feel qualified to help. "I have considerable doubts about the jurisdiction of the military commission," he wrote to Royall. "A judicial determination of the proper location of the line between military and civilian tribunals seems highly desirable." It was a gratifying letter, but of no practical benefit. A young lawyer whom Chafee recommended also considered himself disqualified, and after a few more tries Royall stopped looking for outside help. He realized that he would have to act himself.

The Supreme Court had adjourned for the summer; its members were vacationing in all parts of the country. And the Court had not been called for a special session since 1920, when it convened to hear a dispute between the states of Texas and Oklahoma which had caused oil to be wasted at the rate of a million dollars a day. There was a chance for Royall, though, if he could convince Chief Justice Harlan Fiske Stone that the present circumstances warranted calling the justices to Washington. Associate Justice Hugo L. Black lived in nearby Alexandria, Virginia. Royall did not know him well, but felt an affinity toward a fellow Southerner and a justice who had spoken forthrightly in decisions bearing on civil liberties. With a minimum of formality— Royall later recalled that he telephoned Black to say he was dropping in—he outlined his problem to Black. For reasons he did not make clear, at least to Royall, Black declined to do anything about the situation. Royall returned to Washington; there seemed no way out. His former law professor, Associate Justice Felix Frankfurter, was vacationing in New Milford, Connecticut, and Royall did not know any of the other justices well enough, even if they had been nearby.

On Monday, the day after his disappointing interview with

Black, Royall opened his defense before the commission. That day he saw a brief item in the *Washington Post* that the funeral of former Justice George Sutherland was being held that morning, and that Associate Justice Owen J. Roberts would represent the Court at the services. Royall hardly knew Roberts, but he did know what he had to do. He went to Roberts' office to wait for him. Briefly he outlined his plans and told of his interview with Black. Roberts suggested that Royall come to his farm outside Philadelphia later in the week, prepared to argue his position; Roberts, for his part, would see that Black was present. Royall· agreed, and said that he would urge Biddle to attend as well so that the prosecution would have sufficient notice and thus have no cause for delay. Royall was aware of the exceedingly sensitive area he was now entering; for sound and important considerations of national security the trial of his clients was being held in secret. The Supreme Court would be open to press and public, and there were obviously matters which could not be discussed there.

After the day's trial session, Royall told Biddle of his discussion with Roberts and of his plans to visit him. He invited Biddle to accompany him. Biddle appeared taken aback that Royall had gone so far, although he had been aware from the outset that an attempt at a civil test was possible. "Let me think it over," Biddle said. Royall grinned. "I hope the President has time to see you," he said. Regardless of whether Biddle did indeed confer with the President or made the decision on his own, he later told Royall he would go. He also said that he approved of Royall's action. He too felt that a Court test of the President's war powers was appropriate in this important case, and he was optimistic that they would be sustained.

Before he opened his actual defense that Monday afternoon, Royall moved for immediate verdicts of not guilty on some of the charges on the grounds that the prosecution had not proved its case. He did not seek acquittal on all charges, but only on the second and third—relieving the enemy and spying. Relieving the enemy, he said, could not possibly apply to one of the enemy. If "it was a crime for a German citizen to help Germany, then every German soldier, if there were an invasion of this country, would be guilty under that section and be punished by death. That cannot be the meaning of it." As for the spying charge, he said, "There must be first some clandestine conduct or some false pretense. Second, it must be in the zone of military operations; and third, it must be with the intent to communicate military information to the enemy." The prosecution had proved only the first of these. Proof that the men planned to commit sabotage did not show that they intended to collect and pass on military information. Even the handkerchiefs with the Lisbon address and the fact that the men were taught the use of secret inks did not show intent to spy; they were part of the sabotage plans, to be used to seek more explosives or money, or to write each other. If Royall seemed to be convicting his clients of sabotage while pleading their innocence of spying, it was for a sound reason. The death sentence is mandatory for spying; there is some discretion in setting a penalty for the other charges.

Because of the nature of Royall's argument, Biddle permitted the response to be made by Cramer, who as the Army's Judge Advocate General was an acknowledged authority on military law. He was "a little surprised at the ingenuity of the argument," Cramer said, which would create "the absurd situation whereby a German citizen in this country . . . who might give dynamite . . . to saboteurs . . . could not be tried" for relieving the enemy. On the spying charge, Cramer reiterated that the Atlantic Coast was a military zone, under patrol by United States Armed Forces. As for intent to communicate, Kerling and Dasch had conceded in their statements that the Lisbon address was to be used to write Kappe. Dasch had even said that he was to report "the exact location of additional new-built industrial centers . . . which are manufacturing war materials." It was a clear admission of intent to spy.

Cramer did not have to say much more. After a brief discussion, the members of the commission agreed not to sustain Royall's motion.

Now it was Ristine's turn to speak for Dasch. To understand Dasch's position, he said, the commission had to keep a single question in mind as he spoke: "Is it possible for a German subject, who is within Germany, to become so dissatisfied . . . that he desires, by whatever method presents itself, to leave Germany in order . . . to fight the ruling power of Germany?" The directing of an affirmative answer to that question was the substance of Ristine's argument. He conceded that there was little beyond Dasch's own statements to indicate his state of mind in Germany; on the other hand, an open expression of his feelings would have been fatal. Once in the United States he showed his true feelings: he did not kill Cullen, and he did call the F.B.I.; and when, later in the week, he went to Washington, he brought all the money Kappe had given him.

Royall then rose to speak on a separate motion to acquit Burger. It was the last in this series of motions, and Royall seemed to be aware that before he could get to Burger's case, he had to express openly a fear which had been slowly growing as the trial progressed. "The prosecution in this case, and I use that term broadly to include the F.B.I. also, has seemed to us," he said, "to take the position . . . that the only solution of this case is for all the defendants to be adjudged guilty, leaving any relief which might be afforded to them to the question of presidential discretion." It was a harsh thing to say, but he reminded the commission that Dasch had been urged to plead guilty with the implied promise of a presidential pardon. "If that is equally applicable to the trial of this case we are just going through waste motions. I am sure it is not. We are not interested—I am sure the commission is not interested—in doing what somebody said in a case down in my country: 'Just give him a fair trial and then convict him.' "

It was a statement in the traditional courtroom manner: the lawyer's wrath turning to softness, dismay to understanding, and, of course, scorn for the suggestion "by the eminent and competent Judge Advocate General that we wait and decide this thing after all the evidence is in." That, he said, was not why the Courts-Martial Manual provided for motions for verdicts of not guilty at this stage of a trial. He did not think the commission intended to disregard that provision, and so he would continue. Aside from the merits of Burger's case, an important reason for granting the motion pertained to the defense lawyers, Royall said. He and Dowell were in the position of defending six defendants besides Burger. It was conceivable that during the trial conflict might develop which would put the defense in the "embarrassing and unenviable position" of having to choose between clients. In a civil court, he would merely have sought different counsel for each defendant, but he could not very well do that here. He asked only that the "reasonable man" provision, of which he had been a "dubious beneficiary" up to now, be applied to what he had to say as it had been to the prosecution.

Royall went on to give specific arguments in favor of a not-guilty verdict for Burger. His was the first confession the prosecution put in the record. It was the one "upon which the prosecution relied to lay the basis of its case" and "if that confession is true, Burger is guilty of nothing under these charges." Further, Burger had been available to the prosecution and the commission for questioning; "the view of a reasonable man must be that if there was any feature of his confession which was subject to attack or cross-examination, he would have been attacked or cross-examined. . . . If that does not convey to a reasonable man the impression that that confession is true, I do not know how you can convey it." In addition, the confessions of the other men corroborated Burger's mistreatment, his hostility to the Nazis and the Gestapo and the mistrust of him by the others. Royall spoke for an hour. It was the longest single speech so far.

But as far as Cramer was concerned, all that was under consideration was the question of whether the prosecution had met the legal requirements for establishing a case against the defendants, he said. Having done so, what Royall and Ristine said should be considered when all the evidence was in. "As a matter of fact," Cramer said, "the evidence shows that Burger, who was a soldier of the German Reich, or at least an agent thereof, crossed into our lines carrying dynamite and other explosives and operated under orders to destroy and sabotage wartime facilities. That in itself raises a clear presumption of guilt. The accused Burger has not in any sense of the word overcome that presumption." Thus, Cramer concluded, there could be no question that a *prima facie* case had been made, and that, he insisted, was all the commission had to decide.

The motions on behalf of Dasch and Burger were rejected as summarily as those for the other six. The trial would run its course. And now it was the defense's turn to try to make its case.

Royall and Dowell had decided to defend their clients without reference to Biddle's order of prosecution. Where Biddle had started with the Long Island group, they planned to start with the Florida group, and they would not proceed alphabetically. Dasch and Burger, with Ristine's agreement, would be the last defendants to speak; Haupt would be first. Now, at last, the eight men sitting against the wall, spectators for so long, were once again to become the leading figures in their own drama.

The formal military procedure called for an explanation to each defendant of his legal rights, of the voluntary nature of his testimony, the swearing in, and the use of his full name. This may have been the first time in Haupt's life that he had need of his: Herbert Johannes Wilhelm Godhelp Haupt. Royall started his questioning gently, almost coaxingly, putting Haupt at ease with the simple questions of birth, address and employment, before proceeding to an account of his travels from Chicago to Germany and back. There were no major variations from Haupt's statement to the F.B.I., but his testimony implied a complete lack of understanding of why all this had happened to him. When he left Chicago, it was with Mexico and perhaps Nicaragua in mind, never Japan or Germany. He had told that to just about everybody who would listen. To him there was logic in turning to a friend, any friend, when he and Wergin ran out of money in Mexico. Even the offer of a job in Japan made sense; it seemed preferable to returning to unwanted paternity and possible disgrace in America. The stories in Japan of Germans who tried to return to the United States were terrifying; far better to train as a sailor. His surprise had been great when he found he was on a ship bound for Germany, but as Haupt told it, the event was not far removed from being shanghaied.

German bureaucracy, especially as personified by the Gestapo, annoyed him. The forms he had to fill out, the visits to the Gestapo—four times one week—the questions to be answered, "how many fillings I had in my teeth, where I got them," were exasperating. Finally came a release of sorts; he met Kappe. But, said Haupt, the blackmail was implicit—his own life would be miserable, his friend Wergin would be in danger, if he did not sign up for the school being run by Kappe. No, he did not know the purpose of the school until after he was there. He agreed to go along because it seemed like a good way to get back to the United States, and he at no time intended to go through with the sabotage plans that were taught there. Except for sabotage, the group was instructed not to harm people; although they had some pistol practice they were told they would not carry arms with them, and there were definitely no instructions about spying. He knew nothing about handkerchiefs with secret writing on them, and he had no way to communicate with Germany. What is more, he had planned to go to the F.B.I. on July 6, when all eight men were scheduled to meet in Chicago. As for his purchase of a car, that had nothing to do with picking up explosives left behind in Florida; it was for pleasure and a honeymoon with Gerda Melind. Finally, the F.B.I. had not incorporated all these declarations of honorable intent into his statement.

Haupt's air of unawareness persisted throughout his testimony, whether questioned by Royall and Dowell or cross-examined by Biddle. He made several startling declarations which said more about himself and the situation he blundered into than all his protests, however sincere. He told of disobeying Kappe's orders by not using an alias in the United States even when he was carrying the draft registration card in the name of Lawrence Jordan. Why had he done this, Dowell asked. "For the simple reason," Haupt said, "that that would be a crime, another crime." When Biddle confronted him with the lies he told the F.B.I. after he had registered for the draft, and asked him why he lied, Haupt responded, "Because if I told the F.B.I. where I had come from—if you tell one lie you have to tell ten to cover it—if I told the F.B.I. where I came from I would never have had a chance. . . ." It was the first indication that Haupt knew the events of the past year had consequences for him.

Throughout the cross-examination, Haupt held to his basic story, and for all his inexperience he remained steady under Biddle's persistence. To break down Haupt's declarations of innocent intent, Biddle had to show discrepancies between Haupt's testimony and what he had told the F.B.I. Haupt said there was really no discrepancy; he had told the F.B.I. that he was not going through with the sabotage plan, but they had perversely omitted it from his statement. Why, Biddle wanted to know, did Haupt not say anything at the time about this important question. "Did you remonstrate with them because they had not put the whole truth into this?" he asked. "No," said Haupt, "I thought that is the way they wanted it." "Oh," Biddle said, "you were not giving the statement as it was; you were trying to give it to them the way they wanted it?" Haupt stood his ground. "No," he said, "they phrased the wording of the statement, and many times

171

when I wanted to change it, they said, 'It doesn't make any difference.'" He had told the F.B.I. the story exactly as he had just told it, Haupt said. It was clear to him, at least, that the F.B.I.'s not getting it straight was one of those things that people like him were up against all their lives.

Only once, when asked why he did not report the sabotage plot at once, did Haupt falter. He was nervous, he explained, and did not want to be bothered until July 6. Why not, Biddle asked, and Haupt's answer may well have been the understatement of the trial. "Because," he said, "if I would be picked up by the F.B.I. then I would have been in trouble, which I am now." Also, on that date he knew where all of the others would be. If he reported them before then, and not all were rounded up, his life would be in danger; "the Gestapo had men here. They had men here before we came."

Fear for his own safety was one of two themes in Haupt's testimony; the other was group loyalty. Haupt insisted that the other men did not intend to commit sabotage. How then, he asked, could he go to the F.B.I. and say, "Here I am. I am an American citizen and I come with three saboteurs from Germany and they want to blow up the United States." He would, he said, "be a lovely fellow to . . . save my neck, and have these men shot. After all, I became acquainted with them in Germany, and they are not hoodlums, and I did not want to be a rat, either." Biddle obviously did not think much of this explanation, but he could not dilute it and went on to other matters. Biddle's surrender followed one last attempt to determine Haupt's feelings about the July 6 deadline he had set for himself. Haupt had mentioned his marriage plans. "Were you going to have your honeymoon after July 6 or before?" Biddle asked. "After," said Haupt. "You thought, of course, that the F.B.I. after you had given the confession, would say, 'Go off on your honeymoon'?" Biddle asked. It was quickly apparent that this was just what Haupt had thought. "If I went up to the F.B.I. and told them the whole thing and laid it clear before them," he said, "there would be no reason to be guilty of anything." Incredulously, Biddle tried again: "And just go off on your honeymoon?" "Yes," Haupt said simply.

Haupt's testimony did not help his colleagues. He mentioned that Kerling had once told him about a girl in New York who would go with him to bring the explosives back from Florida, and did not seem to be aware he had damaged Kerling's case. In the same way, he conceded that his parents, his uncle and aunt and the Wergins could not help but know the nature of his assignment, thus providing the basis for later charges against them.

To support Haupt's narrative, the defense introduced James Stewart Eagen, the president of Simpson Optical Manufacturing Company. His appearance was brief; he had not seen Haupt since he left for Mexico. All the defense wanted to know was whether Haupt had applied for reemployment, and to this Eagen could truthfully say, "Not through the office." Mrs. Agnes Jordan told of Haupt's calling on her to ask for news of her missing son. No, she said, in response to questions from Biddle, he had not discussed anything else except having been in Mexico and that he had straightened out his draft status. This was to have been the end of Haupt's defense. Royall had subpoenaed Haupt's mother and his uncle, Walter Froehling—both brought from Cook County Jail in Chicago—and Gerda Melind, but had now decided not to call them. Just as all were agreed to move to Neubauer, Haupt whispered to Royall that he would like his mother to testify.

Erna Haupt, a short, pale, good-looking woman, spoke so softly she had to be urged to raise her voice so that members of the commission, just a few feet away, could hear her. What she had to say neither helped nor hurt her son. She confirmed his leaving for Mexico, and his return. She was extremely vague on details, and said she knew nothing of her son's activities except for registering for the draft and trying to get his old job back. She seemed to be saying that, as a mother concerned for her son's well-being, she really cared about only those two things. Both defense and prosecution treated her gently, and excused her after the briefest of questioning.

Mrs. Haupt did refer to Gerda Melind, and this made Royall decide to call the "Lady in White" after all. Her testimony showed little concern for Haupt, but a pronounced tendency to keep her own reputation as untarnished as the facts would allow. In making the point that Haupt had not told her anything about the sabotage plan, she undoubtedly helped him, but it was apparent she was not doing so out of affection. She had taken his ten dollars for the blood test, but "I wanted to bide for time," she said. "I wanted to talk to him a little more about where he had been." That conversation never took place, because, as everyone there knew, she did not see Haupt again until she entered the trial chamber.

The defense of Herbert Haupt ended on this rather inconsequential note. Royall did not call Haupt's uncle, nor any of the other people he had seen in Chicago; and the prosecution, confident of its case, did not see any merit in more witnesses.

The trial now picked up speed. Neubauer was in the witness chair for just two hours, Thiel little more than an hour. There was not much they could add to their statements to the F.B.I., and neither could, without danger to themselves, call as witnesses the people they had seen since their return to America. Despite the strong case against them, Royall followed the pattern he had established for Haupt: these men had no intention of going through with their instructions, there was no indication that they were spies, and there was the patent fact that they had committed no act of sabotage by the time they were arrested.

Neubauer's defense was, nevertheless, most likely to be understood by a military commission. His response to one of Royall's questions could have been uttered in any army. "As a soldier," he said, "you are not supposed to think; and I did not. I just got the order and I didn't know what for." Even when he was told the assignment was sabotage in the United States, what, after all, could he do about that? "Kappe was a lieutenant, which in Germany is quite a high superior above me," he explained. "There was nothing I could do. I had the order from my regiment to report to him." Trapped as he was, Neubauer said he was relieved that Kappe's instructions specifically ruled out killing or harming Americans. It was not quite clear how this would be avoided in line of sabotage activity, but on railroad work, for instance, he said, they were to watch only for freight trains. "We should take care that we didn't put any dynamite on any track if there were any passenger trains passing." He did not say how they were to keep from hurting the people who manned freight trains.

Despite the fact that these instructions made the assignment seem less unpleasant, and that not once in all the training was he told to seek military information, he had his doubts about the whole affair. "When I found out I was going as an agent over to the United States. I surely didn't like it," he said. "In the first place, my wife was born here in the States, and the family of my wife is here in the States; and another thing, if you have been a soldier or are a soldier, you don't think much of an agent or a saboteur, and I surely didn't like it—didn't like to see me—see myself in a position like that."

Neubauer claimed that he did try to talk Kappe out of using him because of his record with the F.B.I. as a result of the Lekala incident, but Kappe paid no attention. After the discovery of the gold certificates in Lorient, Neubauer said, he and Kerling tried to get Kappe to cancel the voyage, but Kappe was adamant. From that time on, said Neubauer, his nervousness was noticeable to everyone as his doubts about the trip increased. Three or four days before the submarine landed at Ponte Vedra, he broke one of Kappe's instructions and wrote a letter to his wife, advising her to apply for a return to the United States on one of the Swedish vessels that was exchanging American and German civilians and diplomats. He even showed the letter to Kerling, he said, who did not object to it. His nervousness increased each day in the United States; although not fond of alcohol, he bought a bottle of rum to calm himself. He was afraid he would be recognized in restaurants and hotels. And he had no desire at all to go through with the sabotage plan.

This tale of entrapment did not move Biddle. With minimum preliminaries he had the history of Neubauer's membership in the Bund and the Nazi Party, and steered him to his cover story and cover name. Neubauer made no effort to deny that he had both. This established, Biddle wanted to know why Neubauer never told the F.B.I. that he had no intention of going through with the sabotage plans. Neubauer's answer was as simple as his explanation of how he got involved in the first place. He could not tell the F.B.I. because he was afraid word would get back to Germany and cause reprisals against his family. Biddle quoted a sentence in Neubauer's confession to the F.B.I.: "I admit I came to the United States with this group for the purpose of committing acts of sabotage and might have done so if the opportunity arose." That was not true, Neubauer said, because it omitted the last part of the same sentence: "[Haupt] and I felt that
175

we would not have a bit of a chance to commit any sabotage."

Thiel, like Neubauer, also told of being trapped. He had gone into the sabotage plan when his mind was quite unclear, after hearing that one brother had lost an eye in the battle of Rostov and another, especially close to him, had been killed in the Donetz Basin. It was at that time Kappe and Dasch spoke to him "about how nice it is for us fellows who know the United States" to go back there and do something for the Fatherland; even without knowing what the assignment was, Thiel agreed. He thought it was for propaganda purposes, and was dismayed to find after he got to the school that he was to be trained in sabotage. By then it was too late to do anything about it. Doubts about the whole plan recurred, but he did not feel he could discuss them with the others. "I always hoped something would come up to prevent me from going back to the United States," he said.

He never did know much about how the plans were to be carried out. "I was just following orders," he said. Neither he nor anyone else had done anything about sabotage, nor intended to for at least three to six months. In fact, Thiel said he was now certain he would not have gone through with the plans even then. As for not telling the F.B.I. that he had no sympathy for the sabotage plan, "I didn't want to tell the whole story. I thought it would, like you say, be printed in the papers."

Biddle apparently thought even less of Thiel's defense than he did of Neubauer's. He had no trouble getting an admission that Thiel had pledged his loyalty to the party and to Hitler. Perhaps most damaging to Thiel was his answer to Biddle's question, "Before you were apprehended did you make a decision to go to the F.B.I. and report this whole thing?" "No, I did not," Thiel said. Biddle could have stopped then, but he managed one more basic point. He asked Thiel about Ernest Zuber, who had started sabotage training with the others but was not sent to the United States. Thiel's answer was exactly what Biddle wanted. Zuber, who had once been at Ellis Island for illegally entering the United States, "was afraid to come back," Thiel said. "He knew that his fingerprints and his pictures [were here], and I think Kappe agreed that he go back to the Army." Biddle's meaning was clear: if Zuber could get out, Neubauer and Thiel could have too; and there was the implicit warning to Royall that it would do no good to use this defense for the defendants yet to come.

Kerling, as the leader of the Florida group, warranted a more careful examination. Like the previous defendants, he said he had doubts about the sabotage plans. His doubts, however, came from a sense of realism, a profound disrespect for the quality of the men on the assignment and, later, in the United States, an understanding of the obstacles in the way of effective sabotage. He did not plead a change of heart about Germany or the Nazis, nor did he try to evoke pity for being forced into an assignment he did not want. In this he turned out to be the most forthright of the prisoners, and his answers implied a conviction that had the other seven been more like him they would not have been caught and somehow would have carried out their orders. Kerling was a man who knew his mission had failed, was prepared to face the consequences, and did not intend to inform on his colleagues.

His only complaint was that of mistreatment at the hands of F.B.I. Agent Donegan and of being kept up all night answering questions. The ordeal, according to Kerling, continued for the next few days, when with no sleep he went with F.B.I. agents to Florida to recover the buried explosives. They walked a great deal, the water in the hotel was bad and he came down with dysentery. Under Royall's questioning, Kerling said he did not think the F.B.I would ever have found the boxes without him.

Kerling said he had been reluctant to join the sabotage plan, but once committed to it he did not see how he could leave it without being considered a coward. For a member of the Nazi Party's Old Guard that would have been tantamount to treason. As a German, he said, he wanted to do his duty.

Biddle must have realized that Kerling had more strength of character than the previous witnesses; he went to greater efforts than he had with the others to show Kerling's essential loyalty to Germany. Kerling did not deny that he was still a member of the Nazi Party, but in answer to the direct question, "You are a loyal Nazi, aren't you?" he would not give Biddle the affirmative reply he wanted. "I would say I am a loyal German," he said. But he did not like what had happened to the party after the Roehm purge, and he had no use for the Gestapo. Biddle repeated the question. "I can say I have tried to be a loyal party member until I got into this thing," Kerling said, "but when they used me—used their power they held over me through that, I doubt my loyalty." In the end, Kerling's own words on paper became the strongest evidence against him. Biddle read into the record the letters Kerling had written Abigail Johnson. As late as the previous November, two weeks before Pearl Harbor, he had referred to America as being the "prey of a small group of Jews," had said, "I am here in Germany and doing my duty" and "we are in for a struggle for life and death." After that, it hardly mattered what Kerling said about his loyalties, or his doubts.

Before Kerling's defense was completed the two other women in his life appeared as witnesses. Neither said much to help him; if anything, Hedy Engermann, without meaning to, helped the prosecution. Marie Kerling had not even seen her husband, since he had been arrested on his way to her, but Hedy had changed money for him and had made up her mind to travel with him to Chicago, Cincinnati and Florida. The mention of Florida in this context became, for the prosecution, clear proof of Kerling's intent to get the explosives and carry out his assignment. The trip with Hedy was a forthright admission; it did not seem possible to interpret it as a sentimental journey to the scene of the first days of their romance.

The testimony of Heinrich Heinck and Richard Quirin in their own behalf sounded as if their hopes had long since vanished. They appeared for only about an hour each. Perhaps they suffered from following their colleagues, who had already told of their desire to get out of the assignment. They were also victims of their own personalities.

Heinck conceded his Bund membership and acknowledged that he had returned to Germany because of the wonderful things he had heard about the country at Bund meetings. "I thought I would just as well go over and try it," he said. There was disillusionment after his arrival, and he found himself in trouble when he openly compared conditions in America with those in Germany. While this may have won him some sympathy with the commission, his next statement wiped it out. He admitted, which none of the other witnesses did, that he knew before he went to the sabotage school that it was for the purpose of "stopping production of the American factories." Even when he amended this to "slowing down production," it was too late. When, a few minutes later, he announced that he "never had any intention of going through with it," it sounded hollow. Except for a passing mention of this feeling to Quirin, he could not invoke the name of a single person to whom he had expressed these views.

For Biddle, cross-examination was almost too easy. Heinck had known what the school was about; he had used a false name and address at the Martinique and later at the West Side rooming house; he had been a Bundist in America and had joined the Nazi Party before returning to Germany. Biddle was even able to make Heinck's expressed antipathy to the assignment appear to be motivated by distrust of Dasch rather than anything else. Heinck all but conceded this in what, if true, was the only instance in the case of genuine foresight. Heinck said he had had a hunch about Dasch's becoming a turncoat and had told the F.B.I., "I had a funny dream last night. I saw Dasch standing in the F.B.I. office and he told about everything."

Quirin did not make a much better impression than his friend. Unlike Heinck, he said he did not know the purpose of the training program at Quenz Lake. "I was more interested in getting to America than I was in the work I was supposed to do at the moment." In fact, "I was uncertain about myself during the school already. Since I never knew nothing about explosives, and when I found out how it works I was really afraid of the stuff, and I felt sure I could never do anything like that." But he did not confide these thoughts to anyone except to Heinck after they had met Burger and Dasch at Grant's Tomb. Then, he said, "we started to talk about having hopes that it was all over, that we was not going to do anything anyway."

Under Biddle's questions Quirin seemed to wilt. He had not only been a loyal Nazi, he said; he thought he still was. No, he had not made any plans to give himself up to the F.B.I., but if Dasch had come and told him about his plans to do so, "I would have gladly sided with him." Nor could he deny his statements to the F.B.I. that he did not make any effort to get out of the sabotage assignment once he knew about it. On the submarine, and later in America, he started to have doubts, but he had not resolved them when he was arrested. Quirin's was as sorry a performance as Heinck's. Once more each had only the other to support him, and it was painfully clear by the time the two men were back in the prisoners' row of seats that it was not enough.

Dasch's defense was based on a single undeniable fact; he had voluntarily gone to the F.B.I. and revealed the sabotage plot. It was true, as the prosecution contended, that he had waited nearly a week to do so, but unlike the six defendants who preceded him, who had said they intended to, planned to, or considered reporting to the F.B.I. or not going through with the plan—Dasch had acted. It is a commentary on his personality or, as Dasch believed, on his ordeal since he had left the United States for Germany sixteen months earlier, that he could not invoke his potential strength on the stand. George John Dasch was probably the poorest witness he could have had in his own behalf.

To begin with, he had not once conceived of the possibility that he would be tried with the men he had turned in. On the contrary, he had expected praise and reward; there had been a dream of contributing to an anti-Nazi propaganda program in America. The F.B.I. offer, or his interpretation of that offer, for a short prison term if he pleaded guilty, when he felt his innocence so strongly, had been disturbing in the extreme. At the trial, for the first time, as he sat with the other defendants, "the discovery that I brought these men face to face with death was chilling and unsettling." (It is possible that, despite his preoccupation with himself, the intensity of their hatred was by now also chilling and unsettling.) He was also critical of the way Ristine handled his case, and it is probable that he expressed some of this to Ristine during the trial. A better lawyer, he said, "could easily have upset the crazy case that was concocted by the prosecution."

The "crazy case" was simply that Dasch was as guilty of the four charges as the other defendants in that he not only participated in the plan from the start, but was a major figure in its planning. Despite this, it already seemed likely that Dasch would receive a lighter sentence than the others because of his help to the F.B.I. Whether Dasch knew this or not, he sat in the witness chair determined to prove himself completely innocent of all charges. Because of his own emotionalism or a lack of understanding with Ristine, Dasch seemed unable to limit himself to short, direct replies. His testimony was as verbose as his statement had been. His answers, even to questions sympathetically put by Ristine, were rambling and often irrelevant. The result was foreseeable to all but Dasch; he gave the impression of protesting too much. His replies became so disconcerting that Biddle objected and, in one of the few times in the trial, was joined in his objection by Royall. "I think this witness is so unresponsive to the questions and is so wasting the time of the commission," Biddle said, "that I do not think it would be inappropriate if the commission directed him to be responsive and answer the questions. We will be here for a week if this kind of thing goes on. I have never heard any evidence like this in my life." Royall was upset because "I do not know what he is going to say about these other defendants," and as a result could not tell from the question when to object. After Dasch made a particularly long reply, even McCoy lost patience. "We have had statements ad lib," he said, and admonished Ristine to ask direct questions which would bring replies, not lengthy statements.

Nevertheless, Dasch, with Ristine's questions to lead him, was able to emphasize points in his original statement to the F.B.I. which his lawyer realized might have gone unnoticed during the two-day reading. Out of these Ristine chose to show that Dasch had never been a member of the Bund and had actually been anti-Nazi until the time of his mother's visit to the United States in 1939; that he knew he had to fight Hitler almost immediately after he arrived in Germany, and when Kappe tapped him for the sabotage school he realized that this was the opportunity he had been waiting for; that it was he who had talked Kappe out of arming the men who were coming to America, and he who had suggested that no sabotage be attempted until the men had been in the United States several months. The reasons for this delay, Dasch testified, were that he did not know exactly when he himself would be sent to America and that he needed time to plan for his eventual betrayal of the plan. "I wasn't sure of nothing," he said. "I had to plan and work ahead."

With the supporting evidence which Ristine introduced— a deposition from Colonel Kramer that Dasch had called him at the Pentagon the same morning he reached the F.B.I., the appearance of F.B.I. Agent McWhorter to tell of Dasch's Sunday night call in New York—and perhaps helped by his own unfortunate appearance as a witness—Dasch gave the impression of a deeply troubled man. It was even possible to believe that he meant to save the United States from potential danger. Ristine emphasized his nervous state and its palliative, the consecutive hours at a card table. But that calm was only temporary. "At the time I went to Washington, well, my mental state was very much in a fog," Dasch said. "I was tied up in knots, and I had a hard time to remember names and dates and instances, and Mr. Pie Traynor was very kind of helping me along, and things came back slowly. I had nothing written down. I had it all in my mind, and little by little it came out—words and names and instances and dates, and so on." Despite his condition, he said, everything he had told the F.B.I. was substantially true.

To counteract this view of Dasch as the cooperative, if understandably upset, informer, Biddle brought him back to his original role in the sabotage plan. Thus he could emphasize Dasch's partnership with Kappe in order to prove that his intentions were not inspired by anti-Nazi feelings at all. Dasch conceded that he drew up plans for sabotage in the United States, a five-page memorandum which brought him compliments from Kappe and others in Abwehr II, and of which he still seemed quite proud as he told it to the commission. The inspiration for his work—he admitted he was not an expert in military sabotage—came from American broadcasts he had monitored while working at the Seehaus, mainly from the American radio commentators Martin Agronsky and C. L. Sulzberger, whose accounts of sabotage in Yugoslavia by anti-Nazi elements were particularly adaptable. Despite Biddle's insistent questioning, Dasch denied that he had any role in selecting the other men for the sabotage school or that his position with Kappe carried any great responsibility. He maintained, as he had from the start, that his primary purpose was to return to America, and to do that he went along with all of Kappe's suggestions.

And now Biddle arrived at what was to be the prosecution's major point on the difference between Dasch's intentions and his performance. "Why didn't you go right away to the F.B.I.?" Biddle asked. The answer, showing strange memory lapses and expressed in tortured English, may have carried a stronger sense of truth than if it had been a rehearsed speech.

> Dasch: *I had three reasons, sir. May I explain all three reasons?*
>
> Biddle: *Surely. Do them quickly—all three.*
>
> Dasch: *All right. First of all I was a mental and a nervous wreck. I was so glad that I was here. And, second of all, I had to be human, and that is mainly—I had to be human.*
>
> Biddle: *And third?*
>
> Dasch: *Just one second. Why I had to be human—I have got to explain that to the commission. I knew why I came. I studied every other possible one to find out a reason why they came here. I knew this boy—what's his name here?*
>
> Col. Dowell: *Burger.*
>
> Dasch: *Burger—why he came here—but I wasn't quite sure why this little kid Haupt came here, a boy who has remained in Germany only four or five months, who had his mother here and had lived here in America. I didn't know why he came here. I could not at any time run to the police and at the same time take this chance away from the kid to prove why he came here. That would have been merely for the sake of my own self-protection. That would have been the rottenest thing in the world. To be a real decent person I had to wait. I had to give every person a chance to say what I had to say. That's the reason.*

He never did list his third reason. What Dasch also omitted, and what Biddle did not pick up, was that, except for the arrangements with Burger, Dasch did not do the "human thing." He had turned in all the others without giving them the chance that he insisted was their due. Despite the status that Dasch had in the case, no member of the commission asked him any questions. When Dasch left the stand, after little more than two hours of questioning, he had a deep sense of dissatisfaction. "It was not," he said later, "my idea of an honest American trial."

Although Burger had not made the open break with his companions and actually gone to the F.B.I. as Dasch had, his defense was in many ways easier to state and to support. To Americans, Burger's problems in Germany easily translated into an anti-Nazi attitude, although, as he could have told the commission, many loyal Nazis hated the Gestapo. His descriptions of his colleagues and his knowledge of the school and the explosives were of more use to the F.B.I. than Dasch's statement had been. In addition, he conducted himself on the stand in a crisp, military fashion.

Under Royall's questioning, Burger assured the commission that his original statement was correct, that he had no desire to change anything in it. Royall then led him briefly through the points of his life best designed to impress his listeners. He had become an American citizen of his own choice—the only one of the eight defendants who could say this—and he had joined the National Guard in the two states where he was eligible to do so, and received honorable discharges each time—documents which Royall read into the record. He had returned to Germany solely because of the difficulty of finding work in the United States during the depression, and while in Germany he had made no effort to renounce his American citizenship. He had lost it, of course, by virtue of being drafted into the German Army in 1941, but that had not been a voluntary action. He quickly sketched his disillusionment with the Nazi Party, his troubles with the Gestapo, and his efforts to leave Germany. For a man in his position, an illegal escape would have meant serious trouble for his family. He did not have to be more specific to invoke a vision of torture and concentration camps for those he left behind. For this reason, unlikely as it might seem to his listeners, he had to wait for an opportunity to leave Germany by legal means. When, at last, that chance came with the sabotage mission he grabbed it.

As further evidence of his intent, he could show the use of his own name while in the United States, and that he carried papers with German writing which he did not try to conceal. Burger used no heroics; he did not claim he had specific plans to report to the F.B.I. "I couldn't plan anything," he said, "because I did not know the conditions over here." By the time Dasch had confided in him and made the telephone call to the F.B.I. in New York, it seemed perfectly reasonable to let his appointed leader take charge. From that time, even though Dasch delayed, Burger felt that he had accomplished what he set out to do.

So carefully did Royall develop through Burger's answers the picture of a man who gave his all to stop the saboteurs that Burger very nearly carried it too far. "You asked me if I held anything back or made a false statement," he said to Royall. "To a certain extent I did." It turned out that Agent Lanman had asked him if he had any relatives in the United States. "I said no," Burger said, "but there is a distant relative, some old lady of seventy-five years, I think she is, and they call it over here second cousin." By itself, this naïve evidence of honesty conveyed the proper touch. Royall stopped Burger at this point; any more might have been ludicrous.

Biddle cross-examined Burger without expressing any of the sharp doubts he had in questioning Dasch and the other defendants. Even in a lengthy dialogue with Burger as to why he preferred to leave Germany on a sabotage mission rather than to sneak out by way of Switzerland, Biddle seemed finally convinced of Burger's insistence that any other way "would have meant the arrest of my people." Biddle's response, "We always come back to that," might almost have been made by Burger himself. The only real conflict Biddle could find in Burger's testimony was his avowed faith in Dasch to report to the F.B.I., after he had indicated distrust of Dasch at the sabotage school. Burger explained that the views were based on different matters; when Dasch showed his desire to turn in the others, Burger had no doubts about him at all.

Burger also provided a strong support for Dasch's defense. He described his own sense of Dasch's intentions as far back as the early days at the sabotage school, and because he expressed himself less emotionally than Dasch, his version appeared more forthright. His feeling that Dasch was not the loyal Nazi he appeared to be increased from that time, Burger said, and was confirmed by Dasch's performance with Cullen on the beach. He was therefore not completely surprised when Dasch made his feelings known at the Governor Clinton. Nor was he especially disappointed that Dasch did not go to Washington at once. "He was in no state of mind to make any plans," Burger said. Burger had objected to the long card-playing session, but he had also realized that it had a good effect on Dasch. "I noticed that his hands did not tremble any more, as they did before, and that he was easier in his way of speaking, too." Dasch had said roughly the same thing, but somehow it was more credible coming from Burger.

Burger's answers must have struck a responsive chord

with McCoy. The commission president asked him more questions than he had put to any other witness. One question led to a statement by Burger which supported the entire defense position. None of the eight men could really trust any of the others in the situation they were in, Burger explained. He was therefore surprised to find "here in the courtroom that almost none had the intention of carrying out any orders." Yet, he said, as he thought back, it was not really that surprising. "There are several small instances where you could more or less feel" this attitude, he said. "There is no fact I could tell you or no—well, I can't prove it by anything. There is, for instance, a remark Kerling made in Paris when we were standing near the Navy Ministry and the guards—the German guards—marched by. He was standing next to me, and he asked me, 'Listen. What do you think about your group?' and I answered, 'Well, I don't really think very much of my group. I know Heinck—Henry—he is not a hundred per cent saboteur, as you may call—he really isn't; and, on the other hand, George Dasch is not an ideal leader for a mission like we have orders.' I explained that to him, and Kerling answered, 'Well, there will be a way to get out.' Now I see, of course, these remarks in a very different light as at that time. Everything means something now."

Whatever the new meaning, Burger, with this diffuse statement—coming as it did after a series of businesslike responses—must have given the other defendants one of the few occasions for hope out of all the proceedings up to then. Aside from this, McCoy seemed more interested in details of Burger's relationship with Hitler, as if this were a phenomenon separate from the trial. Yes, said Burger, he knew Hitler intimately at one time and had participated in his first grab for power. Although he had sworn allegiance to Hitler then, and again when he was drafted into the Army, that loyalty no longer existed, had died, as he had said before, during the purge in which his friend Roehm had been killed. McCoy had one final question, and in light of the defense taken by all eight men, it was a most pertinent one. "Do you remember," he asked Burger, "whether or not Kappe told you to confess in case one or all of you were caught?" "No, sir," said Burger. "On the contrary, in case anyone got caught we were not to tell anything. That was understood. That was understood from the beginning."

Shortly after 4:00 P.M. on Monday, July 27, Dowell rose from the defense table and said, "If it please the commission, the defense rests." As he resumed his seat, Ristine stood up and said, "The defendant Mr. Dasch rests his case." It had been twenty days since the trial started, and its sixteenth day in session.

PART IV
PUBLIC VERDICT

Chapter 11
Equal Justice Under Law

Whatever Royall had accomplished in the military court-room on behalf of his clients during the past week, he had achieved a major victory outside. He had brought about an event even rarer in American history than this secret trial itself. On Wednesday, July 29, the Supreme Court of the United States was to convene in special session to determine whether President Franklin Roosevelt was within his rights to deny the defendants access to the civil courts, and whether the trial in Room 5235, Justice Department, was legal under the American Constitution.

Royall's legal and philosophic basis for insisting on a test of the President's proclamation and order was a decision by the Supreme Court of the United States in 1866 in a case which is known as *Ex parte Milligan*. The substance of Royall's argument derived from that earlier Court's ruling that a civilian could not be tried by a military commission unless martial law had been declared or the regular courts were not functioning. In a larger sense, Royall was also seeking affirmation of a memorable sentence in the same decision: "The Constitution of the United States is a law for rulers and people, equally in war and peace, and covers with the shield of its protection, all classes of men, at all times and under all circumstances." By arguing that this declaration of democratic justice was applicable even to enemies of the nation in time of war, Royall was exposing it to one of its most rigorous tests.

That he was able to cause the Supreme Court to hold a special session meant that Royall had won his philosophic point. Whether he would win the legal one, the right of his clients to trial by civilian jury, would not be known until the members of the Court heard him and Biddle debate the issues, starting promptly at noon Wednesday. The arguments

188

of these two articulate men went beyond the guilt or innocence of the accused men in whose name the case was made. "The case," Walter Karig, correspondent for the Newark, New Jersey, *Evening News*, wrote, "utterly transcends that of providing justice for the Nazi prisoners. They are merely guinea pigs in a great laboratory of jurisprudence." The test was on an issue basic to the structure of democratic government at a time when that structure was in grave military danger: whether in total war the nation had to suspend some traditional principles to assure victory and, if so, whether making that sacrifice meant that victory would be achieved at too high a cost. It was as much a moral problem as a legal one; Biddle invoked Justice Oliver Wendell Holmes, who said that "public danger warrants the substitution of the executive process for the judicial process"; Royall's position was that "all alien enemies, no matter what their status, are entitled to enter the courts to protect their liberty."

The actual question the Court would decide was whether to grant Royall's request for a writ of *habeas corpus*, which would have the effect of taking the prisoners from the jurisdiction of the military commission and putting them on trial before a civil court. That he managed to force a Supreme Court hearing was testimony to Royall's determination as well as to his legal skill and, in the last stages, to the Court's and Biddle's cooperation.

On the previous Monday, when Royall began his defense and obtained Justice Roberts' promise to see him, he had known that he must inform the military commission of his intention to bring about a civil court test. Accordingly, the next afternoon, as McCoy was about to adjourn for the day, Royall announced that he had a matter of "ten or fifteen minutes" to bring up. He was an optimist; the discussion lasted an hour. The eight defendants were taken from the courtroom, and Biddle and Royall approached the bench. McCoy seemed mystified. "Do I take it that this is an argument or a statement?" he asked. "No, it is not an argument; it is relative to publicity," Royall said. McCoy was still uncertain. "A statement in connection with the procedure?" he asked. "And procedure," Royall conceded.

Royall outlined the story of his participation in the case, his doubts as to the validity of the President's order and proclamation, and reminded the commission that he had put those doubts on record. Now, he and Dowell had prepared papers for an application for a writ of *habeas corpus* to test that validity, and he wanted, "in an abundance of caution," to inform the commission of his intentions. Royall handed McCoy a copy of the legal papers he intended to use. He made it clear that he was not seeking the commission's advice on whether he should present them, but only an opinion as to whether their contents violated secrecy. It would not be respectful, he said, "to ask you what course we should take . . . there is no desire on my part, and I do not think on [Dowell's], to pass the buck to anybody on that."

Royall was right about Dowell, although not aware until then how painful the decision to go along with him had been for an old soldier. At Royall's invitation to dissent from anything he had said, Dowell said he would "add a few words." His brief address must have been raging within him since he was first put on the case. It was also the statement of a courageous man struggling with his conscience. "Colonel Royall has been trained in the law, and I have been trained as a soldier for forty years," Dowell said. "I cannot get it out of my mind, probably because of my training, that my duty as a soldier is circumscribed by the orders I receive from our Commander, in this case the Commander-in-Chief of the Army of the United States, who has detailed me to act as defense counsel before this commission. I am in the embarrassing position of feeling that way about my military duty. The moment this commission has ended, I am under orders to return to my proper station and go on with my duties as a soldier. I have to do that, because I do not know of any other way to be a soldier than to obey the orders I receive.

"On the other hand, a duty has been imposed upon us as defense counsel to do everything legitimate and honorable in the interests of our clients. . . . Circumscribed from going before any other tribunal, if these orders are to be taken strictly, we earnestly and honestly and seriously sought instructions, interpretations, permission to do the thing that we conceive to be the honorable thing to do in the interest of our clients. Frankly, I do not see a way out yet. . . . If the publicity angle was out of the way, I would be considerably more courageous, but we have the very earnest words of our authority that publicity will injure our national cause, our war effort. As a soldier I cannot bring myself to the point of doing that."

If Dowell had not entirely resolved his doubts, Ristine had. It is likely that he was influenced by a growing certainty that Dasch stood a better chance if he remained apart from the other seven defendants in all aspects of the case. He construed his orders, Ristine told the commission, as authorizing him "to appear before this commission and do everything I can, honorably, to protect Dasch's interests," but he added that he did not believe this meant seeking a remedy in any other court. He would not join in the appeal to the Supreme Court.

Dowell's and Ristine's words had changed the course of Royall's simple presentation, and before he could return to it he felt he had to make his own position clear. He was not critical of Ristine, and certainly not of Dowell, "for whom I have just about as sincere admiration as I have for any man I have ever met." Whatever their decisions, he said, "I am going to do what I told the President I was going to do . . . unless somebody orders me specifically not to do it, because that is what I conceive my duty to be." Despite his repeated assertions that he simply wanted the commission's opinion as to whether he was violating secrecy, Royall had to make his point again and again. Cramer wanted to know whether he was asking the commission's advice on his civil action; Biddle wanted to know whether he was asking the commission to remove any oath of secrecy. At last, after Royall made one final, almost exasperated, explanation that it was the question of secrecy alone which bothered him—"I am not asking anybody to take any part of my responsibility. I will do that and suffer the consequences"—McCoy asked to see the petition for the writ. The members of the commission then retired to another room to discuss the question. Their decision was that they did not care to pass on the matter; Royall was once more on his own.

Royall's appointment with Justices Roberts and Black was scheduled for Thursday, which did not leave either Biddle or Royall much time to prepare; they both put in a full day before the commission on Wednesday. The next morning, accompanied by Cramer and Dowell, they took an Army plane to Philadelphia, where they were met by F.B.I. agents who acted as their guards. Black had taken the train the night before. Roberts was a charming host as well as a sympathetic listener. In keeping with the life on the farm in which he showed such pride, his guests lunched on cheese, crackers and milk. After he heard Royall, supported by Biddle, urge a Supreme Court test, he suggested that while he and Black talked the matter over with each other, and by telephone with Chief Justice Stone, the visitors make a tour of his farm. It may well have been the only relaxation any of the lawyers found in the course of the strenuous days which had gone before and were still to come. When they returned from their bucolic stroll, the answer was ready: Stone would call a special session of the Supreme Court for the following Wednesday. Royall had won a major victory at this Pennsylvania farmhouse.

The military commission kept Royall and Biddle occupied all of Friday, but at their request the Saturday session was adjourned at midday, immediately after completion of Dasch's defense, to give the two attorneys a little time to get ready for what each knew would be their most important confrontation in this case. On Monday evening, soon after McCoy had recessed the commission, the Supreme Court of the United States announced that it would convene a special term to receive at open session petitions for writs of *habeas corpus* "on behalf of certain persons now being tried by a military commission appointed by the President." "The astonishing announcement," the *New York Times* said the next morning, "came without the slightest advance indication." At five forty-five, Charles Elmore Cropley, the Court clerk, handed out the brief announcement without comment. It was a "smashing climax" to the trial, wrote Fred Pasley of the *New York Daily News*. "Its historical significance is that it pits the authority of the Supreme Court directly against that of the President."

Although there had been little information about the trial in the press until the Court's surprising announcement, there had been strong reminders of its importance. Two weeks earlier, on July 13, Biddle had announced the arrest by the F.B.I. of fourteen men and women, nine of whom were American citizens, who had helped some of the eight saboteurs. They were, of course, the Haupts, Froehlings and Wergins, the Jaqueses, Cramer, Faje, Leiner and Hedwig Engemann; Mrs. Kerling and a man named Ernest Kerkhof, who, the F.B.I. said, had been "intimately associated" with her, were also being held. Hoover said that they had "given shelter to the saboteurs and . . . furnished them assistance which would have aided the foreign agents in their sabotage activities in the United States." It had taken the F.B.I. three weeks to round them up; Biddle announced that they would be prosecuted immediately. The day after their arrests were made public, the Justice Department reported a large volume of mail asking that the death sentence be sought in each case, and an increasing number demanding that the eight saboteurs be executed at once.

A week later the public was treated to an intragovernmental squabble involving the men on trial. It started when the *Washington Post* ran a story from New York which opened, "It was an old vest—and a Coast Guard intelligence squad that knew what to do with it—that trapped the eight German spies now on trial for their lives in Washington." The vest, the story said, worn by one of the men who landed at Amagansett, was the clue which led the Coast Guard, through laundry markings, to identify its owner, and to learn what he looked like and who his friends were. When this was turned over to the F.B.I., the *Post* report said, the F.B.I. was able to track down the eight saboteurs and their fourteen accomplices. Furthermore, despite acknowledging "this useful aid," J. Edgar Hoover had asked the Coast Guard commandant to discipline the officers for "holding out the vest." It was a neat story, with the right touch of detective fiction and implicit criticism of the F.B.I. for a dog-in-the-manger attitude, but it just wasn't true. There was no official comment on the *Post* story from either Coast Guard or F.B.I. officials, but that afternoon, other papers ran stories attributed to anonymous sources which were critical of the Coast Guard. It had withheld evidence for "several days"; it had failed to search the railroad station at Amagansett, where the Dasch group had been until nearly seven o'clock the morning they landed; Coast Guardsmen had handled the evidence so much it was impossible for the F.B.I. to get fingerprints; and the F.B.I. was not notified for thirty-six hours after the landing. It was clear to Washingtonians that these stories were leaked by someone in the F.B.I., and that in some respects they were as excessive as the *Post* story, so obviously leaked by someone in the Coast Guard. The feud ended as it had started, anonymously, its major victims being the reputations of the two squabbling services.

Two days before the announcement of the Supreme Court special session, Americans had received a more pointed reminder that the saboteurs were still in their midst. On July 25, the F.B.I. announced a "nationwide hunt for three expert German saboteurs." Several hundred thousand posters containing the photographs and descriptions of Walter Kappe, Joseph Schmidt and Rheinhold Barth were distributed to post offices and other public places. Although it was stated that the three men were not actually known to be in the United States, a request from Hoover to all police agencies and the public to help in a manhunt was not one to be ignored. On eastern Long Island, which was excusably self-conscious about submarine landings, three men resembling the descriptions of Kappe, Schmidt and Barth were immediately seen on the Montauk Highway trying to hitchhike a ride to Bridgehampton, a few miles west of Amagansett. The F.B.I. checked and said there was "no foundation to the report," but a nine-state police alarm had already been broadcast. Barth was seen at Noyac, not far from Bridgehampton, and somebody in Lakeview, Long Island, remembered that a paperhanger named Barth lived there. Unfortunately, he owned a copy of Hitler's *Mein Kampf*; he was questioned for five hours before being dismissed. In the Bronx, two girls said a man in Army uniform with a striking resemblance to Kappe, but calling himself Joe, had approached them. Before the week was out, and while the Supreme Court was in session, reports on the three men came from many sections of the United States, including quite a few from the Washington, D.C., area. They were never found, simply because they never left Germany.

If nothing else, the story of new saboteurs on the loose exaggerated the reaction of the public to the Supreme Court announcement. Now, added to what many called a "farcical trial" which had already lasted too long, there was the spectacle of the highest court in the land giving the saboteurs a hearing. The Meridian, Mississippi, *Star* called the procedure a "burlesque" and said that "America is disgusted with the idiocy of this 'spy' case." The *Detroit Free Press* reflected a large segment of public opinion in an editorial which said, "Realism calls for a stone wall and a firing squad, and not a lot of silly holier-than-thou eyewash about extending the protection of civil rights to a group that came among us to blast, burn and kill." The Communist *Daily Worker* agreed with newspapers it normally considered its foes. "The unprecedented action," the *Worker* said, "is in itself a victory for the enemies of America and the United States." This also gave the paper a chance to shoot at one of its favorite targets, Attorney General Biddle. The Supreme Court intervention, it said, was an example of "Biddleism," the work of a man "who preaches 'civil liberties' for American fascism while he slaps at labor and ignores lynchings."

Inevitably a certain amount of criticism was directed at defense counsel. Personal attacks were made on both men by the press and in letters. Because he carried the brunt of the case, Royall was more often criticized. Not surprisingly, one of the sharpest attacks came from a newspaper in his home state of North Carolina. The *Charlotte News*, in an editorial entitled "A Braying Ass," said, "There will be those who will want [Royall] thrown in with the accused and made to stand trial himself." It ended with the sentence, "Speaking for his country and its highest principles, he made a perfect ass of himself." A later edition on the same day made two minor changes in the editorial. The title was now "Stretchout" and the last line read, "He made a sideshow barker of himself."

The letters which Royall and Dowell received showed as much indignation, and frequently more imagination. "From the way your friends are talking," a North Carolinian wrote Royall, "I would suggest you remain in Washington when this war is over." A woman from California sent him a dime to buy one of the prisoners a cigar to increase his enjoyment of the mockery he was making of the United States. She regretted she could not send enough for all eight men because she was using the balance to buy defense bonds "to pay your salaries, to defend your distinguished guests, and to secure their 'rights.' " She was sure, she added, "that the wounded men of Bataan will understand. It is one way to kill Hitler. He must be dying of laughter right now."

There was also articulate support for what Royall was doing, and for the Supreme Court's response. Influential commentators, among them Arthur Krock in the *New York Times* and Raymond Moley in the *Chicago Journal of Commerce*, saw the whole thing as "a fine service to a democracy at war." "Whatever disposition the Court shall make of the grave issues presented to it," Krock wrote, "the fact will brighten the American history of a time when Cicero's cynical apothegm—'inter arma silent leges' [in war the laws are silent]—is the rule in almost every other land." The Supreme Court session, Moley wrote, "reminds all people—peaceful people, hot-headed people and overzealous officials—that the Constitution lives and is operating." The *Dallas News* said that "justice is served by testing and making certain step by step that the procedure in this case is in accordance with our time-honored principles." And, in censure of the *Charlotte News*, newspapers in North Carolina and elsewhere in the South not only supported Royall, but chastised his critics for their ignorance. The *Richmond Times* "rejected" the *News* attack on Royall "as unwarranted and unfair." The Montgomery *Alabama Journal* called the *News* editorial "vitriolic" and "a great injustice to a man performing a distasteful duty and trying to be loyal to the code of ethics of his profession."

Besides these public expressions, Royall and Dowell received letters from other lawyers, many of whom they had never met, expressing great admiration for their skill and zeal in defending unpopular clients. Laymen also wrote in support, indicating some efforts at understanding their unenviable position. Many were of the tenor of "hope your clients get shot but admire what you are doing." Royall heard from a Jesuit priest whom he had once met on a train and from a woman in New York who recalled that "my grandmother was your laundrywoman in Goldsboro," and who wanted to express her pride in his work on behalf of justice. A seventy-year-old man from Alcoa, Tennessee, one of the saboteur's prime targets, supported Royall and Dowell because he was against capital punishment. Many of the letters were, as was to be expected, motivated by sympathy for Nazi Germany; these were turned over to the F.B.I. for investigation. There were also letters and telegrams of advice—some of it useless and some obvious—including one signed "Hater of Nazis but Lover of Justice."

As Americans debated the Court's extraordinary meeting, Royall was putting his case in order. Under American law, the Supreme Court does not hear most cases directly, but only on appeal from a lower court. Therefore, on Tuesday, the day before the Court was to meet, Royall made his formal application for writs of *habeas corpus* for his seven clients to Justice James W. Morris of the District Court of the United States in Washington. Although it was in open court, the press was not aware of this action until it was announced the next day. Royall did not make a lengthy argument in his own behalf; it was almost as if he were afraid to win this plea. A victory here would have done him little good; the prosecution might have ignored a ruling contrary to the President's proclamation, or if it appealed, the appeal might have been delayed until after the trial was over and the sentences carried out.

Biddle argued for denial of the writs as a matter of course; by now, he was looking forward to the Supreme Court fight with great confidence. To no one's great surprise, Justice Morris denied the seven applications. Royall had conceded, Morris said in his brief decision, that the petitioners had landed from a German submarine with explosives, for the purpose of committing sabotage. "In view of this statement of fact," he said, "it seems clear that the petitioner comes within the category of subjects, citizens or residents of a nation at war with the United States, who by proclamation of the President . . . are not privileged to seek any remedy or maintain any proceedings in the courts of the United States."

While Royall and Biddle made their *pro forma* appearance before Justice Morris, the Chief Justice of the United States and the eight associate justices were returning to Washington as well as they could under the restrictions of wartime travel. Justice William O. Douglas had the longest way to go. He was vacationing in Oregon, some three thousand miles away, and was unable to arrive in time for the first day's hearing. He did attend the second day and took part in the Court's decision. Justice Frank Murphy, who had been granted a four-month leave of absence from the Court in June to enter military training as a lieutenant colonel, was reached by an Army field telephone hanging from a tree near Dilworth, North Carolina, where his unit was on maneuvers. He was back in Washington in time for the opening session, but disqualified himself from taking part in a case involving the question of military authority. This did not prevent him, however, from placing a chair behind the heavy red curtains and eavesdropping on the entire proceedings.

Justice Murphy was far from alone in wanting to hear the case argued. As the Court's opening hour of noon approached on one of the Washington summer's hottest and most humid days, crowds began to gather in front of the classical façade bearing the words "Equal Justice Under Law." "Like movie fans," the correspondent for the *Baltimore Sun* wrote, "people lined up at 9 A.M." Some three hundred, the Court chamber's capacity, and the largest audience in the room since the Court had first occupied it seven years earlier, were finally admitted to find places on the red-upholstered mahogany benches. Many of the spectators seemed to have been attracted by the hope of seeing the defendants, although the Court's announcement had clearly said they would not be present. Their absence, the nature of the arguments, and the bad acoustics of the Supreme Court chamber had an effect on the merely curious; by midafternoon attendance had dropped. But the press, Hoover and other F.B.I. officials, government attorneys, wives of lawyers and judges, and many ordinary citizens remained to the end. So did a dozen F.B.I. agents who, two hours before Stone opened the proceedings, placed themselves in strategic seats around the chamber.

The care with which Royall, Biddle and their staffs prepared their cases in so short a time was remarkable. Both men impressed not only newspapermen and other spectators, but the sharp-minded justices who, sitting, as former Justice Sutherland once said, like "nine black cockroaches in the Temple of Karnak," have on occasion been merciless to the ill-prepared. The briefs presented by the two opposing lawyers were thoroughly documented. Among legal authorities, statutes, the Constitution, the Articles of War, the Hague Convention and political and legal history, Biddle cited forty-eight separate court cases and Royall sixteen. In a few instances the same case was invoked by each to make an opposite point. Of all the cases cited, none was quoted more often, nor received as much attention in the oral arguments, as that of *Ex parte Milligan*, which one justice called "a landmark in American liberty."

It was fitting that the Milligan case should have been the key to the legal argument. It shared many similarities with that of the saboteurs, and although there were great differences, too, certain principles were common to both. Lambdin B. Milligan was a resident of Indiana during the Civil War, and an outspoken opponent of Abraham Lincoln. As a member of the Order of American Sons of Liberty, he carried on activities inimical to the North. When he was caught, he was charged with communicating with the enemy, conspiring to seize munitions of war, to liberate prisoners of war and resisting the draft—all this within the military lines of the United States Army and the theater of military operations. His crimes, in general, were similar to those charged to the present defendants: giving aid and comfort to the enemy, communicating with the enemy and violating the Laws of War. Milligan was tried by a military commission, which had been established following Lincoln's proclamation suspending the writ of *habeas corpus*, and was sentenced to death.

Lincoln had not yet signed the death warrant when he was assassinated. President Andrew Johnson approved the sentence, and Milligan was then scheduled to be hanged. Whereupon several lawyers, motivated by the issues in the case rather than any sympathy for Milligan, came to his defense —without pay, according to some historians. It was their belief "that a citizen living under his own rooftree, outside the zone of conflict, was entitled to the right of trial by jury." The Supreme Court was unanimous in awarding Milligan a writ of *habeas corpus*. Civilians, it ruled, had a right to trial in civil courts unless "ordinary law no longer adequately secures public safety and private rights." In the years since the decision, *Ex parte Milligan* has been extolled by some lawyers as second only to the writ of *habeas corpus* itself as one of the great safeguards of American liberty; others, especially in view of the growing scope of World War II, thought it might be unrealistic to apply it under conditions of modern, total warfare.

Precisely at noon, the black-robed judges entered in pairs and solemnly took their places as the audience rose to hear the traditional cry of the Court clerk that "the Court is now sitting." The short ritual was a reminder, if any were needed, that these black-robed men and this Court were the constant link between American past and present, between Presidents Lincoln and Roosevelt, between civil war and world war.

Besides the drama which is inherent in sessions of the Supreme Court, there was added this day a human incident of a kind which is exceedingly rare in these proceedings. Chief Justice Stone looked down from the bench and said, "I have been informed that my son . . . was assigned to participate in the defense. Of course if that fact were regarded as ground for my not participating in the case, I should at once disqualify myself." It was unbelievable, of course, that a man of Stone's integrity would be swayed by the presence of his son on the defense counsel's staff. Major Lauson H. Stone had been assigned to Royall and Dowell by the War Department, and had as little choice as they about serving. Royall had foreseen possible embarrassment to the Chief Justice and had not employed young Stone in the *habeas corpus* proceeding. Biddle told the Chief Justice that his son had assisted solely in the presentation of the defense case before the military commission, "and therefore counsel for both sides join in urging, Mr. Chief Justice, that you sit in this case." When he heard Royall's "we do" as concurrence in Biddle's statement, Stone said, "You may proceed," and the case was under way.

As counsel for the petitioners, Royall was first to present his case. In the written brief which he had filed earlier in the day, Royall had argued "that the conduct of the petitioners as shown by the evidence is nothing more than preparation to commit the crime of sabotage. There was no overt act. . . . Furthermore . . . none of the alleged criminal acts . . . were committed in the zone of military operations." "It would be strained use of language," Royall said, to consider that an unarmed Coast Guard patrol made Long Island a zone of active operations. In neither Florida nor Long Island were "military engagements or combat of any kind in progress." As for suspension of *habeas corpus*, Royall said, 'Congress alone and not the President had that right, and then only in cases of rebellion or invasion, according to the Constitution. The President's order also violated the Articles of War by providing for the admission of evidence which had "probative value to a reasonable man." This phrase, which had given Royall such a difficult time before the military commission, was, he said, contrary to the provision of the Articles which said that "only the rules of evidence generally recognized in the trial of criminal cases" could apply in military tribunals. The President had allowed the commission to make its own rules "as occasion requires," whereas the Articles of War state that he must prescribe those rules himself. And those rules, as Royall's sixteen days before the commission convinced him, were "a much greater departure from the ordinary procedure of Courts-Martial than were the rules . . . in Hawaii immediately following Pearl Harbor, when there was a critical emergency and a specific declaration of martial law."

But all of this was not really as pertinent as the precedent established by *Ex parte Milligan*, which, Royall said, after seventy-six years was still specific: "Martial law cannot arise from a threatened invasion. The necessity must be actual and present; the invasion real, such as effectually closes the courts and deposes the civil administration." The present danger could be met without upsetting this principle, he said. "If there is a feeling that the penalties for wartime sabotage and espionage are not severe enough, Congress can, of course, promptly remedy this situation as to future cases. Therefore, a decision in favor of the petitioners here could leave no inference with our enemies or others that persons guilty of sabotage or espionage would in the future incur less than the most severe penalty."

But beyond the fate of the men on trial stood a principle. "It is trite but still true," Royall said, "to say that the soundness of any system of government proves itself in the hard cases where there is an element of public clamor. Such circumstances test the real ability of a government and its judicial system to protect the rights of an unpopular minority."

As he rose to make his oral presentation and to answer the incisive question of the justices, Royall was calm and self-confident. It was only his second appearance before the Supreme Court, but he knew what he was likely to face. His deep voice was the only one that could be heard clearly throughout the room, and his manner and bearing were impressive. His handling of questions from the bench, especially the many technical ones put by his former law professor, Justice Frankfurter, was skillful. "It was just like old times," Royall told reporters later, "with the professor crowding me to the wall, and my holding out to the last."

Frankfurter was the first questioner, and throughout, the most persistent, although his initial discussion was not on the issues, but on the technical point of the Court's jurisdiction because the case had not come to it through normal channels, that is, through an Appeals Court, but directly from a District Court. If this was a precedent, he said, "the Court might be deluged with cases." Royall argued on the grounds of urgency because the military trial was about to be concluded, and he was supported by Biddle. The discussion, which lasted an hour, ended when Stone said that the issue did not have to be settled at once.

Although the justices had access to the transcript of the closed trial before the military commission, they made it clear that they were not sitting to decide the guilt or innocence of the prisoners. There was also an awareness that Royall would have to be circumspect about discussing specific testimony before the military commission. Nevertheless, there were a number of things which he could say, and around which much of the questioning revolved. In response to queslons by Justice Jackson, Royall agreed that the men were landed from a submarine operated by the German Government, but said that they did not constitute an "invading force" because many of the men, "with varying degrees of corroboration, stated that they were using this as merely a means of escaping from Germany . . . and that they had no intention or purpose to commit any acts of sabotage or violence." Even so, Jackson said, "I suppose that if anyone had seen them landing, he would have had a right to shoot them. It would not have been murder; it would have been justifiable." If that were true, Jackson continued, "at what point and by what act did your men cease to be in that status and acquire the right to be tried by a civil court?" The right to shoot them on landing was not denied by Royall, but once "they got into the ordinary commerce of human beings in the country," he said, "you could not shoot them." Jackson asked, "That is like the case of a criminal whom you might shoot at in order to stop the commission of a crime, but when he has committed it, he has a right to trial?" That was exactly it, said Royall, "except that I do not concede the crime; I am conceding only the appearance of a crime."

Jackson noted Royall's defense of the rights of enemy aliens in wartime, and asked what distinction Royall drew between American residents who, though natives of enemy countries, showed no hostility to the United States, and Royall's clients, who apparently did. Royall refused to make a distinction on their rights to be legally tried. Once the discussion was reduced to near absurdity when Justice Byrnes asked Royall whether it was his contention "that if the Fuehrer and seven Generals of the Army of the Reich should land from a submarine on the banks of the Potomac, having discarded their uniforms, they are entitled to every right you have discussed." And Royall had no alternative but to say that "my argument would have to carry that fact, and does."

Frankfurter was his sarcastic best in pushing Royall to defend his interpretation of a theater of military operations. Royall had just reiterated his views on the military status of the East Coast. "Cannot the enemy determine what the theater of the operations is by being the aggressor?" Frank-furter asked. "If a parachutist should come into this building or near this building, would this not be a theater of operations?"

"I would think it would be, sir," Royall said.

"Well," asked Frankfurter, "why was not [the East Coast] made a theater of operations by the landing of the U-boats?"

"They came unarmed," Royall said. "They came with explosives of course—" Before he could complete his sentence, the audience broke into laughter at Frankfurter's quiet comment, "I would like to know what 'unarmed' is."

The point, Royall maintained, was that in this case "the men came ashore with the explosives and buried them and left, and were apprehended at varying periods." Now Jackson interrupted. "They did not go to any agency and say 'We got away from the Germans. Thank God we are free, and we will tell you where we buried them.'" No, Royall said, they did not; if they had "there would not have been this litigation." Both Jackson and Frankfurter continued to press their point, which was, after all, a key one in determining the President's powers as Commander-in-Chief.

"It is not your contention that the President should wait until these explosives are set off before we do anything with these persons, whatever they are, invaders or not?" Jackson asked.

"We are not dealing with the question, may it please the Court, of what he could do to repel them or—" Royall said. It was a fine point, and he was having difficulty completing it.

"He has taken them in possession," Jackson interrupted, "and you say that is illegal and that we should release them?"

"That is right, sir," said Royall.

"What I do not get," Jackson said, "is how it is to be expected, if they were doing what you admit they were doing, that there would be complacency on the part of the Army or the F.B.I."

At last, Royall managed to convey his position. "No, sir," he said, "we are not arguing for complacency any more than we would argue that if a man is on a murder rampage we should be complacent. He can be apprehended or he can be killed; but it does not deprive him of the right to go into a civil court."

Royall was asked about the President's ruling that only two-thirds of the members of the military commission were needed to vote for conviction, and quoted the Articles of War which specifically said a unanimous vote was required for the death sentence and a three-quarter vote for a prison sentence of more than ten years. Then under that, Stone said, the commission could condemn the men to prison. "Well," Royall answered, "it happens that with seven members, two-thirds and three-fourths do not work out the same. I shall have to go back to fractions. . . . I think there is a difference [of one]." Jackson could not resist. "You have to have a fraction in either case," he said, "and I do not know how you could have a fraction of an officer." Chief Justice Stone did know. "Not unless you dismember him," he said, which ended that line of questioning.

It was nearly four in the afternoon, late by Supreme Court standards, before Biddle came forward to answer Royall. His brief had run twenty pages longer than Royall's, but much of this was taken up by the texts of the President's proclamation and order and a historical survey of military trials of "unlawful belligerents." Like his prosecution before the military commission, the Attorney General's brief was tough and pragmatic. "The United States and Nazi Germany are fighting a war to determine which of the two shall survive," he said. "This case is no more than a small skirmish, but on an important front. It is part of the business of war." His arguments were eloquently phrased and, given the situation of a nation still adjusting to the demands of war, undoubtedly had a strong effect throughout the country as well as in the Supreme Court. "The great bulwarks of our civil liberties— and the writ of *habeas corpus* is one of the most important— were never intended to apply in favor of armed invaders sent here by the enemy in time of war. A jealous regard for this . . . writ has been and should be maintained, to prevent prosecutions for political opinions, and possible abuses of military power in periods of great stress and high emotional feeling. But no such inroads will result from denying the privilege to belligerent enemies charged with breaking through our lines to commit hostile acts." These men were paid agents, acting under German orders, he said, enemies "in as practical a sense" as parachutists, but because of the nature of their offenses they could not be treated as lawful belligerents.

As for *Ex parte Milligan,* "by no stretch of interpretation" could its doctrines apply here, Biddle said. "Milligan never wore the uniform of the armed forces at war with the United States. The petitioners did. Milligan was a resident of Indiana. He did not cross through the lines and enter into a theater of operations. The petitioners [did]. . . . Milligan was charged with the commission of military offenses at a time when invasions gave their slow forewarning months in advance. In the year 1942, we have had concrete experience with the swiftness of modern warfare. Experience—which should be plain by now—has demonstrated that the theaters of operations which existed in 1864 are not the theaters of operations of 1942. Wars today are fought on the total front, on the battlefields of joined armies, on the battlefields of production, and on the battlefields of transportation and morale, by bombing, the sinking of ships, sabotage, spying and propaganda."

As for quibbles over what constituted a theater of operations, military orders were not needed as proof. The sinking of merchant ships off the East Coast and the fact that two submarines could land on the coast were proof enough. "We know that our whole East Coast is a theater of operations in substantially the same sense as the North Atlantic or the British Isles." Biddle also took detailed exception to Royall's charges that there were technical defects in the creation of the military commission. Royall's objection to the two-thirds vote for conviction did not apply to military commissions at all, but only to courts-martial. The commission's right to make its own rules could not be challenged; practically every court had the right to make its own rules. Thus the question of the "reasonable man" provision was not even involved here. In his brief Biddle was attempting to keep the Supreme Court's attention focused on the major issue: Was the President acting properly in causing these men to be brought to a military trial?

Biddle stepped forward to defend the position he had outlined. Today, his white linen suit, normally unobtrusive in summertime Washington, contrasted sharply with the khaki uniforms of lawyers on both sides of the bench. He had taken these few steps many times before, and was thoroughly familiar with Court procedure. As had happened with Royall, he did not speak long before he was closely questioned by the bench. His opening remarks—"the United States and the German Reich are now at war. That seems to be the essential fact on which this case turns"—set the tone of his argument and he seldom deviated from it. In response to questions from the bench he repeated his contention that "when war is declared the rights of enemies to relief in court is largely dependent on the discretion or will of the sovereign." He was less certain of what constituted the kind of unlawful act which military courts alone could try. "Suppose," said Justice Black, "there had been some landings. Several months thereafter a citizen was picked up on the street and it was charged that he belonged to that group. Where would he be tried?" This, for all practical purposes, was Haupt's situation, Biddle said, and therefore the answer was by a military tribunal. "Suppose," Black now said, "that there had been some trouble in a plant and a man had been accused of trying to interfere with work in a defense plant, and it was said that in some way he had received instructions from a foreign country. Under the order would he be tried by a court-martial?" This was, perhaps, too long a step for Biddle to take. "It is right on the edge," he said. If production were consciously stopped by enemies of the United States under the conditions in this case, then he had no doubt that military law prevailed.

Where the line is drawn is, of course, the paramount consideration in law, and now Jackson picked up from Black. "Where is the line?" he wanted to know. Biddle did not know, but he did know that this case was within the line, no matter where it was drawn. Strikers illegally stopping production would face a civil trial, but if they were acting under the direction of a foreign country "that would tip it over" if the President had issued a proclamation covering that circumstance.

As for the legality of the President's proclamation, Biddle went back to a law passed by Congress in 1798, which was still in force. It seemed likely that it was the basis for the President's proclamation in the first place. "Whenever there is a declared war," the law read, "and the President makes public proclamation of the event, all natives, citizens, denizens, or subjects of the hostile nation . . . shall be liable to be apprehended, restrained, secured and removed as alien enemies." There was no doubt, Biddle concluded, that the President had the authority to bar such people from the civil courts.

At 6:00 P.M., before Biddle could complete his presentation, Chief Justice Stone adjourned the Court for the day. It was one of the longest sessions in the Court's history.

Before the Court reconvened the next day, Royall and Dowell met Frankfurter's technical objections; they filed an appeal from Judge Morris' decision in the District of Columbia Appeals Court. That done, the two men entered the chamber for what they now knew was their last chance to win this case. After Biddle concluded, Royall would be permitted a rebuttal argument; the rest was up to the Court.

Almost at once on the second day it became apparent that Biddle wanted more than Court approval of the President's proclamation and order. Frankfurter asked him why the Court was discussing this case if, as was Biddle's view, the proclamation denied such discussion. "Is it your view that . . . we should at once say that we cannot listen to any more talk?" That was his view, Biddle said, "but I hope that you will listen to more talk, for this reason: I think that the case of *Ex parte Milligan* is very bad law and that its effect not only on the courts but on the Army is harmful. I hope very definitely that even should you decide that the proclamation stands in the way of any further action, you may think it advisable to consider whether now you shall not, at least, overrule that portion of the opinion of the majority in *Ex parte Milligan* which says that where civil courts are sitting . . . there can be no trial by military commission." Jackson reminded Biddle that he had argued the day before that the Milligan case was so different from the present case that it did not provide the precedent which Royall had suggested. "That is true," Biddle said. "You can satisfy all the requirements of this case without touching a hair of the Milligan case; but this petition would not have been in this Court except for the Milligan case." Frankfurter interrupted, "You want to touch the head as well as the hair?" Biddle's response was, "Yes." As the questions continued, he may have sensed that he was asking more of the Court than it was prepared to give. When Jackson asked him if he thought the Court should consider overruling the Milligan case, Biddle moved back from his first position. "That is a matter of the policy of the Court," he said, "whether [it] thinks it is important at this time to knock out a case which obviously by its implications interferes with the appropriate execution of orders of the Commander-in-Chief."

"Unless you show where it interferes," Jackson said, "we

do not know what you want to do. The difficulty I have in deciding a case in the dark . . . is just that. If we are to set aside the Milligan case, we ought to know what we are setting it aside for." Biddle replied that it was "profoundly impractical" to say that military commissions could not be set up unless martial law had been declared or the courts were closed. "It is preposterous," he said, "for the law to be that the President could not take proper steps to repel and capture attacking enemies because he had not closed his own courts by proclamation."

Royall's rebuttal was brief and, for the most part, involved with answering technical questions raised by the Court on aspects of the Articles of War and the laws of war. But intensive questioning came from the justices, who sought Royall's own definition of a zone of military operations. He had repeated his contention that nothing done outside such a zone could be tried by a military tribunal. Whereupon Jackson wanted to know, "Where is this war if it is not along the Atlantic Seaboard?" "I have heard it is across the water," Royall said; and to Jackson's immediate question, "This side of the Atlantic where all these ships have been sunk is not a theater of operations?" Royall maintained, "The coast is not a theater of operations."

"I still do not quite get your distinction there," Black said. "What about the planes that fly over foreign countries and drop bombs and destroy property far removed from the scene of battle?"

"If it was a military plane, that is generally accepted as a means of fighting or of combat," Royall said.

"A submarine is, too," Black said.

"A submarine is, but these submarines in this case did not do anything but transport," Royall said.

"But all the plane does is transport a bomb," Black said.

"Yes, but the submarines just transported men. A plane would be an instrument by which bombs immediately would be put into operation. The submarine transported men so that in the future they could put something into operation," Royall said.

"Your distinction is one of time," Black said.

And Royall, like Biddle before him, was faced with the question of where a line is drawn. "If you take the theory that everything that was done that might aid the enemy makes it a theater of operations," he replied, "you reduce the thing to an absurdity. If that were true, a strike in a war plant could be tried by a military commission sitting in judgment over the strikers, if there is any pretense that they did it in violation of any law with any ulterior intent. . . . I would draw it at a place between the airplane and the men who landed to commit sabotage."

Justice Frankfurter, as he might have done at Harvard Law School, summed it up for his former student. "You say," he told Royall, "that this is essentially a procedural problem, namely, what agency, what tribunal, and under what safeguards a charge of guilty should be determined. And you say that there are specific provisions in our Constitution, as well as implications from our form of government, which assure the ordinary criminal trial except . . . in active war areas where there is a shooting going on, or by agencies that themselves bring the shooting to the non-shooting country. Is that about a fair statement?"

"That is substantially what our contention is," Royall said. "That is exactly what the Milligan case holds."

Just before 4:00 P.M. Thursday, when the Court adjourned, Royall quoted once more from the decision of *Ex parte Milligan*. It was, as it had been from the start, the soul of his argument in this room. At noon the next day the Supreme Court would announce its decision and call this extraordinary session to an end.

But the trial before the military commission would not wait for that. At 10 A.M. Friday the seven generals would hear the final arguments for and against the eight prisoners. Until the Supreme Court ordered otherwise, that trial was still in progress.

Chapter 12
Death Watch

Final arguments in military trials follow a pattern as precise and as formal as a ballet step. The prosecution is permitted an opening statement, after which the defense sums up, the prosecution returns with the last word—and the trial is over, except for the verdict. The knowledge that the Supreme

Court would deliver its decision at noon could not help but affect the Friday-morning session. McCoy announced that he would call a recess at 11:45 A.M. to permit both sides to arrive at the Court on time. Meanwhile, there was the case at hand.

Cramer made the prosecution's opening statement, a brisk, confident summation which contained no doubts as to how the commission, and, by implication, the Supreme Court, would decide. "This has been a most unusual case," the Judge Advocate General said. "It is the first time a military commission has met in seventy-seven years. . . . It is still more unusual because of the fact that, for the first time in my knowledge, at least, every one of the eight defendants has claimed that he did not intend to do this, and while admitting that he did all these things, they came through simply to get out of Germany. In other words, they claim that instead of being invaders, they are refugees. I will make it unusual in one other sense—my opening statement will be brief."

Cramer kept his promise on brevity. The happy word "refugees" with which he ridiculed the defense was almost all he wanted to say. In less than ten minutes he reviewed what the prosecution had taken ten days to show in support of the charges, and he concluded, "The prosecution submits upon that evidence that we have made out a case for which we ask on each of these charges and specifications a finding of guilty, and a sentence in these cases of death."

Royall could not be so simple nor so brief. As an experienced courtroom lawyer, and therefore a realist in sensing the mood of a jury, Royall by now had few illusions about the probable outcome of the case before him or, for that matter, the one before the Supreme Court. In the face of this it was important that he make his position abundantly clear, and his arguments as forceful as he could, even at the expense of laboring the obvious. He had to remind the commission that the Supreme Court argument was a separate matter and "in no sense" a challenge of the members of the commission or of "their ability or wisdom or fairness." He had to say also that in order to vote for conviction they "must be satisfied beyond a reasonable doubt that the accused is guilty." Otherwise, they had to vote an acquittal. Nothing in the President's order altered that. And he had to tell them that, except for the spying charge, they had discretion on the matter of punishment. Since he was contending that the spying charge had not been proved, he was, in effect, making his strongest plea to the commission, not so much to acquit his seven clients, but to withhold the death sentence.

"We believe," he said, "that these men have done nothing, if we take every word and every inference of the prosecution's contention to be correct, that warrants the infliction of the death penalty. They did not hurt anybody. They did not blow up anything. . . . If it be said that their intentions were bad . . . the law has always drawn a distinction between what a man intends to do and what he does." On this he could refer to his own experience. It was probably just as well that the trial was secret; that segment of North Carolina which had felt betrayed because of his defense was sure to be distressed at his choice of examples. "It happens down in my country," Royall said, "where a certain part of our population is a little more criminal-minded than the other part, and it is not infrequent that our courts are filled on a Monday morning with cases involving assault with intent to kill; frequently secret assaults. . . . Here is a man who shoots another, and if his marksmanship had been good he would have been electrocuted. . . . He generally gets about eighteen months or two years, sometimes three or four years. The law has drawn that distinction for hundreds of years. . . . The law considers not merely the intent of a man, but the result and the accomplishment, in determining what the sentence will be. And that is written into every law, in the Courts-Martial Manual and in the criminal statutes of every state and the United States."

Even taking "the prosecution case to the limit," Royall said, and admitting that the defendants did intend to commit sabotage, the fact remained that "they did not do it." He spun variations on this theme throughout his defense. A man with enough explosives and the intent to blow up Madison Square Garden when it was full of people would not be given more than five years, if he did not carry out his plan. So here, too, "these men may have planned something . . . they prepared to do some things which, if accomplished, might have been terrible. But they have not done it." Even "the fact of war" could not change that. Wartime had to be given some consideration; he understood that. "But do not let it destroy our entire perspective of just exactly what has happened."

Dowell followed Royall to deal specifically with the technicalities of military law which he felt favored the prisoners.

He used the technicalities to support the theme "they did not do it," as if this fact alone had to cut through everything else to reach the consciousness of the commission. The Courts-Martial Manual said that "mere preparation to do a criminal act" did not constitute an attempt, and, where Royall cited Saturday night gunmen in North Carolina, Dowell used the Manual's own illustration of a man buying matches to set a haystack on fire. "Buying the matches is not an attempt," he said.

Furthermore, said Dowell, as he and Royall had maintained throughout, the prosecution had not established the essential elements of a charge of spying—actually obtaining or endeavoring to obtain information to send back to the enemy—and, as before, they denied that the area the men crossed was a military zone of operations. "The fact that some of these men went to Chicago and were found there did not make Chicago a theater of operations." That being the case, and there being civil laws to cover these offenses, the commission should abide by the intent provided under civil law. Royall took over from Dowell and enlarged on this point. Espionage was seeking information about an industrial unit; spying was seeking actual military information. No matter what the prosecution maintained, it had not proved the offense of spying.

Royall concluded just before the recess. Whether or not anything more had to be said in this case would be known in a few minutes.

The Supreme Court session lasted exactly four minutes. As soon as the justices were seated, Stone picked up two typewritten sheets and started to read the decision, which is called *per curiam*—by the court—and in the absence of a specific dissent, indicates unanimity. The first three of those minutes covered a brief review of the legal steps taken by Royall and Dowell, and a pause for the passage of a low-flying airplane whose roar obscured Stone's words. Because of time, Stone said, the judgment in the case would be given now, and a full opinion—which would give the reasons for the decision—would be issued later.

The heart of the decision came in the last minute. "The Court holds," Stone said, "that the charges preferred against petitioners . . . allege an offense or offenses which the President is authorized to order tried before a military commission. That the military commission was lawfully constituted. That petitioners are held in lawful custody for trial before the military commission and have not shown cause for being discharged by writ of *habeas corpus*. The motions for leave to file petitions for writs of *habeas corpus* are denied. The orders of the District Court are affirmed. The mandates are directed to issue forthwith."

This done, Stone adjourned the Special July Term of the Court. The press reported Biddle as "elated" but had no direct quotation from him. "The Supreme Court has spoken," was all Royall would say. There was no other road now but the one he had taken in the commission's chamber. Royall and Biddle had still to finish the trial that had been started nearly a month earlier by the now-approved Presidental proclamation.

"I want to talk to you briefly about the individual cases," Royall said when the commission met again. He seemed to be aware of how little could be said for some of the men beyond what the record already showed. But he went down the list, concisely but sympathetically. Kerling could not tell the F.B.I. he had no intent to commit sabotage; he was an Army man who took his orders seriously. But there was the fact that he had marital problems in the United States and, whether or not that was his motive for coming over, there was enough in his story "to raise a doubt . . . as to whether he would actually have carried through this thing." Heinck was "a fellow who follows orders." He could not have embarked on a sabotage program on his own initiative, and when he realized that neither Dasch nor Burger was going to do anything about it, he was pleased. Quirin had more initiative and more ability than Heinck, but he did not commit any act, "and there is at least an uncertainty as to whether he ever would have done so." Neubauer was also a follower, and had been wounded in battle. It is unlikely that he could have acted by himself. And of the five men he was discussing now, perhaps the one with the least grasp of the entire situation was Thiel. He was, Royall said, "as they call it in the mountains of North Carolina, chinking wood, to fill in between the chinks of log cabins." He did not even know, within a thousand dollars, how much money he had been given. With the spying charges unproved, these men were

213

not guilty of any offense which should be punished "with extreme severity."

If Royall seemed to be tacitly accepting a guilty finding for these men, hoping by his argument to win a prison term for them, Ristine was under no such restraint. His argument for Dasch, which followed Royall's summation for five of his clients, sought a complete acquittal on all charges. He started with the proposition which "eminent counsel for the prosecution" could not dispute, "that it was Dasch who came to Washington and who laid this case with the F.B.I., with the solution appended thereto." He reviewed Dasch's history, emphasizing those points which supported his claims that that had always been his intent. There were many such points, of course, although unfortunately without anybody's word but Dasch's to help lend credence. Ristine had to answer the prosecution's questions: why did Dasch wait so long to tell, and was it not more likely that fear of being caught after the appearance of Coast Guardsman Cullen had caused him to go to the F.B.I.? Ristine's answer was that far from being afraid of Cullen, by permitting him to live instead of killing him, Dasch showed the courage which carried him through the rest of his firm resolve. "Everything he did—everything—" Ristine said, "is consistent with the prearranged, thought-out plan on his part to come back to the United States and expose the whole thing and not carry it out." Correspondingly, none of it was consistent with a plan made on the spur of the moment after being seen by a sentry. "If Dasch can think that fast and change his mind that quickly and thereafter consistently carry out that plan—well, he is just a greater actor than I believe it possible for him to be."

On the matter of taking so long to report to the F.B.I., Ristine said, Dasch needed the six days to rearrange his mind and figure out how and what he could do. "You know, gentlemen of the commission, it seems as if he were a little bit precipitate as it was, because what do we find? We find, in spite of what he did . . . that he is on trial here with all the rest of the defendants." Besides, Dasch had called the F.B.I. in New York on the day after he landed, and it was the fault of the F.B.I. that it was not efficient enough to connect his call with the news it already had of the landing. Finally, when the F.B.I. did have Dasch in hand, the surest indication of the trust its agents had in his story was their offer to seek a short sentence if he would plead guilty in court. If the F.B.I.

believed Dasch, obviously the commission could.

"What are we going to do in a case like that?" Ristine concluded. "Is there one of these charges that can stand on the face of an intention on his part, before he left Germany and ever since, to do what he has done in this case? Why, I submit, gentlemen of the commission, that every one of these charges must fail, if that be true, and that there is but one just and fair finding that you can bring in, and that is: 'We find the defendant Dasch not guilty of every charge and every specification.'"

The last session of the trial started at 9:30 A.M. Saturday, a half hour earlier than usual, in the hope that the arguments could be concluded before the lunch recess. The members of the commission were planning to start weighing the evidence immediately, and even to work through Sunday in order to get their verdicts to the White House quickly. There was now a natural urge to conclude the trial, even though McCoy had throughout, including these last hours, repeatedly told lawyers for both sides that they should take all the time they required. Royall took him at his word and devoted more time to the defense of Haupt and Burger than he had for the other five.

Royall started boldly. He knew it was likely that the prosecution would point out inconsistencies among the various statements of the defendants, and he tried to weaken the effect of that possibility. He admitted at the outset that there had been some variations. "We cannot run away from that fact," he said. "But that is not confined to the defendants. I have a list, which I would be glad to give to the commission, of thirty-seven inconsistent statements made by members of the F.B.I. in this trial." This did not mean he wanted to try the F.B.I., he said, nor was it meant in criticism. He pointed it out "only to illustrate that even honest and competent men, as the F.B.I. men clearly are, can have differences in recollection even when they keep a minute record of it themselves." He gave only two examples—conflicting versions of whether Dasch had been promised a reprieve and whether Donegan had ever been alone with Kerling after the alleged slapping incident. All he wanted the commission to do, he said, was to keep from giving too much weight to possible inconsistencies in the stories of his own clients.

In arguing for Haupt, Royall laid great stress on his youth

and, of course, on the unique and peculiar circumstances of his leaving America. "He left here because of some difficulty with a girl," Royall reminded the members of the commission. "We are not trying him for that. He has probably proved himself guilty of some unlawful or immoral conduct in connection with [Gerda Melind]. She did not say that he promised to marry her, but he got in trouble and skipped out. That is a bad thing to do, but it happens every day. The girl, of course, deserves sympathy. She was a widow, and it was unfortunate. But it has happened many times before. It is not a terrible crime. If he had seduced her under promise of marriage, it might have been more reprehensible. She became pregnant, and he did what many other twenty-one-year-old boys would have done; he left and went down to Mexico."

The emphasis on Haupt's thoughtlessness was to help make clear that he did not leave Chicago with the intention of going to Germany, that, indeed, everything that happened to him from the time he left home might have happened to any young man. He could not be judged by the criteria used for mature men, Royall said, and the rest of his adventure was proof. Haupt had every reason to come back to America from Germany and Kappe's proposal cleared the way. Once back in America, he moved around quite openly. And if he did not immediately go to the F.B.I. and tell his story, it was because he was waiting until everyone was together on July 6. "Well, now that is his story," Royall concluded. It had been corroborated by the evidence, considering the circumstances, he said, and therefore warranted the commission's special attention.

From innocent youth, Royall had now to switch to knowledgeable maturity. His argument for Burger emphasized anew the apparent straightforwardness and frankness of the man. He reminded the commission of Burger's willingness to appear as a prosecution witness and of how Biddle made no effort to undermine his statement. He cited Burger's mistreatment at the hands of the Gestapo as the strongest possible motivation for leaving Germany and the corresponding need for leaving legally. Where Haupt had done what any boy his age would have done, Burger was represented as doing "what any man would do." Thus, Royall said, "there is no doubt at all in our minds that the defendant Burger, regardless of concern with any other case, should be found not guilty of those charges." Royall did not mean by this that Burger should be permitted to roam free. "Of course, he will have to be interned," he said, "but there is plenty of procedure to intern him. He is an alien enemy and the Government is interning most of them."

With that, and a short summing up of his recommendations, Royall's defense was complete.

Cramer's closing argument began with vigor and confident humor. "After listening to the arguments . . . of the defense," he said, "it seems to me that their idea of the proper specification to be brought before this commission would have been worded somewhat as follows: 'In that, Burger and all the rest of these defendants, with intent to defraud the German Government, did, in Quenz, Germany, in about the month of May, 1942, unlawfully pretend to said German Government that they, well knowing the said pretenses were false, and by means thereof, were saboteurs, and by means thereof did fraudulently obtain from the said German Government the sum of $180,000 in money, four or eight boxes full of explosives, and a free trip across the Atlantic in a submarine."

Having had his fun, Cramer reverted to the serious prosecutor. The actual charges had been proved, he said, and these men had to be punished. There had been testimony that other saboteurs were being trained to come later; the punishment of these men would be the best possible deterrent. He agreed with Royall that the men did not do any sabotage work, but his appraisal of that fact reached, naturally enough, quite an opposite conclusion. It was enough that they had come through military lines for the purpose of committing the sabotage, he said. The only reason they did not act was that they were caught by the F.B.I. No other reason stood up. If Royall could quote each man to the effect that he lacked intent, Cramer could quote each one to the effect that he did. Kerling: "At the time of my landing I intended to follow my instructions." Heinck: "During the evening [at Faje's apartment] it was mentioned that we had come to the United States on a German submarine." Quirin: "I consider myself an agent of Germany." Neubauer: "I came to the United States . . . for the purpose of committing acts of sabotage." Thiel: "Would probably do some of these things." Cramer did not quote Haupt directly; he had harsher words for this young man, whom he did not consider misled at all. He had lied to Gerda Melind when he left Chicago, and he had spent most of his time trying to evade the draft when he returned. As far as Cramer was concerned, Haupt's claims of innocence were no more to be believed than those of the others.

What it came down to, he added, was whether the commission should accept "their own self-serving declarations." He could understand it if one had denied intent to commit sabotage, "but when all eight of them come in and have the same excuse . . . it becomes a situation where nobody can ever be convicted . . . if he says he did not intend to do it. If that kind of excuse is to be accepted, there is no use prosecuting." This was by way of a conclusion on these six men and an introduction to his words on Burger and Dasch. Despite the contentions of these two—Burger's hatred of the Gestapo, Dasch's dislike of Hitler—they were in the good graces of Kappe, "who I presume was not the dumbbell that these men would have you believe." Cramer could not conceive it possible "that a man with Kappe's ability and the position he had would seek to take an outfit of this kind and send it abroad—an expedition of this kind, constituting simply eight morons, as you might say, who had no intention of going through with this at all. Kappe was smart. He knew his men."

The turning point, said Cramer, was on the beach at Amagansett, when Dasch realized "that the best thing to do was to run for cover." He and Burger got together, "and that is the reason, probably, why their stories coincide, each corroborating the other." If Dasch had been honest in his intentions, Cramer said, and had gone to the F.B.I. that Sunday night instead of just calling, there would have been a chance to catch the submarine off the Florida coast.

Despite the harsh words for Dasch and Burger, Cramer implied—and it was the first time this was done by the prosecution—that there might be some leniency for "one or two of these defendants" who helped the prosecution. But this was not a matter for the commission to decide, he said. The only question was whether or not the men were guilty. "What they had done to assist the government may amount to little, or it may amount to a great deal; it all depends on the circumstances, which are not before this commission, and of which this commission can know nothing at all. . . . I respectfully urge the commission to take into consideration the old maxim of courts; that clemency is a matter for the appointing authority and is not a matter for the court. . . . For that reason, we ask for a finding of guilty under each specification and a sentence of death."

Biddle did not have much to add to Cramer's presentation. He had even hesitated to say anything, he said, in view of Cramer's "admirable analysis" and because "the facts speak for themselves, and speak loudly." As it was, he limited himself largely to quoting testimony in support of the spying charge, to further impress on the commission that only a death sentence was proper punishment and to counteract Royall's argument for a lesser penalty. His point was simply that the eight men "came with the means and instructions to communicate and intended to do so." Therefore, if the commission believed "that these men were behind the lines for the purpose of sabotage and, in addition, for the purpose of spying, I think your obligation is to find for [the death penalty]. I think that that is mandatory."

A few minutes before one o'clock, although all the arguments were made, McCoy called a recess rather than an adjournment. There would be one last meeting after lunch, a precaution in case either side had any final matters to present. If, as expected, nothing more was to be said, he would adjourn, and the members of the commission would start at once to consider their verdict. The session was called to order at 2:24 P.M. After McCoy said, "The prosecution and the defense having nothing further to offer, the commission is closed," it was adjourned at 2:25. The trial was over.

The seven generals remained in session the rest of Saturday and all day Sunday. President Roosevelt, to whom they were to deliver their decision, was in Hyde Park that week end fully aware that the actions he had started a month earlier were now about to reach a climax. He had not been surprised at the Supreme Court denial of the writ for *habeas corpus*, and he had an opinion of his own: he hoped the commission would recommend death by hanging. Under his order, he had to determine the time and place of execution. On Sunday he seemed impatient. "It's always hard for generals to act as judges," he said to Hassett, "and I hope they don't string it out too long. They ought to bring in a verdict just like a jury, and I don't see why their report should be a long-drawn-out one." Hassett said he thought a page should be enough, and the President agreed, although he expected a wordy report, generals being that way.

On Monday morning the military commission reached a verdict and summoned the defense and prosecution counsel and the prisoners to tell them so. They did not say what the verdict was; the President would make that announcement. It was a brief meeting. Biddle was out of Washington and so did not attend. Royall, for whom this was the last official day on this assignment, was questioned by reporters as he left the Justice Department. "We have no further responsibilities in this case," he said. "We are leaving." A few hours later, a squad of workmen came to remove the partition which separated his and Dowell's office from Biddle's, and to take down the wooden barricades from the corridor outside Room 5235 and the heavy drapes which hung inside. By the time the three thousand pages of trial transcript and the commission's findings had been delivered to the White House that afternoon by McCoy, Cramer and a few members of the prosecution staff, the room was ready to be used as an assembly hall once more.

Stephen Early, President Roosevelt's press secretary, said it was unlikely an announcement would be made that day, and since no one else connected with the case would say anything either, correspondents had to continue to speculate. Neither Early nor anyone else mentioned that the President was not in the White House that day. He was still at Hyde Park, intending to take the overnight train back to Washington. In midafternoon an Army plane brought him the commission's report, which he started to read at once. That day, too, he signed the bill authorizing an "appropriate medal of honor" for J. Edgar Hoover for his role in rounding up the eight men.

While waiting for official word from the White House, the press mingled fact and fancy to a degree that not even normally rumor-filled Washington had experienced. By now, most reporters were writing without reservations that Dasch would escape the death penalty. A few suggested that Burger and Haupt would receive no more than long prison sentences. Speculation centered on the method of execution, and papers quoted military authorities on hanging versus shooting. One reporter pointed out that the District Jail, where the prisoners were held, was ideal for either. An old dining room had a sufficiently high ceiling to permit a gallows large enough to hang all eight at one time; the prison wall was of concrete and would make the proper backdrop for a firing squad. And if it came to it, the writer added, the jail was also equipped with an electric chair. A report that a load of lumber had been delivered to Fort Myer, an Army camp just across the Potomac River in Virginia, led some to believe that hanging was most likely—and, appropriately, on military soil.

A general feeling of impatience was aggravated on Tuesday, when President Roosevelt, relaxed in a tieless white shirt and seersucker trousers, told his regular press conference that "I am now in the process of reviewing the evidence, which is voluminous. I will have finished within two or three days." In answer to a request for comment on the length of time the trial had taken, the President said that the American processes of justice operated that way. He did not doubt that under similar circumstances Americans caught in Germany would have been summarily shot, but in the United States the preservation of society was carried out by legal means, which, he added, take time. He was pleased to see that most press comment had pointed that out. He adroitly avoided a question designed to get him to indicate the verdict. When a reporter asked him "who fixes the sentences," he simply replied that he had a report and a verdict from the commission. And, finally, when he was asked whether he was putting everything else aside to consider the case, his response was a brisk, "Oh my, no."

Despite his last answer, the President received only three callers on Wednesday and did devote most of his time to reviewing the transcript and the commission's recommendations. As an avid reader of detective fiction, he must have been especially interested in the accounts of a plot that failed, written, as it were, by its participants. On Thursday the White House still had no comment, although Jack Vincent filed a story for International News Service saying flatly that all eight men had been found guilty, and that if there were to be any reprieves they would come from the President. Other correspondents could only report that the President was conferring with legal and military experts.

On Friday, Vincent wrote that all but Burger and Dasch were to be executed in the electric chair at the District Jail. Hassett, acting as press secretary for Early, denied that this was so, and later, at his press conference, the President merely said that he had not yet completed his review of the case.

International News Service ignored the denial, and took the White House response as an indication that the six doomed men had been given a twenty-four-hour reprieve. In his story that night Vincent did not retreat from his initial position, but speculated that the delay was caused by the President's reconsidering his decision on Haupt. For the rest, he quoted "official sources" as saying that the District Jail had turned over all its facilities to the military and that "all arrangements for the greatest mass execution in Washington's history were completed." He reported that inside the jail Dasch and Burger were being kept away from the others for fear they might be killed by one of the condemned men. In the jail wing where the men were kept, he said, a large number of armed troops, supplied with a small arsenal of submachine guns, machine guns, hand grenades and tear gas bombs, were guarding the prisoners. Unarmed soldiers had been placed in each man's cell to prevent suicide attempts, and cell lights were kept burning all night. The men were chain smoking to the point where they were given loose tobacco to roll their own cigarettes because their regular ration was used up.

There is no way of checking Vincent's account of life inside the prison, but if it was as accurate as the story the White House denied, it is quite likely a true description of the last hours of Quirin, Theil, Heinck, Neubauer, Kerling and Haupt.

Despite the White House denial and the President's statement, newspapers and press associations were by Friday afternoon assigning reporters and photographers to watch the District Jail. That day, too, there came a report from Cairo, New York, that the official executioner of the state of New York "was mysteriously absent from his home," which led to a theory, never confirmed, that he was on his way to Washington to supervise the executions. At three o'clock Saturday morning, three American soldiers and a British sailor arrived at the door of the jail in a taxi and demanded admission. They had come to volunteer as a firing squad "to save the government some money on electricity." They were firmly turned away by a guard, but remained long enough to have their pictures taken by news photographers.

Finally, at six o'clock, as a cold, dank dawn broke over the ugly stone building, Major Thomas Rives, deputy provost marshal for the District of Columbia and a former superintendent of the jail, walked to the entrance. He nodded silently to the reporters, but refused to answer questions. A half-hour later, Rives's superior officer, Brigadier General Cox, and an aide, arrived. Behind them were three Army automobiles, their passengers of officer rank. A little before ten, a Catholic priest, Father Daniel O'Connor, chaplain of the reformatory at Lorton, Virginia, entered the jail. Several Army chaplains and doctors followed soon after, and one guard broke regulations by telling newspapermen that six stretchers had been delivered by an Army ambulance. Shortly before noon, as the rain began to fall steadily, Dr. A. Magruder Mac-Donald, the District of Columbia coroner, came to the door. He was the last official seen to enter. Rumors that J. Edgar Hoover, Biddle and members of the military commission were also inside the jail, could not be verified. At the White House, Early had told reporters, "There is still no news for you," but to those maintaining their vigil at the jail there were no longer any doubts that the executions were about to take place.

Inside the jail, Rives had ordered a ban on all telephone calls, even from the public booth, except those made on approved, official business. By late morning the lights in the jail wing where the execution chamber was located were turned off. Reporters had been told that the dimming of the lights would be a certain sign that the electric chair was in operation; now, even that advance indication had been removed. With the coroner's arrival, Cox and Rives checked their watches with the prison clock, and the three men walked to the room next to the execution chamber. A large sheet of one-way glass separated the two rooms, permitting witnesses to see the executions without being seen. Two dozen chairs had been placed there earlier. From them there was a clear view into the execution chamber itself, a bare room twelve by sixteen feet, brightly lighted and incongruously painted a pastel yellow, dominated completely by its sole piece of furniture, the electric chair.

The room had not been used for a year, and its ceiling ventilators had to be supplemented by several extra fans to clear it of its musty air. The chair had been made of red oak in the jail's carpentry shop eighteen years earlier, when electrocution replaced the gallows; it had been recently refurbished by new generators and other electrical equipment to increase its voltage. It worked by two electrodes, one fastened to the condemned man's leg, the other to his head. Up to this day it had been operated twenty-four times, and until a special room was built in 1940, had been kept in an alcove of the jail's dining room, its brass electrodes visible to the prisoners eating there. This had been considered shocking by a group of visiting officials and had been stopped.

The six men who were to be brought to the chair had awakened early and had been given a breakfast of scrambled eggs, bacon and toast at seven. They ate well, as they had during their entire imprisonment, and were taken to their cells on "death row," about a hundred yards from the execution chamber. Just before walking those last steps the men were visited by a barber who clipped their hair short and shaved the calf of one leg. The procedure for each man entering the chamber was the same; he was bound securely to the chair with straps around his waist, arms and legs. A rubber mask, with slots for nose and mouth, was slipped over his head. (Prison humor had it that some years earlier a condemned man, hearing the same mask was used for all executions, protested that this was unsanitary.) The mask was followed by a metal helmet containing a small sponge dampened by a salt solution. Another sponge was attached to the calf of the shaved leg. When the electrodes were in place, the executioner left the room for a tiny cubicle with a small pane of one-way glass. From there he could watch as he turned on the electricity. He had two switches, in case one failed.

Prescisely at noon Saturday, August 8, as a practice air raid siren keened through the city, the first prisoner was brought to the electric chair. The pledge of secrecy kept officials from telling the order in which the men died, although there was a jail precedent for proceeding alphabetically in multiple executions. One witness did say later that they went unaccompanied by a chaplain, and without flinching, although each appeared to be in a "stunned, confused, trance-like state." At one-twenty it was over; it had taken just fourteen minutes a man. Two executioners, who received fifty dollars for each death, and two assistants, who received twenty-five, had worked swiftly. All had gone "smoothly, without a hitch," according to one official. As soon as Coroner MacDonald pronounced the last man dead, someone telephoned the White House.

None of this was known, of course, to the reporters who had been waiting outside the jail. They had been breaking the monotony by feeding ham sandwiches to a stray dog they called "Jake" and mentally measuring the distance to the nearby Gallinger Hospital, which had public telephone booths, and to which they expected to run when they had definite news to report. At one twenty-five, two Army ambulances drove into the jail yard, and at about the same instant a reporter came dashing up to shout that the White House had just announced the executions.

The official statement was curt, its words speedily transmitted to the nation's press; some papers had it in print before the six bodies were removed from the jail. "The President completed his review of the findings and sentence of the military commission . . . which tried the eight Nazis saboteurs," it read. "The President approved the judgment of the military commission that all of the prisoners were guilty and that they be given the death sentence by electrocution. However, there was a unanimous recommendation by the commission, concurred in by the Attorney General and the Judge Advocate General of the Army, that the sentence of two of the prisoners be commuted to life imprisonment because of their assistance to the Government of the United States in the apprehension and conviction of the others. The commutation directed by the President in the case of Burger was to confinement at hard labor for life. In the case of Dasch, the sentence was commuted by the President to confinement at hard labor for thirty years. The electrocutions began at noon today. Six of the prisoners were electrocuted. The other two confined to prison. The record in all eight cases will be sealed until the end of the war."

The President had ordered the executions carried out without advance announcement in order to avoid crowds of curiosity-seekers. Now, the official news brought a few of the curious to the jail, although the rain undoubtedly kept many more away. Several convalescent patients from Gallinger Hospital watched while their hospital robes got drenched. From a nearby roof a group of young women huddled under a single umbrella. A woman who lived in the neighborhood said she had come because she had two sons in military service and wanted to learn first-hand that "those Germans have been put to death," and that she would be "glad to help carry out the sentence if they'd let me." It was two hours after the White House announcement before the Army ambulances left the jail yard. During that time many of those who had witnessed the execution left the jail, often one at a time. None offered any comment to the waiting reporters. "Mum's the word," Cox said, putting a finger to his lips and smiling. "I'm sorry, I can't tell you a thing," said Father O'Connor. "Nothing to say, boys, nothing at all," said Coroner MacDonald.

At three o'clock, reporters looking through the jail door saw a blanket-covered stretcher carried from an elevator. As they watched, the silent performance was repeated five more times, at intervals long enough to permit the elevator to rise and descend. Suddenly, at three-thirty, the gates to the jail yard were opened and twenty soldiers took up positions on either side of the entrance. Some carried shotguns, others held submachine guns or rifles. As soon as the soldiers formed a line which met the approval of a lieutenant in charge, two ambulances rolled out of the yard, slowly at first because of the slippery pavement and the crowds pushing on both sides of the driveway. Once on the street itself, the ambulances picked up speed. Behind them, a dozen cars followed, their horns blaring to keep traffic from cutting them off from their quarry. These carried the newspapermen, staying with their story. At Walter Reed Hospital, the Army's medical center, guards permitted the ambulances to enter, but immediately leaped forward to prevent the others from following. It was then five minutes past four, and for some of the newspapermen the end of a twenty-four-hour watch.

Earlier, inside the jail, Burger and Dasch had been brought back to their cells from a protracted period of exercise. When they passed the empty cells which had that morning held their colleagues, they did not have to be told what had happened. In Chicago, Mr. and Mrs. Haupt were in Cook County Jail waiting to be tried for treason. The prison warden and the United States Marshal took it on themselves to keep the news of their son's death from them, and from the Froehlings, Wergins and Jaqueses, who were being held with them. The Marshal conceded, though, that they would probably get word through the prison grapevine. A reporter found Gerda Stuckmann Melind after she had been told the news, but she had no comment other than that she planned to stay at her beauty parlor job all day. In New York, Helmut Leiner, Anthony Cramer, Hermann Faje and Hedwig Engemann, who had seen or talked to two of the guilty men, were also being held for trial for treason or knowledge of treason. Mrs. Kerling and her friend Kerkhof were in jail, too. All six undoubtedly had the news from prison sources. Rome Radio broadcast that "Roosevelt's blood purge continues" and the German radio quoted a Foreign Office spokesman as saying that the execution was "a serious event whose consequences enemy countries could not ignore." He hinted that reprisals would follow which Germany's enemies would not "be entitled to criticize."

By the following week the story of the saboteurs had ceased to make large headlines. Biddle's plans to proceed with indictments of those who helped the eight men, and his ideas for strengthening the civil laws against saboteurs were duly carried in the press. By then, the story of the landing of United States Marines on Guadalcanal was on page one of American newspapers.

In mid-October, nine weeks after their death, the six executed men made news again, when Washington reporters discovered that they had been buried in Blue Plains, the District of Columbia's Potter's Field, a grim piece of land overrun with weeds and colorless grass, near the Home for the Aged and Infirm and the Industrial Home for Colored Children. Unpainted wooden boards served as headstones. They bore no names, but were numbered 276 to 281, to correspond with Health Department records. The six graves were in a new plot at Blue Plains, separated from the bodies of the other unclaimed dead by a five-foot wire fence of a type called "anti-sabotage" by its manufacturer.

Chapter 13
Postscript to Pastorius

Peter Burger and George Dasch, the sole survivors of Operation Pastorius, were held in the District Jail in Washington for a few weeks after the executions of their six colleagues. They were then taken to the Federal Prison at Danbury, Connecticut. In October, the treason trial of Mr. and Mrs. Hans Haupt, Mr. and Mrs. Walter Froehling and Mr. and Mrs. Otto Wergin began in Chicago. The government's major witness against them was Peter Burger.

His appearance gave credence to press reports after the

executions that he and Dasch had won their lenient sentences as much by a promise to testify against the fourteen men and women held by the government as by their assistance to the F.B.I. Nevertheless, Dasch did not testify. He has claimed that he refused to cooperate because the Justice Department wanted him to lie on the witness stand. It is more likely, after his testimony on his own behalf, in which his tendency to ramble was disconcerting to his own lawyer as well as the prosecution, that Biddle was hesitant about permitting Dasch to appear for the government. Whatever the reason, it did not prevent Burger from supporting the prosecution's position.

Burger did not tell, perhaps was told not to tell in a public trial, many details of the events leading to the arrest of the eight men. Neither his role nor Dasch's in assisting the F.B.I. was mentioned. Instead, he outlined Operation Pastorius, from the school at Quenz Lake to the landing in the United States, and the objectives for sabotage in the country. His testimony, supplemented by that of F.B.I. agents and others, convincingly brought Haupt's part in the sabotage mission to a jury of nine women and three men. Other witnesses testified that the defendants were aware of what Haupt was planning, and that they had helped him. All six were found guilty; the three men were sentenced to death and the three women to twenty-five years in prison and $10,000 fines. These sentences were not carried out, however. After appeals, the women were found not guilty, Wergin and Froehling were sentenced to five years, and Haupt to life imprisonment and a $10,000 fine. The other Chicagoans, Mr. and Mrs. Harry Jaques, were never tried for holding Neubauer's money; they were interned and later sent back to Germany.

In the course of two days on the witness stand, Burger made a convincing witness for the prosecution. His face "bore a gray pallor, and his gray suit accented this dullness," one reporter wrote. "The only dash of color in his dress was a flaming red tie against his white shirt." He spoke vividly when describing the sabotage school and its goals. But when the defense lawyer asked him if he was promised immunity for testifying against his colleagues before the military commission, Burger drew himself up stiffly and in a haughty voice replied: "I may remind you, sir, that you are speaking to a German soldier. The U.S. Government respected me by not offering any promises. I expect the same of you, sir." And once he made a reply which, perhaps better than any he made at the military trial, indicated where his loyalties really lay. "Do you know where Herbert Haupt is now?" the defense lawyer asked Burger. "I understand he gave his life for his country," Burger said. The lawyer seemed uncertain about the response, and asked Burger what country that was. "I meant my own country," Burger said. "Germany."

This kind of slip did not prevent Burger from appearing again soon afterward in the New York trial of Anthony Cramer, Thiel's friend, who was sentenced to forty-five years in prison. The case was appealed to the Supreme Court, where the verdict was overruled because intent was not proved. Cramer later pleaded guilty to "trading with the enemy" and was sentenced to serve six years beyond the three he had by then spent in prison. Burger was not needed for the other trials. Hermann Fajc pleaded guilty to trading with the enemy by taking Heinck's money, and was sentenced to five years. Hedwig Engemann and Helmut Leiner pleaded guilty to charges of misprision of treason—hiding knowledge of the act. She served three years; he was sentenced to eighteen, but was paroled in 1954. Mrs. Kerling and Ernest Kerkhof were never tried, because they had not seen any of the eight men.

On October 29, 1942, Harlan Fiske Stone, the Chief Justice of the United States, delivered the full opinion of the Supreme Court in *Ex parte Quirin et al,* the name by which the case of the "enemy belligerents" has gone into the law books. It was three months after the Court heard the arguments on Royall's plea for a writ of *habeas corpus,* and ten weeks and two days after six of the men had been executed.

The opinion affirmed the responsibility of the Court "in time of war as well as in time of peace, to preserve unimpaired the constitutional safeguards of civil liberty." It took exception to the government's view that "no court can afford the petitioners a hearing." Neither the President's proclamation nor the fact that they were enemy aliens, the Court said, "forecloses consideration by the courts of [their] contentions that the Constitution of the United States . . . forbid their trial by military commission."

Stone himself considered this the most significant sentence in the decision; "I am afraid the opinion was not good literature," he wrote a friend. "I hope you noticed that [it] flatly rejected (as unobtrusively as possible) the President's comment that no court should hear the plea of the saboteurs. That, I thought, was going pretty far."

"Constitutional safeguards for the protection of all who are charged with offense are not to be disregarded," the Court said, "in order to inflict merited punishment on some who are guilty." But neither, it added, could the detention and trial of the accused "be set aside by the courts without the clear conviction that they are in conflict with the Constitution or the laws . . ." The Court decided it did not have that "clear conviction" and was thus able to justify a trial by military commission.

The Court arrived at its decision without having to upset the safeguards inherent in *Ex parte Milligan*. The reasons for the difference between that case and *Ex parte Quirin* were carefully outlined. By agreement and practice, the Court said, the law of war not only distinguishes between the enemy's armed forces and its civilian population, but between lawful and unlawful combatants as well. Lawful ones are held as prisoners of war when captured; unlawful ones are subject to trial and punishment by military tribunals. Spies, of course, are the classic example of unlawful belligerents, but others who enter enemy territory in civilian clothes to commit "hostile acts involving destruction of life or property" are just as unlawful. Royall's argument that the men had not actually committed an illegal act when arrested—although he made it more forcefully before the commission than before the Court—was not considered applicable. "The offense was complete" when the men passed defense lines "in civilian dress and with hostile purpose."

Judicial decisions, by definition, cannot please everybody. When legal scholars looked into this one more deeply, there was strong disagreement about how boldly the Court had really acted in August. One law professor wrote that "the Supreme Court stopped the military authorities and required them, as it were, to show their credentials. When this had been done to the Court's satisfaction they were allowed to proceed." Another legal expert said the Court was more like "a private on sentry duty accosting a commanding general without a pass." And one of the country's outstanding experts on constitutional law said the decision was "little more than a ceremonious detour to a predetermined goal." The pro-Roosevelt press regretted that the Supreme Court did not give broad sanction to the President's war powers; anti-Roosevelt editors regretted that the Court did not define a limit to those powers. But when the opinion was published, the Russian defense of Stalingrad, the slowing down of Rommel in Africa, American and Australian victories in New Guinea were hopeful signs of progress in the war. For most of the public, the Court's opinion was hardly pertinent to the more dramatic and poignant matters of wartime life and death.

Yet the issues raised by Royall and Biddle will be pertinent if there should be another war. The word "total" as applied by Biddle and others to World War II would be drastically revised in atomic warfare. Although some members of the Supreme Court believed, as Stone said, that "the civil safeguards of the Constitution [are] irrelevant to military affairs in the actual conduct of war," all of them did guard the right of the judiciary to determine that relevancy. Holding to that right is important to democratic life as much in war as in peace. Both Biddle and Royall have in the years since the trial speculated independently on its possible outcome if it had been brought up after the war, as Milligan's was; it is conceivable that in peacetime the President would not have been upheld on the use of a military commission to try the eight men. Merely by hearing the appeal, despite the President's order, the Court may have done as much as is possible in wartime.

Despite the Court's approval of it, there is, in retrospect, an inconsistency in the government position; taken to its logical conclusion, even a trial before a military commission should not have taken place. Once the eight men were arrested and their confessions made, a summary trial and immediate execution in secret would have conformed with Biddle's concept of total war and with wartime practices toward spies or other "unlawful belligerents." A short communiqué after the fact would have done as much for the nation's morale as the publicity generated by the actual announcement. The secrecy about the means of capture, which was important to the F.B.I. and the War Department, would have been more tightly maintained than it was. The Germans would not have known, as they had to, by the unofficial stories and press speculation, that Dasch and Burger and the coincidence of a Coast Guardsman at Amagansett were responsible for the failure of their sabotage plans. They would have been left to worry about flaws in their methods.

And Americans would have been spared the spectacle of justice being openly disputed. It is unlikely, given the state of the war in mid-1942, that anyone would have questioned a decision that eight captured Nazi agents, landed by submarine from Germany and equipped for sabotage, had been put to death.

Not having taken that course, the government was vulnerable to the strong defense made by Royall, although it was obviously not anticipated when the President's order and proclamation were issued. Royall acted, as Roger N. Baldwin, director of the American Civil Liberties Union, wrote him, "with courage . . . on an issue of vital import . . . [and] many defenders of civil liberties are greatly in your debt. . . ." By raising the issue, Royall, of course, took his own position to its logical end; partial justice is often as bad as none at all; therefore, once the government had ordered a trial of any sort, all the force of the law pertaining to trials had to be invoked.

In losing his fight, Royall won enormous esteem. Soon after the special session, Justice Frankfurter, back once more in New Milford, Connecticut, sent him a note. It was shorter than some of the questions with which Frankfurter had taxed Royall during the Court session. "My dear Kenneth," he wrote. "Now that the grim business is over, I should like you to know how greatly I esteem the admirable manner in which you discharged the difficult and incongenial task entrusted to you by the Commander-in-Chief. You were in the service of both War and Law—and you served both with distinguished fidelity." Justice Jackson, who had disagreed with Royall, wrote that "it is not unjudicial to say to you that you have acquitted yourself like an officer and a gentleman in a most difficult situation . . . an impressive demonstration that the right to counsel in our democracy is neither a fiction nor a formality."

Perhaps even more amazing to Royall in defeat was the view of the men he defended. Not long before they died, the six condemned men drafted a statement. Kerling instigated it and, not surprisingly, refused to let Dasch and Burger sign it. "Being charged with serious offenses in wartime," the statement read, "we have been given a fair trial. . . . Before all we want to state that defense counsel . . . has represented our case as American officers unbiased, better than

232

we could expect and probably risking the indignation of public opinion. We thank our defense counsel for giving its legal ability . . . in our behalf."

Although there were rumors that Royall's career would be harmed because he had embarrassed President Roosevelt and Secretary of War Stimson by his defense, they were completely unfounded. In December 1943, he was promoted to brigadier general, a rank in keeping with new responsibillities in the Army's Fiscal Division. Perhaps the most subtle testimony to his legal skill came from the Judge Advocate General; Cramer asked Under Secretary of War Robert Patterson to appoint Royall as his assistant. But Patterson saw another future for Royall. In 1945 he named Royall his special assistant in charge of legal and legislative matters, and by the end of that year, when Patterson became Secretary of War, Royall was made Under Secretary. In July 1947, he succeeded Patterson as Secretary of War in President Truman's cabinet, and after helping in the reorganization of the Armed Forces, became the nation's first Secretary of the Army, a post he resigned in 1949 to return to private practice.

By the time Royall became a member of the Cabinet, Biddle had left it after serving with distinction for nearly four years as Attorney General; he resigned on Roosevelt's death but did not leave until June 30, 1945; he was named United States member of the international military tribunal at the Nuremberg trials of the Nazi leaders, and returned from Germany to a retirement made active by participation in politics, public affairs and writing.

Early in 1943, after Burger's courtroom appearances for the government, he and Dasch were transferred from Danbury to the Federal Penitentiary at Atlanta, Georgia. In 1945, Dasch was moved to the Federal Penitentiary at Leavenworth, Kansas. The two men did not see each other again until early April of 1948, when they were brought to Fort Jay on Governor's Island in New York City, from where they were deported to Germany. On the recommendation of the Justice Department and with President Truman's approval, their sentences were ended after five years and eight months in prison.

A military ship deposited them at Bremerhaven. In Germany, they were placed under some restrictions—a form of parole—but these were gradually lifted. Burger faded into the anonymity of postwar Germany and little has been heard of him. In 1953, a series of articles entitled "The Invisible Front" appeared in the weekly German picture magazine *Der Stern*. Among other stories of Abwehr activities during the war was a version of Operation Pastorius. All the documents pertaining to the participants after they landed in the United States were still classified secret at the time. Although some of the incidents and conversations reported in *Der Stern* were completely fictitious, the only possible source for some of the other material was Burger, who in the series was never once identified in the plot's betrayal. The implication was strong that the saboage plan would have worked if Dasch had not given up. More than that, Burger, in a letter to the editor, suggested that Abwehr leadership consisted of fools or traitors. Colonel Lahousen, the head of Abwehr II, and Admiral Wilhelm Canaris, chief of all Military Intelligence, were both considered suspect by the Nazis; thus this would not be a difficult theory for Germans, especially those who are still pro-Nazi, to accept.

Burger's acts can be viewed as having a certain consistency. Disillusioned by what he considered the betrayal of the original Nazi program and of the party's Old Guard, he had nevertheless found a way to survive Hitler's purge and Gestapo degradation. He had learned to keep himself alive in situations far more complicated and sinister than the one he met in a hotel room in New York on a hot Sunday in June when he faced George Dasch and weighed, as he must have since Cullen's appearance at Amagansett, the chances for the sabotage plan's success and his own survival. Perhaps Burger's letter to *Der Stern*, his contribution to its articles, and his emotional response of "my country, Germany" at the Chicago trial, are the only clues which will ever be available to the motives and loyalties of a man who helped convict his comrades, but expected the respect due a German soldier. Just as he had been inclined to feel that his life and Germany's would have been better if Roehm and the Old Guard Nazis had held power, he could still feel that Germany would have been capable of brilliant sabotage if only the right men had been in charge.

Dasch's case is more puzzling than Burger's. The actions and intentions of this unhappy man have baffled both Germans and Americans. *Der Stern* dealt more harshly with Dasch than with any other person connected with Operation

Pastorius. He was singled out as the informer who caused the death of six comrades in the performance of their duty. The publication of his picture and the highly prejudicial account of his deed started a spate of abusive stories in the German press, which he found himself unable to stop or counter. Dasch, who had not attained the status and reward he expected in the United States for revealing the sabotage plot, found himself cast as a villain in Germany for doing so. He tried unsuccessfully to obtain a pardon from the United States Government and to be permitted to return to the country. And in 1959, before the official transcript of the military commission trial was made public, he wrote a book to explain himself. It adds little to his defense, and it contains some inconsistencies and conflicts with his statements to the F.B.I., many of which can be attributed to an inevitable lapse of memory after seventeen years, and to the human tendency to impose consistency and reasonableness upon a troubled and confused past.

The essential questions in Dasch's case are when and why he determined to reveal the German operation to American authorities. The cynical view is that in Germany and the United States, Dasch was ever the vacillating opportunist. His ambition for a position higher than waiter had been frustrated in the United States. Even the prospect of citizenship had not held him when it seemed that his efforts might succeed in Germany, although his job qualifications were based on a largely invented version of his life in America. In Germany he made good in a way—work in the monitoring service, and then leadership in an important mission. Perhaps the chance to return to the United States opened an even greater vision for a man who had so recently managed to seize opportunity. In both his book and his F.B.I. statement, Dasch says that he was familiar with the Abwehr file on the Sebold case and its destructive effect on German Intelligence operations in the United States. He could have seen himself as a second Sebold; and he may have imagined that a defection in wartime would be much more valuable and better rewarded than one in peacetime. Or, there is the prosecution's even simpler contention that Cullen's appearance on the beach was the turning point for Dasch.

Dasch himself has continued to claim that he decided in Germany to destroy Operation Pastorius, and that his reasons were a profound shock and distaste for the realities of Hitler's Germany, and a revelation that his true ties were to a democratic America. In his book he provides affidavits from Germans that he expressed these sentiments even before going to the sabotage school at Quenz Lake. But neither Dasch nor his harshest judges seem to have understood that, short of official punishment, there could never be unassailable and objective proof of anti-Nazi convictions in the police state of the Third Reich, and that even affidavits may be suspect.

Dasch's actions and statements give the impression of a man whose imagination and ambition were beyond the ordinary, while his personality and character prevented success time after time. He seemed totally unaware that his offer to improve and direct American propaganda to Germany—which he raised in his first discussion with the F.B.I.—would not be welcomed as further proof of his anti-Nazi feelings. Instead, it was taken as an indication that his informing was just one more calculated effort by a man whose political persuasions seemed so quixotic; Dasch was too naïve to foresee this interpretation. It is this failure to anticipate and accept the risks or possible pitfalls of his acts which emerges from his story. For a man without toughness of mind, the harsh fate which was his because he was considered a renegade by many people on both sides of the war has left Dasch hurt and bewildered.

On December 10, 1942, one day shy of the first anniversary of Germany's declaration of war against the United States, the F.B.I. turned over to the Tresury Department the sum of $174,588.52. It represented the total of the money found on the eight men, and in the coffee tins, under the rugs and behind the radiators in the homes of their friends. The exchange was barely mentioned in the press. There was no need to; Operation Pastorius was long dead. And with it, too, died the German desire to mount a major sabotage offensive in the United States. At the time it was conceived, the plan was logical in terms of the Nazis' military superiority in Europe. But not long after the failure of the saboteurs, Hitler and the German High Command had to contend with major defeats in Russia and Africa. It is not likely that any new plans from Abwehr II, even had they been suggested, would have received a high priority. Late in 1944, Abwehr I did manage to place two spies on the Maine coast, but they were also picked up by the F.B.I. No other attempts to send saboteurs or spies to the United States during the war are known to American authorities.

When the news of the failure of Operation Pastorius was announced, Colonel Lahousen made a brief note in his diary. "Since early morning," he wrote, "radio reports continue to come from the United States . . . that all participants in Operation Pastorius have been arrested. . . ." No one can know how Lahousen and Walter Kappe reacted beyond the normal emotions of anger and disappointment. Lahousen himself said after the war that he had never had much enthusiasm for the sabotage mission, and it is possible that he was relieved to devote his attention to European objectives. Lahousen was a victim of the Gestapo-Abwehr rivalry, but lived to testify for the Allies in the Nuremberg trials. Less is known of Kappe's eventual fate, although he too survived the war. It seems probable that the collapse of his mission led to his reassignment to less glamorous duties than Intelligence, but as he looked back on Operation Pastorius, it must have been hard for him to see where he had failed. Schulz and Koenig were dedicated and excellent teachers of sabotage; the Abwehr laboratory supplied weapons of the highest proficiency; Barth and the gentlemen of I. G. Farben provided technical details about railroads and the aluminum industry; Kappe himself supervised the most minute of details and, except for a mistake about some of the American money, overlooked very little in the machinery of the plan. What he overlooked, and where the sabotage mission had eventually to fail, was the nature of the men who were selected to carry it out.

Aside from Dasch's role in starting the F.B.I. on its quick roundup of the other seven men, and even leaving aside the results of John Cullen's accidental discovery at Amagansett, it is hard to believe that Operations Pastorius could have succeeded under any circumstances. Sooner, rather than later, one or more of the saboteurs—Haupt by talking too much or Heinck by his fondness for the bottle, for example—were likely to have exposed themselves. In the months before they were scheduled to start actual sabotage, the F.B.I. was almost certain to have tracked down some of the eight men. The F.B.I. had records on Neubauer and Kerling from their *Lekala* adventure and knew that they had returned to Germany; they and Thiel, Quirin and Heinck were also vulnerable because of their membership in the German-American

Bund, whose files the F.B.I. knew so well. Haupt's cablegram from Japan was in F.B.I. hands; and so were the names of the German and Japanese nationals, including Dasch and Thiel, who left on the *Tataku Maru* on March 27, 1941. It seems probable that one of the eight men would have been arrested fairly quickly; given their personalities, it is just as probable that none of them, except perhaps Kerling or Burger, could have maintained his alias and fictional autobiography.

The general tendency during the war to attribute to Germany the superman qualities which its own propaganda proclaimed must have made it hard for American authorities to believe that this strange group of men could have been chosen for so important an assignment. The kindest thing that can be said for Walter Kappe is that they probably represented the best he could find. In his Nazi arrogance he would not have believed that most of the Germans who left America to serve Hitler's Third Reich were the least qualified to do so.

Acknowledgments

Nearly all the material in this book is based on the testimony at the secret military trial of the eight participants in Operation Pastorius, the hearing before the Supreme Court of the United States, F.B.I. records, and some unpublished letters and documents relating to the case. In addition, a number of books contributed fresh data as well as bases for understanding some of the people and events. Among them were:

Total War and the Constitution, Edward S. Corwin, Alfred A. Knopf, 1947.

Eight Spies Against America, George J. Dasch, Robert M. McBride Co., 1959.

Memoirs: Ten Years and Twenty Days, Karl Doenitz, translated by R. H. Stevens in collaboration with David Woodward, World Publishing Co., 1959.

The Uprooted, Oscar Handlin, Little, Brown and Co., 1951.

Off the Record with F. D. R. 1942-1945, William D. Hassett, Rutgers University Press, 1958.

German Military Intelligence, Paul Leverkuehn, translated by R. H. Stevens and Constantine FitzGibbon, Praeger, 1954.

Harlan Fiske Stone: Pillar of the Law, Alpheus Thomas Mason, The Viking Press, 1947.

The Rise and Fall of the Third Reich, A History of Nazi Germany, William L. Shirer, Simon and Schuster, 1960.

The Meaning of Treason, Rebecca West, The Viking Press, 1947.

There have also been discussions of the case in many law journals. Of these, the most useful for this book were those in the *American Journal of International Law* (January 1943), the *American Political Science Review* (December 1942), *Cornell Law Quarterly* (November 1942 and September 1943), the *George Washington Law Review* (February 1943), *Harvard Law Review* (January 1943), *University of Pennsylvania Law Review* (November 1942, December 1943 and March 1944) and *Washington Law Review and State Bar Journal* (November 1942).

In the course of assembling the material I was particularly helped by Robert E. Wick and Jack Keith, Jr., of the F.B.I.; Francis Biddle; and Kenneth C. Royall. None of them is responsible, of course, for any errors in the use or interpretation of the material they provided. Jerry Korn and Gordon

Manning, good friends who also happen to be good editors, gave freely of their skills. And as they have done for so long, my wife, Kartherine Sharp Rachlis, and my children, Stephen and Christopher, provided encouragement and incentive while the book was being written.

E. R.